C000090079

BLYTHE, J.
SOLDIERING ON

ABE

30 JUL 19

13 AUG 200

3

22. OCT 19

12

SOLDIERING ON

A Soldier's War in North Africa and Italy

John Blythe

940.5481

N. Y. C. C.

6 APR 1990

COUNTY LIBRARY

065

Hutchinson

LONDON · SYDNEY · AUCKLAND · JOHANNESBURG

To Elsie

This edition first published in Great Britain
in 1989 by Hutchinson,
an imprint of Century Hutchinson Ltd
Brookmount House, 62–65 Chandos Place,
Covent Garden, London WC2N 4NW

Century Hutchinson Australia (Pty) Ltd
89–91 Albion Street, Surry Hills, NSW 2010

Century Hutchinson New Zealand Limited
187 Archers Road, P O Box 40-086, Glenfield, Auckland 10

Century Hutchinson South Africa (Pty) Ltd
P O Box 337, Bergvlei 2012, South Africa

First published 1989

Printed in Hong Kong

Copyright © John Blythe

ISBN 1 86941 044 0

Contents

Thoughts Upon The Desert

Sand-bound and sand-girt,
Sandstone its sod.
Who made the desert?
Surely not God.
But somebody made it
And painted its tones,
Spread it and sprayed it
And scattered its stones.
Somebody plucked it
Of plant and of frond.
Somebody sucked it
Of stream and of pond.
Or was it born naked,
And scorched to the core?
Barren and baked
Flat and forlorn?
But let us not quibble
Or argue or guess,
Lay the blame on the devil
And let him confess.
For arid its acres and stony its shell,
It is not our Maker's this sample of hell.

Lin Rowell
'A' Troop

Preface

In writing *Soldiering On* I set out to relate the day to day business of being a soldier on active service, and I hope that, by portraying events as I saw them, readers will gain an insight into how we thought, how we behaved, and how we came to terms with the problems we faced during World War II fifty years ago.

I did not have access to notes or diaries, relying only on memory, so allowance should be made for the passage of time. However, place names and dates were checked against the *Official History of New Zealand in the Second World War 1939 — 45 'Divisional Signals'* produced by the War History Branch of the Department of Internal Affairs Wellington. The modified maps in the book were also reproduced courtesy of the Department of Internal Affairs and I am indebted to the Pictorial Reference Service of the National Library of New Zealand for all but three of the photographs.

To my family, who provided encouragement and assistance, and to the following people who allowed me to use their material I owe grateful thanks: Sergeant Alan Boyd for putting me in touch with Lin Rowell whose verse 'Thoughts on the Desert' appears at the beginning of the book; Les Cleveland's graphic lines from 'The Iron Hand' which match so perfectly the situations described; the estate of the late Alan Moorehead, war correspondent, for permission to use copyright material; David Hill who read the early manuscript and made suggestions; and finally, First Officer Malcolm McDonald, Gulf Airways (Bahrain), whose initiative resulted in this book reaching the publishers.

Winged Sandals

Hermes, the son of Zeus and Maia, the
messenger of the gods, commonly figured as a
youth, with the *caduceus* or rod, *petasus* or
brimmed hat, and *talaria* or winged shoes.
Identified with the Roman Mercury which is
the insignia of the Royal Corps of Signals.

Chapter 1

The War I Started

Wellington — Trentham Camp

The year was 1938. There were six of us if one excluded the chap behind the desk. He had not been very forthcoming anyway, simply checking our names against a list and motioning us to sit down. Covertly we studied one another. All male, all in our early twenties. What the hell was it all about?

Speculation was interrupted as the door opened. Perhaps another lamb to the slaughter? Not quite, for this bloke was older and there was something military about him. Perhaps his stance, the way he held his shoulders? The fellow behind the desk nodded and got up and left the room. The newcomer, from the middle of the floor, introduced himself.

'I am Lieutenant Philpot of the Royal New Zealand Navy.'

Philpot wasted no time in indicating that what he had to say was highly confidential and must not on any account be passed on to family, employer or friends. There was also some mention of the Official Secrets Act. He had our complete attention as he went on to explain the reason for the meeting.

Because the international situation was bad and we were living in troubled times with risk of war, the New Zealand Government had decided to establish a nucleus of people trained to handle confidential communications passing between themselves and the Secretary of State for Dominion Affairs in London. Some of this information would be sent by cable in the General Telegraphic Code but much of it would be in high grade cipher, particularly if war eventuated. There would in that event also be messages in Navy codes from warships and from radio transmitters in the Pacific Islands via the radio station on Tinakori Hill.

Philpot concluded by asking for our home telephone numbers and directed us to return to our jobs and say nothing to anybody. He was quite emphatic about this and such was his manner there were no questions.

As I walked down the steps of Wellington's General Post Office where the briefing had taken place, I was wondering, 'Why me? Why have I been selected? What's the Post Office got to do with this cloak-and-dagger stuff? What will I say when the boss asks what took place?' Back at the office my clam-like attitude did little for my promotional prospects but eventually matters settled down.

It was a month before I heard again from Philpot.

'No. Say nothing to your employer. Just report to the Navy Office at Defence Headquarters on Monday as I've directed you.'

So instead of going to work after the weekend I turned up at the Navy Office where Philpot put the six of us through extensive training in handling codes and ciphers over a period of two weeks.

At the end of the course, which had been conducted with typical Navy thoroughness, Philpot wound things up by again telling us to keep our mouths shut when we went back to work. His message must have struck home because the six of us adjourned to the St George Hotel in Boulcott Street for a few beers and not a single word was spoken about what had occupied our time over the previous few days. I do recall, however, leaving the hotel thinking about Philpot's final injunction. It was all very well for him to tell us to keep our mouths shut but I had been missing from work a fortnight and the boss was sure to demand an explanation.

As events proved, he did not disguise his irritation but I had a distinct feeling that he had been tipped off not to probe. It was more difficult to satisfy workmates but as the days passed the incident was forgotten.

The following year the international scene deteriorated rapidly. German youth were drilling and marching in great numbers and we heard for the first time references to Blackshirts and Brownshirts. Pictures appeared in the newspapers of Hitler's stormtroopers goose-stepping with raised fists before great multitudes, and tanks were depicted rumbling down the Unten Den Linden. It was not at all reassuring when the British Prime Minister, Chamberlain, clad in morning suit and carrying an umbrella, walked around like a clucking hen, trying to make soothing noises. Against Hitler's tanks and screaming rhetoric he was too low-key to be convincing.

I arrived home one Saturday to learn that someone had been phoning but would not leave a message. Next weekend was the same but this time there was a telephone number which I rang to be told curtly to make myself ready and a car would call for me. I was boarding in Brooklyn at the time and the Ministerial limousine with chauffeur certainly received some curious looks. Mildly embarrassed but enjoying the experience, I took possession of the back seat. God knows what the driver thought, but he kept it to himself as we drove through the city streets. We pulled up at Defence Headquarters where an orderly conducted me to a room in which flying personnel in mufti were sitting around talking. The atmosphere was markedly more relaxed than the Navy Office in the same building, and spotting an interdepartmental cipher on a shelf amidst sundry files and papers, I thought possibly air-crews and clerical duties might not be a good combination from a security point of view.

Nothing much was happening and none of my contemporaries from the cipher course was there. In fact it was all fairly light-hearted and at half past four a Group Captain sent out for pies. At eight o'clock we all went home.

Next weekend was almost a repeat performance. Another Ministerial limousine. No wonder my landlady was bemused! Every week-day morning I gobbled my breakfast and ran like hell to catch the No. 7 tram as it rattled down the steep Brooklyn hill, so weekends presented something of a contrast.

However, a picture was emerging. Hitler was moving military forces into adjacent countries and peacefully annexing them — the Rhineland, Austria and Czechoslovakia — and he was doing it each weekend. That's what caused the flap on Saturdays and Sundays.

This time the car carried on to stop at Parliament Buildings where I was introduced to Carl Berendsen, Permanent Head of the Prime Minister's Department and future ambassador to the United States. With his dark bushy eyebrows and rasping voice, pipe-smoking Berendsen was a vibrant personality and a little intimidating on first acquaintance. The sign on his secretary's door read 'Imperial and Foreign Affairs', and it seemed to me that from costing clerk at the Post Office Stores on Fryatt Quay to Government House Staff in the House of Parliament on the hill was a move up in more ways than one.

That weekend was the beginning of a new existence. Whatever the story was that was passed around to explain my absence from work I never did find out. My new boss was a Mr James, slim, with dark greying hair parted in the middle, horn-rimmed spectacles and formal manner, but with a lighter side too. Second Secretary to the Governor General, he had been detached from normal duties to take charge of the cipher section, bringing with him two under-secretaries from Government House. There was also the Commercial Manager and the Transport Principal from the Post Office, who had been trained earlier by Philpot. Four of my contemporaries made up the team and work was divided into shifts around the clock.

From the Commercial Manager I learned that when the cipher nucleus was first envisaged, the Post Office, as a communications department, had been considered the best source from which to recruit staff, and that the small group of people originally trained had been top executives. However people at this level could ill be spared so subsequently it had been decided to utilise Post Office cadets with University Entrance from separate branches, so presumably that was how I had come to be selected.

Whether by accident or design (but probably the former), the cipher room was more appropriate to a film set than as a place to work. It was large, carpeted, and every wall was shrouded in heavy olive drapes. Four desks were ranged together and covered by a green baize cloth. A tall carved wooden Speaker's chair, seemingly still to contain a presence, faced the desks. No daylight penetrated, but weak bulbs in the high ceiling glowed dimly and desk lamps burned day and night.

Nobody came to clean the room and it was an eerie place, high up there in Parliament Buildings. On occasions when I was alone at night, I would gaze at the Speaker's chair and feel its incumbent eyeing me. Sometimes, just for the hell of it, I would sit in the chair and look at my own empty one. The whole thing reminded me of that old film, *The Phantom of the Opera*. Lord knows, Parliament was large enough to accommodate a ghost and sometimes faintly but clearly could be heard the notes of a violin. There was a simple explanation; the sound emanated from the Speaker's quarters.

Our door to the corridor bore a large notice: ENTRANCE TO THIS ROOM ABSOLUTELY PROHIBITED. Some members of the House resented the secrecy which prevailed and it was not uncommon to overhear caustic comments as they passed. We were also a source of confusion to the staff at Bellamys who served us morning and afternoon teas. Four uniformed flunkies carrying white napkins would wheel in tea wagons complete with silver teapots and tureens, a scene which initially made me feel hysterical. Let's face it, costing clerks are not normally accorded VIP treatment and this went on for several weeks. On receiving the bill, Treasury queried it with Berendsen who laughed his head off. From that point onwards, tea was paid for and uplifted by us as we came on duty.

Working in the Prime Minister's Department one would be expected to know the gentleman but I had never seen Michael Savage, though I knew what he looked like. Everybody did, because his baby face hung in every working class home, but the man was ill and continually absent.

Looking back, it is difficult to relate events in chronological order but one evening I was alone, deciphering a most urgent message. As the pieces began to come together, my God! This was it! With quickening heart: 'His Majesty's Government . . . . Germany has attacked Poland 5 a.m., 1st Sep. 1939 . . . .' This was what we had been waiting for! I felt stunned. All those people out there, strangers, family, friends, going about their business while I held this in my hands. Breathing deeply I continued to savour the impact, going quickly out the door, which I presume I locked, and down the stairs like a rabbit to Berendsen.

The days immediately after the declaration of war remain blurred, but activity increased on our front. Uniforms and military braid appeared, as did Major-General Duigan, Chief of Staff. There was a flood of cipher messages and we were dismayed to learn that even the mundane departure of cargo vessels and their contents had to be put in cipher in case enemy submarines were lurking off our coast. The name Freyberg began to crop up in messages and it seemed that he would be the one chosen to lead our troops overseas. It was also clear that we needed more staff in the cipher section and better working conditions, so we moved into more normal rooms where fresh air and daylight prevailed and two young women joined us to handle the typing.

On 24 November 1939 it was announced that a New Zealand Expeditionary Force would be sent overseas, comprising three echelons with reinforcements at intervals to keep them up to strength. Freyberg would be the Commander in Chief and with his brilliant record and as holder of the Victoria Cross he was a popular choice. Fred Jones was the Minister of Defence.

I believe politicians were more colourful characters in those days than they are today, and can still see the tall, solid figure of Peter Fraser, usually in a grey suit, and hear his dour but not unpleasant Presbyterian voice. He was reputed to be half blind. I know his speeches were typed on a typewriter with exceptionally large type and remember him coming out of Berendsen's office one evening; instead of using the door into the corridor, he opened the door of a particularly large wardrobe in our room and tried to climb into it while my companion and I watched slack-jawed.

There was Bob Semple in riding britches, standing lithe and tall outside the Chamber, slapping his booted legs with a riding crop. John A Lee, more red-faced then than later, empty sleeve tucked into his jacket, galloping down the concrete steps by the monument to Bowen Street. Walter Nash with his neat grey head, and suited in good quality cloth. Close up he possessed the air of an old thoroughbred stayer. Gordon Coates, looking like the Army Captain he was. I stood by his grave at Matakohe the other day reflecting on his reaction if he came back to the political scene of today.

We received daily from the Secretary of State in London a special report which kept the New Zealand Government up to date on current events. It was referred to as the DW and covered not only operational matters, but also meetings between foreign ministers with other powers. Some were allies, some neutral; one could only speculate how the latter were going to jump. As the war progressed the DW was looked forward to and became the special event of the day. People commencing a new shift always asked whether the DW had arrived and sat down to read it before commencing work.

The contents made depressing reading, not only because we were in retreat everywhere in Europe, but our merchant shipping losses were enormous; the figures were appalling. The British Navy was suffering also. I recall the poignancy of a report from one of three small destroyers. (HMS *Glasgow* and HMS *Glow-worm* were two of the names.) They broke radio silence to say they were being overwhelmed by superior naval forces in the North Sea but were fighting on. Reports came filtering through and then there was silence. The incident lingered in my mind. The Prime Minister was reported to be suffering from cancer and it all added a sombreness to the scene.

Then Michael Savage died. As a member of his personal staff I was expected to walk behind the casket at the State funeral but in the main entrance to Parliament ran foul of an officious secretary. I don't know why, perhaps I was tired having been up half the night, but I failed to identify myself and went looking for an alternative route to join the assembly. Finding it moving off, I gave up and went home to catch up on some sleep. I must admit to having a thing about Ministers' secretaries in those days after a run-in with one when dining at Bellamys when I refused to disclose information to him.

As the tempo increased, Berendsen and his close associates were virtually living on the premises. To afford them some relief, the cipher officers moved into Berendsen's office about 9 p.m., and carried on doing their cipher work there. This enabled us to man the key telephone and if anything urgent cropped up to get in touch with him. Not infrequently, one would have to wake a tired man in the small hours over something significant, and never once did he not thank one politely.

We were not always busy. There was time to smoke and I smoked a pipe. So did Berendsen. It was said that his wife bought him cheap ones at Woolworths which he burned through at the rate of knots. The drawers of his desk, usually half open, were full of them. If his pipes were cheap his tobacco was not. He smoked the best and if I was short I was not averse to helping myself to a pipeful occasionally. I would sit at his desk in the small hours, puffing away, thinking of people at home in their beds and feeling that I was at the heart of the nation; a kind of Walter Mitty experience for a young man.

At a later stage a senior public servant took over the watch in the early part of the evening to enable us to get on with our work. Answering the phone in his absence one night I was shocked to be confidently asked what the latest news was. The caller was equally surprised when he realised I was not his usual source and quickly hung up. I pondered for two or three days whether to report the incident, but let it slide. After all I was a very junior public servant.

There was another breach. I came on duty one Saturday morning, when the typists did not work, and found a sheet of carbon paper in a wastepaper basket. Holding it against the light of the window I found it had been used only once and was perfectly legible. It showed the names of troopships, the date of their anticipated arrival at Wellington, and the departure date for the next echelon of troops poised ready to leave. As I burned it I reflected what was the use of Fraser, now Prime Minister, stubbornly insisting and succeeding against considerable resistance from Churchill and their Lords at the Admiralty in having the *Ramillies* as an escort. He had argued vigorously that the visit of one of Britain's biggest battleships would not only provide a formidable escort but would also discount a lot of German propaganda and give New Zealand civilian morale a boost. Most of us had never seen a battleship and I knew it would cause a sensation. Here before my eyes was a piece of evidence the Germans would dearly love to get. Anybody could have walked in over the weekend; the typists' room was never locked. Passes to the building had still not been issued. They would come later. Some of the attendants at the main entrance door at Bellamys made an effort but others were pretty casual about who came and went.

Most New Zealanders have little to do with titled people and this proved something of a problem when the United Kingdom High Commissioner, Sir Harry Battersby, adopted the practice of calling in at the office on Saturday mornings to keep himself up to date on events in Europe. We had been directed to address him as 'Sir Harry', but I used to feel that calling him by his Christian name was not only a gross familiarity but that our conversations were grotesque. However orders were orders, so I said 'Yes, Sir Harry' and 'No, Sir Harry' with every second breath, barely holding back a rising hysteria similar to the one the Bellamy waiters used to provoke in me.

More uniforms were becoming visible in the streets and they were not at all smart. Lemon squeezer hats, black clumsy boots and stovepipe trousers were like remnants from the Great War. All the glamour appeared reserved for the aircrews in their fore-and-aft hats with the white flash.

It was brought home to me about this time that there was a war on when entering a bar we ordered drinks which normally took a little time to prepare. It was too much for the barmaid, who had spent all Saturday filling Army throats; she lost her temper and we walked out. The same night we had our first confrontation with the Army as we defended a stairway at a twenty-first party against gate-crashers but fortunately they were too drunk to give us much trouble.

Standing in Lambton Quay with people all around me speculating when the next echelon would leave, I felt bursting with the information locked inside me. So much of it was bad. Coventry had been almost razed to the ground. Churchill had withheld the true facts because he feared civilian morale was not strong enough to want to continue the war and the populace might ask the Government to seek terms with the enemy. At times like this it was asking almost too much to go on remaining silent, but people were very good. Some suspected I had a strange job but no one pried, except the little telegraph boy from my former office. Our notice on the door proved too much for his curiosity one day and he entered our room, eyes widening as he recognised me; the news was all round my old habitat within the hour.

Many of our messages for onward transmission by cable were uplifted by elderly Post Office messengers. One night I was confronted by a poor devil who had a lugubrious face at the best of times. Close to tears, he recounted how he had lost one of our messages on his way back to the General Post Office. It was not particularly secret so we enciphered it again and sent away a very relieved man.

The missing envelope turned up next day, handed in by a member of the public.

The cipher staff were a mixed bunch. Of the original group that trained at the Navy Office, there were only four of us. John Hale, tall, witty, keen on yachting, would become a Spitfire pilot and win the DFC. Laurie Heath, Kilbirnie cricketer, would serve on radar in India. Ken Fish joined the artillery in the Pacific, and Bill Mart also went on to become a fighter pilot and win the DFC. Strangely, we would all survive the war, at least physically.

Initially we believed we would not be allowed into the Services but it was not long before John Hale began to rock the boat. He announced that he was going to join the Air Force come hell or high water and eventually got his way. Having released one of us, Berendsen could not prevent the rest from joining up, and by this time it was accepted that it would not be too difficult to train replacements. In this connection putting a message into cipher undisturbed in a quiet room was not difficult, but apparently very different for tired people in war-torn London. Virtually all inward messages were either mutilated in transit or in the making; it became a challenge to fill the gaps and we took risks at times but were never caught out.

Along with the others I enlisted as a pilot and studied navigation for some weeks in my spare time, so that it was a crashing disappointment one day to receive a bleak rejection notice stating that my right eye was slightly myopic. I had to look up the dictionary to find that this meant light rays focussed in front of my retina instead of on it, but more about that later.

The Navy then came up with Scheme B, whereby anyone with University Entrance could enlist as a prospective sub-lieutenant, so off I went to enrol. Papers had to be filled in which required an employer's signature. The day before applications closed my boss and the Commercial Manager, both ex-Army, talked me out of applying. They reasoned that there was too much class distinction in the Royal Navy and that as a New Zealander I would get nowhere. They were not entirely wrong, but in retrospect it was ludicrous. I was not seeking to carve out a career.

Shortly afterwards I was picked up in the first conscription ballot for the Army and although I was quite pleased about this there were to be times later when it was annoying to be called a conscript and also to have it entered in my paybook. I often felt like pointing out that I had volunteered for the Air Force but what was the use? In the event I was to survive whereas all my contemporaries at the tennis club who enlisted in the Air Force did not.

On my last day at the cipher section Berendsen made a formal presentation and next morning I reported to Buckle Street Army Barracks. Although early in the day, some were already intoxicated and one or two could barely stand up, but good humour prevailed; in fact it was hilarious. One young man was accompanied by his girlfriend, or perhaps she brought him. I listened to her telling a doctor that he was very delicate and would never stand up to Army life. The doctor kept a straight face and listened politely but what a wimp the guy must have been; he didn't open his mouth. Perhaps she was successful because I never saw him again.

There was an out for me had I elected to take it; my left arm had been fractured more than once and the doctors voiced their doubts but after my repeated assurances that it was perfectly all right they arranged an X-ray. The results were satisfactory and a week later I marched from the barracks to the Wellington railway station en route to Trentham Camp. We were a motley mob carrying empty kitbags into which our civilian clothes would go once we were kitted out. Again, some were half drunk and walking parallel with us on the footpath a sodden harpie kept pace shouting, 'Conscripts, conscripts, you bloody conscripts,' but she got back as good as she gave, perhaps more.

One military camp is like another, but for sheer ugliness and cold Trentham would have been hard to beat that winter of June 1941. The thin palliasses we filled with straw did little to insulate us against the cold, and although we spread newspapers under them and covered ourselves with greatcoats it made little difference.

On the first day we filed through an orderly room where questioning began: age, educational qualifications, occupation, who was your last employer? Without thinking, or perhaps wanting to impress, I said, 'The Prime Minister.'

The Sergeant looked hard at me for a moment, then said quietly, 'Because of your educational standard you'll be put into the special training corps for NCOs and future commissioned officers.'

As I considered myself officer material (who doesn't?) I left well satisfied with the interview. What the Sergeant didn't say, at least in my presence, was, 'Here's another smart bastard.' When the list of fatigues appeared my name was at the top to clean the lavatories; whereas others moved off after one day I had the job for a week.

I had previously heard the lavatories referred to as Houses of Parliament and as I cleaned there was plenty of time to reflect that from Prime Minister's Department on the hill to Trentham Camp latrines was hardly moving up. In fact I was beginning again at the bottom. From there one graduated to peeling potatoes under the charge of an old-timer who looked like a potato himself. There was a piece of equipment which supposedly peeled the spuds by friction but wasted fifty percent of their bulk and produced leprous-looking marbles. However, sitting on a sack of potatoes in the sun, it was not too bad a job. Next step up was to the cookhouse where a stint of fourteen hours washing and stacking greasy tin plates without the benefit of detergents was guaranteed to reduce one almost to tears.

The medical and dental treatments had their moments because everything was performed at battalion strength. Standing in a queue approaching a line of medical orderlies and doctors I was unprepared for swab, scratch, swab, hypodermic needle, swab, again the needle, swab, continuing unsteadily with cold perspiration breaking out towards the exit where the Sergeant Major was separating the men from the boys.

'Not feeling too good lad?' He grasped my shoulder and turned me slightly to the right. I nodded mutely.

'Go in there and lie down on the floor till you come right.'

As the room slowly revolved around me I joined scores lying prone on the floor.

Dental treatment, if not so severe, was certainly more colourful.

'Your teeth don't look too bad, I'll just give them a clean.' His genial manner fooled me. At the end there was dental scale and blood everywhere.

'Sorry old man,' he was still smiling, 'But I have so many outside to get through.'

Somebody should have had a go at him, the butcher. As I stumbled out the door my bloodstained shirt brought grimaces in the waiting queues. Next day, however, it was the injections which bothered most until the sergeant drilling us woke to our predicament, apologised and let us stand easy. It was the only apology I ever received in the Army and I value it because, my God, we earned some.

Shooting on the rifle ranges it quickly became obvious that the average Kiwi could not hit a haystack at fifty yards and the instructors were in a fury. I could hear their abuse as they came down the line but when they reached me I discovered that life was full of surprises. I had shot a few rabbits as a boy and as a school cadet fired away a few rounds, but was quite unprepared for the range results when the figures appeared on the notice board. There I was, right at the top of the list. It was the same in the snap-shooting where I had put all five shots through an area equal to that of a fifty-cent piece. 'You should frame this and give it to your girlfriend,' said the delighted sergeant, handing me the punctured disc. But the Air Force had turned me down because the same eye did not measure up to their requirements. Who was fooling whom? But it was no fluke and they put me in the battalion shooting team where I continued to surprise myself.

One evening was devoted to night manoeuvres and we thought it was going to be a lark. It was, but not quite in the way imagined. There are few nights when it is totally dark but this was one of them. We were crawling on our bellies across a paddock in extended order when there was a terrified snort, a series of whinnies, thudding hooves, startled shouts and horrific blasphemies. It was not a large paddock and there were an awful lot of us — about a battalion — and how someone did not get injured I'll never know. We didn't wait for our orders but took to our scrapers, completely routed.

In the absence of reading material at night there was time occasionally to ruminate and it was becoming abundantly clear to me that there was no beauty in the military machine. Bayonets, barbed wire and explosions were threatening and the human body fragile. The system was explicitly designed to erase personality, eliminate intelligence and to mould us into automatons. Every night we spent hours cleaning brass buttons and equipment. It occupied almost all spare time and a night's leave in town had to be equated with reprisals in the morning. You were not supposed to win and I imagine the majority understood this but a few did not. After working for hours with Brasso and cleaning rags, they took to bed with them under the blankets anything with brass attached. Others, perhaps more cunning, coated the brass with a girlfriend's nail polish, an idea which had some merit.

Then there was the awful close intimacy with people with whom one had nothing in common, except the situation we found ourselves in. Later, friendships would develop, but in the beginning what closeness could there be between a tennis-playing clerk and a hill-country shepherd ten years his senior, or the older salesman who nightly kept the hut aghast at reports on the condition of his immovable bowels? Seven, eight, ten days we waited.

On the main parade ground we stood to attention one morning while out in the centre the final rites of a court martial were enacted. As the hat was ripped to the ground from the head of the small figure, and the buttons torn from his tunic, it was like witnessing the rape of a man's honour and I felt soiled. If the incident was publicly staged for our edification it missed its target, just as those officers did, violating one's person by thrusting their faces to within six inches of one's mouth shouting, 'Did you shave this morning soldier?' As one stared back at the little yellow flecks in their eyes, it was difficult not to retort, 'Yes, you stupid bastard, in cold water with a blunt razor, along with a thousand others!'

My girlfriend visited the camp and I could barely wait for her arrival but it was not a good idea; her femininity increased the feeling of entrapment and her departure left a deep depression. We were able to get out of camp on alternate weekends but could never rid ourselves of its encompassment no matter how we tried. Then influenza struck the camp and to make up the numbers I was sent on final leave with a draft due to leave the country. After saying goodbyes to family in the South Island thoughts were grim; wartime farewells possess a unique essence of finality and parting with my girlfriend was prolonged to the last moment. Next day before falling into marching order I stood in a queue to telephone, but what could one say?

The band played as we marched down Camp Road for the last time and there was a surprising degree of formality as former instructors stood to attention in salute as we went by. No longer were we rookies to be bawled at and ridiculed but a New Zealand Contingent leaving for the war zone and apparently warranting respect.

We disembarked from the troop train at Wellington Station and marched to Pipitea Wharf where the *Aquitania* was waiting, all 47 000 tons of her, former pride of the Cunard Line. There were seven thousand in our ranks and not a single friend. Never have I felt so lonely. Towards evening we pulled away, steaming slowly, black smoke pouring from four black funnels, and as darkness enveloped us at Pencarrow Head I stood alone at the stern leaning against the long barrel of the eight-inch gun, looking back.

Chapter 2

Settling In

Cairo

First day out came a big surprise when unexpected mail contained a letter from my girlfriend Claudia. It lifted morale tremendously, being tangible evidence that someone cared. It must have been some document; the voyage lasted five weeks and every day at some stage I extracted it from a breast pocket and slowly read again each phrase, seeking fresh nuances as yogi-like I withdrew from my immediate sphere.

South of the Great Australian Bight in grey seas, two large ships joined us, the *Queen Mary* and *Queen Elizabeth*, both packed with Australian troops. Along with the escorting cruiser they made a fine sight and we felt flattered to be part of such grand company. The huge seas washed

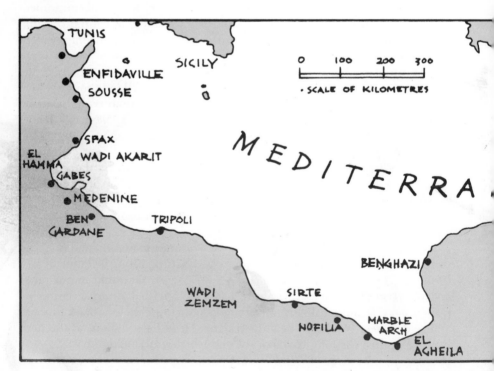

right over their plunging bows, sending sheets of spray even over their towering bridges. Later in calmer seas they loomed at dusk like broad castles in line astern, for we were the slowest ship and led the way, or in the moonlight to port ploughed steadily abreast while I stood guard duty watching for enemy periscopes.

Because of the nature of the convoy and the importance of these ships as carriers we had been warned not to sit on the side rails and assured that if anyone fell overboard the ship would not stop because it could be put at risk. It was surprising therefore to see the lengths to which some people went to secure their own ends. Hammocks had already been strung on all available deck space but some persisted in hanging more on the extremities. I could not bear to watch them as they swung outwards with the ship's roll, suspended over the sea. Hell! You can so easily fall out of a hammock three feet off the ground in your own backyard, trying to get into it.

We spent three days off the port of Fremantle, too big to get close to shore, but a determined few in ways known only to them secreted themselves in lighters replenishing our water supplies. Feted in Perth they arrived back drunk as skunks to be arrested by the guards as they came in over the rails. Although threatened with all kinds of dire punishments more elected to take French leave and suffered the same consequences.

We put into Trincomalee where we were again not allowed ashore but

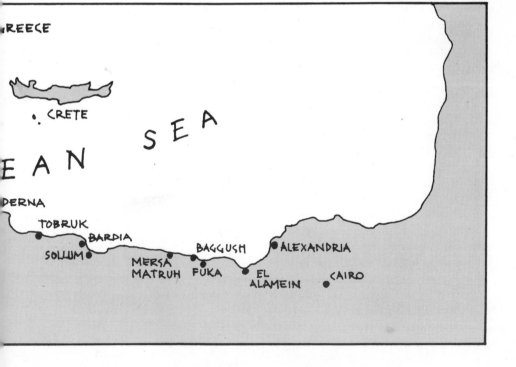

watched with interest a boat come down the tideway; a European in a white pith helmet and a coloured crew lent an exotic touch and made me think of Somerset Maugham.

In the Indian Ocean we showered under a heavy downpour while lightning flashed, and when the ship's crew played fire hoses into a narrow canvas contraption they had set up, we plunged for four strokes amidst the vaccination scabs floating there like giant tea leaves.

We entered the Gulf of Aden and sailed up the Red Sea to anchor in the Gulf of Suez while the *Queens* went on ahead to unload their cargoes. The red mountainous ranges in the light of the setting sun looked biblical in aspect but most of us were too weary of shipboard life to be interested and longed only to get ashore.

Three days later we arrived at Tewfik at the entrance to the Suez Canal. With its milky topaz water and flat desert stretching away in all directions it had an almost stunning effect on us after watching the moving sea. We disembarked to trudge across dusty desert with no food and no blankets and the instruction to find oneself a tent and park the body. I could not sleep that first night, missing the motion of the ship, so lay under the stars and watched the probing searchlights pencil the skies until dawn.

In the morning they rounded us up like sheep to make an incredibly dreary, hot train journey across white desert. There were endless long halts when I think we first began to develop that infinite patience which would be required if we were to survive the years which lay ahead of us and keep our sanity. It was during these stops that idiots, despite warnings about drinking contaminated water, traded for it with Arab urchins appearing from distant buildings with earthernware pitchers. The sergeant drew his pistol and threatened 'to shoot the little bastards' but he was wasting his time.

In the late afternoon we circled the outskirts of Cairo and the tall turrets of the Citadel and reached Maadi Station about dusk where tired eyes stared in disbelief at a Kiwi horseman riding an Arab stallion with the biggest genitals we had ever seen. The Camp proved to be a dusty march a league or so away and we made it in the dark.

At first sight Maadi Camp was a novelty to us. Towards Cairo we could see the tall towers of the Citadel, and to the west the pyramids across the Nile some miles away. If there is a pastel shade of grey-yellow then that predominated, but the desert acted like a screen onto which lights are played. In the mornings these were sometimes pink or salmon, in the afternoon a blinding white, and tinted gold at sunset. Coming from a shower after lunch and before siesta, already sweating again, able to open only one eye in a squint against the glare, we placed the towel over our heads like the hood of a burnous.

Set in open desert the large huts, which could accommodate a platoon, were well dispersed for air raids. They were of block construction to about chest height; above that I could never make up my mind whether the material fastened to the wooden frames was painted hessian or just plain paper, but whatever it was it did the job. Unglassed windows ran along the walls, with wooden shutters which were never closed except during dust storms, and the huts were light and airy. A low verandah ran along the front. Scattered about us were water towers and ablution blocks. (I liked the phrase 'ablution block', having never heard it until I joined the Army.) There were dobe-walled latrines, each with a basin outside filled with dark, strong-smelling Jeyes Fluid into which we thrust our hands, recreation huts — the NAAFI, the YMCA and Lowry Hut — tarsealed roads running black through the sand, and Shafto's scrim-covered cinema, notable for the number of times the projector broke down.

Assembled in the open-air cinema next morning we were briefed on hygiene and the rigours of 'Gyppo tummy', how to conduct ourselves with the Egyptians, and not to think that because Egyptian men walked hand in hand occasionally they were queers. The perils of the Berket, the red-light district, and the risk of venereal disease were emphasised. We were virtually commanded to visit the Museum of Hygiene on our first visit to Cairo.

The food was deadly and that's praising it. I did not smoke but occasionally before going into the mess room for lunch would take a few drags of an issue cigarette to kill my appetite. Those in authority naturally were doing their best but some of our supplies must have been dependent on shipping and it showed. There was also very limited equipment for training and a sneaking suspicion that using broomsticks in lieu of weapons was only

Divisional Signals in Maadi, Egypt, with equipment brought out from Greece.
Alexander Turnbull Library

just being avoided. We were not very far from having our backs to the wall. We had the basics but little more, and stragglers from Crete still trickling in reminded us of past defeats. Notwithstanding this, morale was particularly high. We knew that the New Zealand Division had acquitted itself well even if it had had to turn tail, and the easy bearing and confidence of the sergeants who had fought there impressed us enormously. One seemed vaguely familiar, but so much had he changed it took me a fortnight to realise he had been in the cipher training group at the Navy Office in 1938.

We performed most of our training early in the day and again after siesta. Late one afternoon we were sitting in little groups under the verandahs of the huts dismantling and assembling Bren guns. It was all fairly relaxed and some were almost snoozing when there was a hell of a sharp crack and a shell went down our group from the adjacent verandah! Somebody had not only put a live shell in a Boyes anti-tank rifle but had cocked and fired it. It's a wonder nobody got perforated.

We threw grenades and in the gas chamber I tried to beat the system by closing my eyes and holding my breath but did not make it and came out like the others, coughing and weeping. Then we went in again wearing gasmasks. The gasmasks were an abomination especially when we route-marched at night when they became as hot as hell. There must have been real concern about their being required, judging by the way we trained. Clad in gas capes on manoeuvres, we were sprayed by aircraft flying just above our heads.

The bed bugs were a pest. Reputedly introduced to Maadi Camp by 18 Battalion after a tour of duty at the British Kasr-el-nil barracks in Cairo, they hid in the cane chairs in the recreation huts. Their favourite habitat, however, was the crevices between our bed boards which we frequently upended and beat on the floor while neighbours in adjacent beds, if temporarily free from bugs, watched in amusement. Horrible things, they left welts and always seemed full of our blood.

It never rained and at dusk the setting sun would hang like a golden disc on the horizon, sharply etching in black the three main pyramids. While one watched it would quickly disappear downwards like some stage prop; too artificial to be real. At ten o'clock every night bugles in sad sequence sounded the Last Post in the Northern, Southern, and Central Infantry Commands as the lights went out.

The first day's leave in Cairo was a bewildering experience. Between the Camp and Cairo was a large collection of buildings and streets completely deserted, called the Dead City. Comprising mainly tombs, it was out of bounds to us except on duty in Army transport, for the road led through it. It was a weird experience to emerge into the foul-smelling, busy markets.

Going on leave, one boarded any old green bus to rattle along under beautiful tall flame-coloured trees of the little township of Maadi, between comfortable homes of Europeans, where the houses hid dappled in shade and native gardeners swept dry lawns with bamboo rakes. I looked with interest at the black-clad women walking barefooted and carrying huge loads of firewood or water vessels upon their heads. What wonderful carriage they had. From Maadi we went by train to Babel-uk Station, to walk the last leg into town to the New Zealand Club, past the stinking poultry shop and the café where the hookah smokers gathered and the smell of Turkish tobacco and dung hung heavy in the air.

In the city, the shoeshine boys plagued merry hell out of us, importuning to clean and polish our boots. We brushed them away like flies, and not without difficulty. We realised only later that our white knees gave us away as being new chums. A couple of years later and varnished dark by the sun, I noted that the pink-and-white beefiness of reinforcements freshly arrived from New Zealand, when measured against our lean brown bodies, would arouse slight repugnance; we would watch the shoeshine boys torment them while ignoring us.

We visited the Museum of Hygiene first as directed. Its situation on the outskirts of the Dead City made getting there educational, but inside was a revelation. Mounted on the walls of one room were rows and rows of penises, all in a state of erection. They were all shapes and sizes, in ghastly coloured wax or something similar, and bore hideous red growths depicting the ravages of syphilis and gonorrhoea in horrible Technicolour. It was enough to frighten us immediately, and as for the several bright-eyed Waafs and nurses gazing at them . . . surely it was sufficient to cause permanent frigidity?

Later in the day we went into the brothel area. Everybody did. It was the pièce de résistance and well worth the visit, even if we were only looking and not buying. Besides, we had the vision of the Museum freshly etched in our minds. The area was apparently out of bounds to troops, but nobody, including officialdom, seemed to mind. In the first house I was shocked and slightly outraged to see a passing soldier casually clutch the crutch of a neat young woman in a white trouser-suit, but she did not appear to mind.

Susceptibilities were soon blunted in the second dwelling we entered. Here a girl was nursing an adult dwarf on her lap. As we arrived she unbuttoned his fly and began to fondle his small penis. They both thought it a huge joke. Most of the women stood around in slips or underwear. Not all were young and not all were particularly attractive. Those that were better looking spoiled their looks like others with too much eye-shadow. You had to watch the young ones and guard your back. Three or four of them, surely not older than fifteen, would occasionally leap astride an Australian airman dead drunk asleep in a chair and mimic the sexual act, while their companions coming silently up behind us would viciously swing a stiff palm upwards between our legs. We moved from place to place looking curiously at these women and the odd military client but it finally became too sordid when an attendant passed carrying a basin of Condy's fluid in which floated used condoms. Outside in the street we were immediately surrounded by little boys wanting to sell us 'feelthy pictures'.

'You sleep with my sister? Very clean, very sweet, very nice,' came from the mouths of nine-year-olds.

'You wanna see exhibition zig-a-zig? See woman and donkey?' We washed the taste away with cool beers at tables under gaily coloured umbrellas in an open air café garden.

About this time an incident at the New Zealand Club was being given a great airing. Apparently two drunken soldiers returning to the Club had goosed two New Zealand women leaving the front entrance and there was hell to pay because they were supposedly senior officers' wives. Although this was bad, there could have been underlying reasons, even if the perpetrators were unaware of them. We were subjected to indignities in the Army, enjoyed few privileges and were placed on a lower social scale than officers. In town we encountered every kind of depravity and the Tuis and Waacs could all have stayed at home as far as we were concerned. Rumour had it that below the rank of Major, in the early days, one stood little chance of meeting them socially and underneath our perhaps placid-looking exteriors resentment simmered. The gulf was so wide that I recall later in Italy meeting an approaching uniformed countrywoman and passing her by with eyes front and stony face despite the fact that we were the only pedestrians in the street. The act of these two goons had to be studied in this context.

Sometimes instead of going into town we stopped off at the Maadi tent which was within walking distance, or bludged a ride from Army transport. One was never turned down. The tent was a huge semi-permanent marquee served by European volunteers living in Maadi and a splendid job they did for us. Nestling underneath tall trees adjacent to the swimming pool built by New Zealand troops, it was a delightful oasis. We took every opportunity to swim but never sunbathed for more than ten minutes. Who wanted to sunbathe in Egypt anyway? Shade was what we sought.

There were nights when we performed night picket duty on the water towers which I found an awful bore. I was never quite sure what I was guarding against, but suppose someone could have poisoned the water if it was left unattended. Mounting the formal guard down by the orderly rooms on the main camp road was another chore. Other evenings I walked with a new friend, Don, to one of the recreation huts where we would have supper consisting of a couple of sweet cakes and a cup of tea. I would inveigle him up on to the stage to play the piano to me. Don was small, with a long, sensitive face and was a good pianist. He was hardly the stuff for a blood-and-guts infantryman but underneath was apparently tough and durable like the rest of us. I would sit back and nibble and sip, letting his music drift over me. He had a light concert touch and for some reason, perhaps because of our stark surrounds with not a blade of grass about, his music always held a particular sweetness.

18

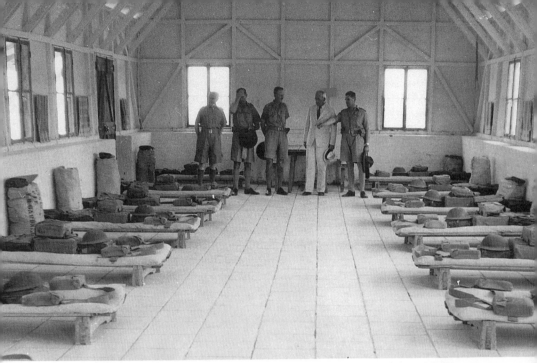

Interior of military hut, Maadi Camp, showing Prime Minister's visit to Middle East. *Alexander Turnbull Library*

As a change from going into Cairo, one day another mate and I boarded the train at Maadi and travelled six miles down the line in the opposite direction to a town called Helwan. Here was one of our main hospitals, a picturesque Chinese garden, and a very fine British canteen where it was said you could eat marvellous pork sausages — tinned, of course. Heavens knows why, but we all had a craving for sausages which were not available in the camp or in the city — at least not the type of sausage we were used to eating in New Zealand. Of such trivia our life was made up, but the sausages along with fried eggs and tomatoes dripping in their own gravy tasted out of this world.

Wandering along at a leisurely pace at peace with myself after the sausages I must have become detached from Len and realised I was alone in an almost deserted street, although there was a European woman about four hundred yards ahead of me. It was then a very large Egyptian in galabieh and sandals, powerfully muscled, stepped out from nowhere, barred my way and demanded money. To say that I was startled would be no exaggeration, but I was also furious at the fear he caused to swell inside me; I was a soldier, was I not? We were not allowed to carry weapons out of camp; he was twice my size, and they were supposed to be handy with the knife. (I knew that very well because my bedmate a week earlier had been picked up unconscious in Cairo with a knife through his lung and his paybook missing. Paybooks could fetch a sizable sum as they were useful for identification and presumably sought by the enemy.) I continued advancing, aware that for some reason the woman ahead had stopped and was looking back. He did not know this. Perhaps he had already tried it on her? With these thoughts in mind and without changing step, heart hammering, I sailed right up to him muttering between clenched teeth and looked him straight in the eyes, 'Go to hell you bloody bastard,' until almost breast to breast somehow I found I had passed him. I did not look back, which was perhaps foolish, but it seemed over before it had happened. It was possible, I thought, that the woman may have been a deterrent. The dark streets of Cairo at night were one thing, but fancy being accosted in broad daylight in Helwan! Up until that time I had always found the fellaheen extremely subservient, but this chap was no suppliant simply begging. This bloke had been full of menace and scared hell out of me.

Further along the street with time to calm down I found myself overhauling a Maori as he came abreast of another countryman leaning against a fence. The latter with a deadpan face said to him, 'Good day, native.' After my little shock it did me good. As a South Islander I had had very little to do with Maoris but this little incident typified their capacity to laugh at themselves. I had the greatest admiration for them. During bayonet practice they would assume postures of the greatest ferocity, faces screwed in hideous grimace, and then with wide grins turn the whole exercise into pure burlesque. We had several of them in our hut in Maadi of whom I have fond memories.

I found myself back in Helwan sooner than anticipated. There was a large prisoner-of-war camp in the vicinity and we were detailed to undertake guard duties for a period. What a dump it was, and what a place to spend your days. Just barbed wire, tents, watch towers and dirty sand. It had the faint, sickly-sour smell associated with all camps in the Middle East; a composite of dried sweat, chlorine and septic tank on the blink. Within two days I was stricken with Gyppo tummy; a combination of nausea and diarrhoea which reduced one to crawling on hands and knees to the latrine every five or ten minutes.

As we recovered, a cheerful young Arab boy brightened our days, bringing with him on the back of a donkey bottles of soft drink wrapped in ice in dripping sacks. Those poor donkeys, with such fragile-looking legs and the heavy loads they carried; they had every right to bray, which they did at times with great gusto. The boy spent a great deal of time with us then one day some fool decided to give him a bath. He fought frantically, shrieking his protests, and as the rags came off revealing pink scars on his sticks of legs I felt ashamed. It was a stupid thing to do and I took no part. He never quite trusted us after that, always stopping on the periphery of our little camp to shout, 'No bath, no bath?', coming forward only after repeated assurances that there would be none.

A good many weapons had had to be abandoned in Greece and Crete, so we were issued with captured Italian rifles and ammunition: further confirmation of our bad supply position. They were unreliable, perhaps even dangerous, and by banging the butt on the ground they could be discharged. It was therefore nerve-racking returning on the blackest night from a day's leave to hear the challenges ring out from the towers, 'Halt! Who goes there?', and to answer, 'Friend.' Back would come the reply, 'Advance, and be recognised.' Knowing that these particular rifles were pointed down in your direction and probably at your gut, you found that several such challenges were usually sufficient to sober you up. It was no play-acting; we were still new reinforcements and deadly serious, and a bullet in the stomach from a panicky guard was definitely a possibility.

I learned something about myself on that guard duty and the shocking effect discipline and brain-bashing can have on raw material. There were a few Germans in a separate compound; they were a surly bunch and we saw little of them — virtually only their heads, in fact, because of scrim placed around their wire. The Italians, by contrast, were in full view and everywhere. Dark-haired and brown as berries, they were short and sturdy. Most were attired only in shorts and sandshoes. They seemed a busy lot; I suppose they had to be, to stop going out of their minds in that place. They spent their days playing football and good at it they were too. They even had uniforms of a kind for each side: black shirts and white shirts, though we could never actually identify a particular side as they swapped the shirts and gear around for the big matches. They also spent hours doing fancy marching in time to their own singing and really catchy stuff it was. From the top of my tall tower I looked down and enjoyed the entertainment. Sometimes as individuals came to urinate at the pipe beneath my tower on the other side of the wire, our eyes would meet when they looked up. Poor devils, I felt sorry for them.

There was an inner wall and an outer wall of wire, and in between guards patrolled in pairs. Each compound was separated in that manner. We were the outer guards and the tall towers were outside the camp, as were our own tents. We had no contact with the inner guards and from a security aspect it all seemed very effective. At the foot of the towers were slit trenches, and in my innocence I sometimes wondered whether in the event of an air raid I would open fire from the tower or descend first to one of the slitties. Goodness me, how naive I was then.

Orders were that there must be no fraternisation and no communication between prisoners in one compound and those in an adjacent one, and these rules seemed generally to be observed. We had also been informed, quite explicitly, that no warning shots were to be fired. We must shoot to kill. One day, therefore, the sight of one group of prisoners facing a similar group in another compound drew my full attention. They looked my way and one standing slightly in advance of the others shouted something and made motions of throwing an article which appeared to be clothing over the wire into the other compound. I shook my head several times but he persisted. Both groups were staring at me now. They were about forty yards away, perhaps a little further. Again he motioned, at which

I raised the rifle, pulled back the bolt and held his head in my sights. If his arm had moved, and if that rifle was firing correctly, he would have died instantly. I knew how accurate I could be and never for a moment doubted I would miss. The two groups shook their fists while I held aim. They'd heard the bolt go back, knew the rifle was loaded, distrusted the damn things probably more than I did, and I obviously wasn't fooling. After shouted insults the groups began to break up and move away from the wire. The chap in front was also walking away. I lowered the rifle. Hell. I was pretty sure it was no plan for escape they wanted to pass — probably only an old pair of shorts. So what was happening to me? I had come close to killing that guy. So close I felt a little sick. There had been no thought involved except that they must not communicate: shoot to kill, if he throws, pull the trigger. The trouble was I was still a new boy, had never experienced the real thing. I was an automaton with my 'Yes sir, no sir, three bags full sir.' As an 'old dig' in later years, after being blooded, I'd have simply turned my back on them for an instant and let them get on with it, no doubt to have been rewarded with cheerful grins and a wave. Bloody war! I had plenty of time after that up on that tower to think about what I had come close to doing.

Signaller of Long Range Desert Group in touch with General Headquarters. Boyes anti-tank rifle behind him. *Alexander Turnbull Library*

Normally I enjoyed the solitude of the towers, both day and night. I enjoyed also a daily swim. Around us was the desert, but about a mile away was a cement factory and two large houses. Each possessed its own huge swimming pool and Don and I went there every day with our towels. One pool was particularly deep and looking down into its mossy green depths I sometimes wondered whether it was wholly man-made. Each pool was available on alternate days. In neither house did I ever see the owners, only the gardeners, but we were certainly grateful for the privilege. A swim once a day and a bottle of soft drink on the way back: we asked for no more.

It was too good to last, however. One morning we were recalled to Maadi Camp and that Saturday morning abomination, the Sergeant Major's formal parade. (Until our officers rebelled, that was.) It was an incredible ceremony. First, outside the huts our officer would inspect us and look down our rifle barrels. Next we would march by platoon into company formation until the full battalion was assembled on the main parade ground. There we would stand rigidly to attention while a pair of cadre staff sergeants goose-stepped again and again across our front. Yes, goose-stepped! Yet we were supposed to be fighting Nazism. Then the Sergeant Major would arrive like a Roman emperor and walk slowly between our ranks, to peer down barrels thrust out, admonishing, putting dozens of us on charges for not keeping our rifles clean. Surely, our officers argued, if the rifles were good enough for them they should be good enough for the Sergeant Major? Fortunately someone in authority agreed and there were no more parades of that nature. Whether this was a tradition in the British Army I am not sure. If it was, then it was something we could do without.

In my youth I had been given to understand that anything British stood for quality and so it was disappointing to find many of the British soldiers in Cairo were on the short side and horribly foul-mouthed. Every second word was the same four-letter one and wearying to listen to in a conversation. They were tough however, and awfully cheerful for no apparent reason. They could also carry a tune better than we could and it was painfully obvious that not only could the Kiwi not fly, neither could he sing. Not all British soldiers were small, however, as we realised later on meeting 51 Highland Division, and later still the bulky men of the First Army in Tunisia. The exceptions of course were the tall Guards regiments, but they cut no ice with us; any outfit that boasted how they moved to slit trenches in step under bombing at Tobruk revealed a mentality too awful to contemplate. In due course I learned to admire the King's Dragoon Guards, the Scots Greys and other regiments, but those were my first impressions in Cairo.

The British officers on the other hand obviously came from another planet and I think they thought so themselves. Tall and willowy, dressed in corduroys and sheepskin jackets, they wore silk cravats, suede desert boots and carried fly swats. Their drawling, high accents and bland assumption that we were socially inferior, of lesser intelligence and lacking formal schooling, aroused our bile. They had their good points and nobody doubted their courage individually, but there were times when listening to their persiflage through my headphones in what were extremely dangerous situations I felt impatient. This kind of nonsense for instance.

'I say Dennis old chap, would you please check the map reference you have just given me, over.'

'Why Nigel, it seems perfectly all right to me old chap, over.'

'Well Dennis old chap, either you are a very brave man or your sums are not good because it places you right in the middle of jolly old Jerry old chap, over.'

A somewhat longer pause, then back came an amended reference.

But the troops we really disliked were the British Military Police or Redcaps, called that because of their cap covers. Some of them were granite-faced thugs so brutal that Freyberg was obliged to enter into an arrangement with their Provost Marshal that offending New Zealanders should be detained by his sadists only long enough for New Zealand military police to arrive and make arrests. Had Freyberg not done this there would inevitably have been ugly scenes involving our units. I recall sitting on a lawn at the Heliopolis swimming pool watching two bathers heading towards the dressing room one day and making a bet with a companion that they were Redcaps. They reappeared dressed and I'd have won the bet if it had been accepted; they needed no uniforms for identification.

Infantry training was becoming monotonous and a notice inviting people to participate in a regimental signalling course in another part of the camp looked like an interesting diversion so we applied and were accepted. We spent the next three months either sitting on our bottoms at the Signal School receiving instruction, or out in one of the wadis at the back of the camp operating radio pack sets. We had three officers with us on the course, and it was interesting to notice that they were no better or no worse than the rest of us and actually fitted in quite well. This was to their credit, because it could not have been easy. We were not impressed by the capabilities of the No. 18 radio sets which had a very restricted range. They were also quite bulky and in an infantry attack would make one pretty conspicuous, especially with the antenna sticking up. One did not however dwell on the thought, 'sufficient unto the day' being largely our motto.

We completed the course in October, 1941, returning to the Central Infantry Command to find that in the interval most of our draft had departed 'up the blue' to join the Division at Baggush, a coastal oasis thirty miles east of Matruh. We wanted to join them but unless the Division were to become involved in action and suffer casualties, our chances meantime seemed only fair.

In the interim, Divisional Signals — who must have been wanting to build their numbers up — invited us to join their unit. This sounded more attractive than remaining in the infantry as cannon fodder; Div Sigs operated their own vans and armoured vehicles, where perhaps they were able to carry a few home comforts. On the other hand, we were not to know they went short on sleep. As infantrymen our chances of survival let alone emerging unscathed from this war could not be said to be good. Putting this to the coterie I knocked around with, and suggesting that Div Sigs would not be at the sharp end all the time as we would be in the infantry, I found them of the same mind. Only Vince elected to turn the offer down and as a consequence lost a leg very shortly afterwards and was invalided home.

So back we went to Signal School where, when attentions flagged, an Errol Flynn type interspersed morse transmissions with jingles about ladies of dubious virtue called Fifi and Lulu. Little did we guess that some day he would be Minister of Defence; there is no doubt that New Zealand possessed then an egalitarian society. Indeed, one of our other instructors was the son of the current Minister of Defence.

One day we were startled to hear that the Division had become involved in heavy fighting at Capuzzo and Sidi Rezegh and that the news was grim. They had succeeded in linking up with the beleaguered troops in Tobruk but in doing so had suffered very heavy casualties. Rumour had it that they had been cut to pieces and while this was an exaggeration there was no doubt that they had been badly mauled in the process; it was sobering to think that if we had not joined Div Sigs our first introduction to desert warfare would have been the holocaust of Sidi Rezegh, where our inexperience could certainly have lessened chances of survival.

Changing the guard at Helwan Prisoner of War Camp. *Alexander Turnbull Library*

From the road in front of the Signal School we watched long columns of infantry marching out as they emptied the Infantry Commands to replenish the depleted Division, thinking that there but for the Grace of God go we. As the Division was still in action it was a solemn sight to watch guys we knew trudging by; a feeling almost of having deserted them, but mixed with relief nevertheless.

Still not ready for us, Div Sigs offered leave. Six of us took off for Jerusalem, a popular trip at the time. We were standing at the Cairo Railway Station with time on our hands when one Ernie insisted he must start his leave with a visit to a brothel before we departed. Against our wishes he took off and just when we had given him up and were about to board the train he returned in a gharry, grinning and exuberant, jumping aboard at the last moment.

It was a long slow journey. Pressed against a Bedouin as we crossed over the Suez Canal I found his garlic-smelling breath almost too much for me. There were hours in the train across the Sinai Desert but it was picture-book stuff with palms and occasional glimpses of blue sea. Then the trees of Palestine, more interesting greenery and the temperature dropping all the time. In fact it became so cold that snow began to fall! Snow in Jerusalem? Yes, the first in twenty-five years. When we left the train it was ankle deep and still snowing.

We booked in at the Hotel Majestic. This was a bit of a misnomer, since it was more like a bed-and-breakfast joint but reasonably clean, except for the paper in the lavatory. Arab toilet facilities and Arab customs take some getting used to. I caught on, only just in time, but not Len! He came back, his usually droll face contorted in rage, swearing furiously.

'That paper in the box in the lavatory. Did you know it had been used?' he roared. I nodded, trying hard not to laugh.

Forewarned that there were too many notices in Jerusalem prohibiting entry to cafés and bars to 'other ranks', we entered a dressmaker's shop as signalmen and after some laughs one warrant officer I, two warrant officers II, and three sergeants emerged; a common practice for New Zealanders going on leave in Palestine at the time. I nearly blew our cover at dinner at couple of days later, realising only just in time that the puzzled British soldier having to repeat himself across the table was actually addressing me. There were times also when I thought the warrant officers in their cups came under close scrutiny from the real thing at adjacent tables, but we got by without incident.

Our favourite haunt was the brightly lit Tulip Bar, where we tried out all sorts of exotic drinks, emerging at closing time to lose our feet on the steep icy cobbled street, and continuing down some of the way flat on our backs. In our relaxed states we suffered no injury.

It was interesting to walk above the original Via Dolorosa and think of Christ carrying his cross; to stand in the Garden of Gethsemane amongst the gnarled olive trees. We climbed the Mount of Olives and gazed speculatively at the footprint on the floor of a tiny chapel where Christ supposedly ascended into Heaven; it looked like concrete to me. From there we gazed down into the open coffin of a Russian funeral cortege wending its way through the snow past the dark green cypress trees beneath us.

In the Mosque of Omar, the Dome of the Rock, before the Holy Sepulchre — it was an odd feeling to stand before that piece of history. The persistence of a priest who nagged at me to present him with my astrakhan gloves brought from New Zealand put me permanently off the Greek Orthodox Church.

On Christmas Day we visited Bethlehem where outside in the street I stopped startled at the sight of a man in robes approaching with a lamb in his arms; an exact replica of one of those biblical pictures I brought home from Sunday School as a child.

A visit to the Dead Sea via Jericho should have been interesting but proved dull, like the weather, the whole place being too much like a superphosphate plant. Standing later before the Jewish Wailing Wall I could not escape the fact that a visit to the Holy City was wasted on people like me; I was too ignorant to really appreciate it. On our last day we hired a large taxi and went all the way to the Sea of Galilee, visiting Nazareth, Jacob's Well, and the cities of Tel Aviv and Haifa. Next morning we left for Cairo.

Chapter 3

Before the Storm

Syria — Palestine — Mersa Matruh

In the desert the fighting had begun to taper off and both sides had gone into one of those recesses where activity on a wide scale diminished; as the BBC used to say in its news bulletins: 'activity in the Western Desert over the last twenty-four hours has been confined to routine patrols.' This summary of the situation did not always go down well with troops who had just 'had the shit shelled out of them!'

Suddenly, routine was broken by the unexpected arrival of the Division, which had been pulled out of the line for rest and refit before proceeding to Syria. Well, that was a turn-up! We wondered whether our little group was ever going to see any action. We had arrived in Egypt in July 1941; it was now January 1942 and we had not got past Sig school. All we had seen were a few bombs dropped on Cairo, whereas many of our contemporaries who came overseas with us were already dead. The fighting had finished in Syria, the Australians had attended to that. Still, it might be interesting. But *Syria?*

Maadi Camp not only bulged at the seams but every bar and dance-hall in Cairo was packed with Kiwis. The latter expression tagged on us by the British was one which for some reason I disliked. Perhaps it was the reminder of boot polish? The Division's headwear differed from ours. They wore sun helmets, whereas we still had our lemon-squeezers identifying us as base wallahs. During their stay, therefore, we kept a low profile.

The Division was gone as quickly as it had arrived. The camp became quiet and empty, boredom set in, and at every opportunity we hitchhiked into Cairo without even bothering about leave passes. Nobody cared. Even the instructors at the school seemed affected with the same lethargy so that when orders arrived to pack our gear and get ready to join the Division we could not get away quickly enough.

It was odd, retracing our steps through the Sinai Desert into Palestine, where Ernie signalled our arrival in Tel Aviv by immediately persisting in taking us on a brothel trip. However our taxi driver was obviously frightened of being picked up by the authorities who were clamping down on prostitution. We sat in the darkened taxi talking in hushed voices while he and Ernie visited one substantial house after another without success. It was like driving around Remuera on a dark night, a feeling akin to being in a pub after legal hours, and after the strident, colourful and unrestrained bawdiness of the Berket area in Cairo, it struck wrong notes. Finally, at the driver's insistence and to Ernie's utter disgust, the trip was aborted. The driver virtually pushed us out of the cab and made off, obviously relieved to be rid of us.

Ernie, with his fair hair, blue eyes and laughter, was one of the healthiest extroverts one could meet and frank about his sexual urges. Some years later I was pleasantly surprised to hear his unmistakable voice again as down the gangway of the Lyttelton ferry came an affluent-looking Ernie, leading his bride by the hand. Observing her rather refined face as he introduced her, I thought that surely she must be in for some interesting experiences and at the very least, a lot of laughs.

We moved into a transit camp at Kefar Vitkin by the sea. It was a pleasant place with salmon-coloured soil, citrus trees, and Israeli girls with the longest of sun-tanned legs. They wore sleeveless blouses and very short shorts of bloomer-like design and as they worked in the fields they made a gorgeous change from the prematurely aged Egyptian women in their black shapeless neck-to-ankle garments and bare feet. We never tired of gazing at them but as they were usually in the company of Israeli men we made no approaches.

The weather was kind and perhaps the Army forgot about us for a little while because the days gradually merged into weeks. We did not mind. It was nice to lie naked on the beach engaged in lazy gossip, or stand on the outskirts of the village watching a children's festival, all the children dressed in white dresses and garlanded with flowers. The Israelis treated us with great courtesy. We were fighting their persecutors. Our little group was perhaps a little tardy in getting there but we were on our way and they were not to know otherwise. In Tel Aviv they stood aside in the bus queues, beckoning us forward. We received smiles everywhere we went and it was good to feel the return of self-esteem.

One day an incident occurred of which I am not particularly proud. Four of us had wandered down the beach away from the camp one morning, carrying towels. Perhaps we had a swim in mind. It was a beautiful day with no wind and the sea sparkled. Two camels were kneeling in the sea facing in to the beach, wavelets lapping them while their owners standing in the shallows poured basins of water over them. I'd always associated camels with sandy deserts, not delightful sandy beaches, but there they were, camels having a paddle in the sea.

'Saeeda,' we said to the men, who replied in kind.

I don't know how far we walked. When you are accustomed to reeling off anything between twelve and twenty miles at frequent intervals you don't take note of it, especially if you happen to be enjoying yourself. Steps which led up a cliff face looked interesting, so we climbed them to emerge in a small courtyard at the top. It belonged to a café at the end of a village street. From the beach it had not been visible and was a pleasant surprise.

We sat in the sun looking down at the sea and drank wine. Two Australians arrived and sat down with us. About an hour later and several wines, it transpired they knew a café in the village where there was beer available. What were we waiting for?

Beer on top of wine is not a good combination, especially if one starts drinking early in the day under hot sun and omits to have lunch. We must have stayed some time because it was now late afternoon. At one stage I stood in the open doorway while a donkey cart passed by. One of our new Australian friends was underneath the donkey, looking my way. His arms were around its neck and his legs were clasped about its middle. I've often wondered how he finally got out of that embrace. Did the donkey stop or did he finally fall off? How did he dodge the wheels? He must have been almost comatose; I know I was.

Soon we were looking for a bus to take us back to camp. The first one we boarded apparently went in the wrong direction and so did most of the wine and beer I had consumed. Horribly aware of the occupant in the adjacent seat shrinking away, I used my towel to mop up. Later, still feeling very ill, I lay in grass at the roadside, aware that I was in Palestine but knowing little else.

Another bus. The right one this time. It was early summer's evening and my companions were still drinking. They passed the bottle to me about a third full and I promptly threw it through the half-open window, much to their disgust. Aware of the disapproving glances of the civilian passengers and hiding behind a scowl I grimly stayed upright with the aid of the bus strap until we reached the camp.

Our accommodation was nothing fancy, just a tent and blankets for sleeping on the sandy soil. Next morning I thought for a moment I was experiencing a bout of the DTs but the great hairy tarantula on the six-inch strip of sand between my groundsheet and my neighbour's was no illusion and had me frenziedly hammering it with a boot. I ground the great loathsome thing to pulp, not without some difficulty because the sand was so soft. I was dry, very dry, so took several long swigs of sweet red wine from a bottle alongside.

'I'll have some of that,' said Eric, who had sat up to watch my struggle with the tarantula. Grasping the bottle he held it up against the bright morning sunlight shining in through the open fly of the tent.

'Gawd,' he said disgustedly. 'Did you drink that?'

He passed it back.

Taking a look inside I found the top three inches of the contents black with bugs, midges and small beetles. What might in earlier days have made me puke had surprisingly little effect. I felt good: after all, it was a survive-or-perish lifestyle we were pursuing.

But our glorious freedom was coming to an end. More troops had been coming into the camp daily from Egypt and there were now enough of us to fill a train. One night we all moved off in boxcars on the final leg into Syria. There was insufficient room sitting on the floor to stretch our legs out fully, so it was a matter of placing them either over or under somebody else's legs, but in army style we were companionable, leaning on each other and reasonably comfortable. Put the same number of civilians in the same boxcar and there would have been hell to pay. We were warm, had water in our waterbottles and our bellies were full. All through the night we jolted along, taking turns to sit by the open sliding door, hang our legs out or relieve ourselves. As we rattled down some of the descents myriads of fireflies rose from grass bordering the line like sparks from our wheels. It was a memorable experience.

In daylight — or perhaps it was the next afternoon — we stopped for the engine to take on water and four of us bludged a ride on the footplate with the good-natured crew. As the huge engine thundered and shook down steep curving gradients, embankments flashing by, I should have been frightened out of my wits but the adrenalin was flowing. We were indeed travelling very fast. Too fast. The weight of boxcars full of troops behind us meant we were virtually out of control and if we had left the line there would have been a murderous pile-up. My mates and I were shovelling coal furiously into the roaring firebox, clutching at any handhold to prevent being flung off as we swayed and lurched from side to side. The grinning train crew, entering into the spirit of the thing and spurred on by our whoops, left us to get on with it.

At the end of the line, at least for that day, was Damascus. As we approached the famous place, claimed to be the oldest continuously inhabited city in the world, I thought of Damascus blades and the incongruity of someone from Dunedin arriving in this manner. My hand was on the whistle lanyard, waking the dead and putting the pigeons — or was it swallows? — to flight. Later, sitting on our gear in front of the station in the sun, with our pith helmets, brown skins, shorts and ankle puttees, I thought we matched the scene. We walked down the street called Strait and later in a gharry on our way to visit the Blue Mosque conducted the usual debate as to whether we should put the driver between the shafts and take the miserable skinny horse in with us.

Next day on the final leg we stopped at Riyaq. Learning there was going to be a lengthy delay, we went for a walk through the town, stopping outside what I thought was a dancehall. Military police at the door were engaged in some kind of altercation with a bunch of turbanned Sikhs from an Indian unit. They were being prevented from entering by the Redcaps but we were waved inside. I had been slow to catch on. It was a military brothel, with a few bored-looking girls sitting around. It was even equipped with its own blue-light ablution centre for hygiene. I do not remember Ernie being with us so we must have mislaid him somewhere. As it was not our scene, after a short look around we walked out. The Indians at the door had still not given up.

Like my memory of the early days of the war, the time in Syria remains blurred. There were wide-open plains, almost desert, dark cedar-covered hills and rushing torrents. Wild-looking horsemen, burnous-covered and carrying rifles, were picturesque in the extreme, even to our no-longer suburban eyes accustomed to the kaleidoscopic polyglot of Cairo with its red fezzes, Camel Corps, veiled women, uniforms of all nations, and scar-faced Sudanese. The Syrian women, black-garbed and nondescript, pattered humbly along behind on arthritic-looking donkeys. A chauvinistic world, this, where women laboured on the roads carrying baskets of stones to fill the potholes while men strutted around them. The village locals wore strange garb, tight-fitting trouser legs and baggy seats behind almost touching the ground. Christ would be born again, or so the story went, this time from a man. The baggy seats were there to catch him before he hit the ground. Icy torrents rushed beneath stone houses and swallows wheeled and wove echelons in the sky as at evening the muezzin climbed the balcony of the minaret to call people to prayer.

The land had recently been fought over and taken by the Australians from the Vichy French. It was stark and violent; fifth-columnists were said to abound but it was full of history and we found it an interesting place.

Baalbek was our destination. The Division was spread out, some at Elaine eighteen miles to the north, some guarding the former French airfield at Talia and a few up near the Turkish border. We were quartered in barracks close to the famous ruins of Baalbek. Previously inhabited by French legionnaires, some of the walls inside had been decorated with their humour and showed a good deal of talent. We roamed the ruins, looked with interest at the Temples of Bacchus and Jupiter and decided that these priests in the Temple of Venus — where they prepared young supposed virgins for marriage — must have had things very much their own way. It was here I adopted a little chameleon which stayed immobile upon my shoulder until any unwary fly came within twelve inches of it. Out would shoot about a foot of tongue like a piece of elastic and the poor fly disappeared. It was upsetting to lose him during the mad flap back to Egypt which was still to come, but just as well; he would have gorged himself to death at Alamein. It would have been interesting all the same to have seen him in action there.

We were posted to Headquarters Divisional Signals where the first few days were occupied building an annex. This was merely a shallow rectangular hole in the ground with a couple of rows of sandbags around the edges and it was difficult to understand why it was a matter of such interest. It seemed to me to be of no great importance and I was bored out of my mind.

From Baalbek we went on manoeuvres to the Palmyra Desert, where never before or since have I seen so many scorpions. One chap was stung

'Good job Kiwi'. *Alexander Turnbull Library*

by a black specimen and as such stings were reported to be fatal, along with medics we watched his survival with great interest. We felt we had a vested interest, since the scorpions were so numerous. I loathed them and although later I would sleep with lizards, snakes, large fleas, rats and sundry other crawlies that made rustling noises in the night, the scorpions took the palm for putting the fear of God in me.

We returned to Baalbek to hear the morale-boosting news of the first thousand-bomber raid on Germany, but had barely got ourselves sorted out when a tremendous flap ensued. Everybody started rushing around bringing equipment up to a state of instant readiness. The camel tanks in all vehicles were emptied and filled with fresh drinking water and drivers worked like dervishes on their vehicles. Word was out that the Division was returning post haste to Egypt because the 8th Army had suffered heavy defeat at the hands of Rommel, but as things had been going well in the desert we did not pay too much attention to this. Some even suggested that perhaps the Second New Zealand Expeditionary Force might be returning home to New Zealand. Whatever the reason, we were on the move again.

Down through Syria, Palestine, across the Sinai Desert, over the Suez Canal and into Egypt; it was a hot, exhausting journey. For four days we drove with the doors of the truck latched out on rods to divert air across our knees and aching bottoms. The Division halted in the vicinity of the pyramids but a corporal and I in a fifteen hundredweight 'pick-up' truck had been attached as radio operators to the Commander Royal Artillery, Steve Weir; CRA for short, or to give him the full title he would assume later: Sir Stephen Cyril Ettrick Weir, KBE, CB, DSO, and bar. He had attended Otago Boys' High School as I had, but there is little between a Brigadier and a signalman to encourage reminiscences.

From Cairo we pursued his staff car, worried whether a tyre which was making nasty thudding sounds, despite efforts to find the cause, would hold together. If we became involved in a wheel change we would be in real trouble because as it was we could barely keep up with the staff car and the CRA had not told us his destination. He never did. It was always a curt 'follow me'.

West of Alexandria, for the first time on the famous, or infamous, Desert Road, I looked with interest at an amazing collection of road signs. But how bleak it was; pleasant enough as you ran alongside the blue Mediterranean, but inland were just tumbleweed and endless arid wastes of sand, rock and grey escarpments shimmering in the distance. Then as we breasted a rise from a flat plain came the stunning shock of blue sea again and white stone houses. Even a few stunted trees; we had arrived at Mersa Matruh.

We went on to park out of sight of the town beneath a high ridge sloping away from the sea and looking down on the Desert Road on which was a flood of yellow transport apparently heading back to Alexandria. It certainly looked like an army in retreat. What the hell were we doing here? The corporal had disappeared and I sat in the truck for some hours feeling lonely and depressed. The sky was overcast and everything seemed grey to match my spirits.

Further up the slope at the crest was a heavily sandbagged armoured command vehicle with very tall aerials. Its siren kept up a continuous moaning, denoting air-raid yellow. This went on and on but no enemy planes appeared. Presumably pickings were too good further up the Desert Road? The only vehicles moving against the flow were the odd New Zealand staff car or truck. As the hours went by their numbers increased and as the Division began to arrive I said to myself, 'This is bloody great, every bastard is running backwards except us!'

Near at hand were old gun emplacements and trenches falling into disuse. Further down the slope was an anti-tank ditch and barbed wire ran round the perimeter of the defensive box we had entered. Without even thinking of mines, I was so raw, I walked down and had a look. It was pathetic.

The ditch was choked with sand and would not have stopped a child's trike.

The corporal finally returned and at dusk we moved over the ridge away from the road and down to the sea, where we halted close to the beach by a large command post dug deeply down into the sand and shored up with sandbags and roofed. Peering down through a ventilation shutter I could see Steve Weir's camp cot set up in one of the alcoves and I thought it would be good if he wanted our radio set up down there in a handy position. What an optimist I was; left to our own devices, the corporal and I dug two shallow slit trenches and sitting on the edges munched our dry rations. Close by, anti-tank gunners were digging their guns in but the muzzles were facing out to sea. Seaborne invasion as well, I thought gloomily.

When the stars came out the gunners ceased their labours. A desert sky at night is magnificent but I wasn't in the mood for admiring it, and as we were on wireless silence so as not to divulge the presence of the Division I took off my boots, placed them under my head in the trench and folded my knitted woollen scarf over them to act as a pillow. Gazing up at the glittering stars, wondering what the morrow held and thinking it had been a tough four days since we had left Syria, I fell asleep.

'Bloody hell!'

An air raid! My first in a target area. I hadn't even heard them coming. They were bombing Mersa Matruh. Us! The brilliant flash and vicious crack of a 3.7 anti-aircraft gun alongside me, which until that moment I had hardly been aware of, levitated me clean out of my trench in much the same way as the scorpions in my blankets at Palmyra. Feeling stupid I got back into the slitty and lying on my back gazing upwards, watched the streams of red tracer fire reaching up into the heavens. I listened to the shouted commands to the toiling gun crew, gaining heart from the fact that somebody knew how to take counter-measures, and tensed to the crashes of the guns around and to the 'crumphs' of exploding bombs. As the ground shook I found it exciting but not particularly frightening.

Adrenalin was flowing, my mouth was dry, but my heartbeat was only a little quickened. A near-miss no doubt would have altered the situation but my reaction to this baptism was interesting and I was not to know it would change with experience. Next morning, surveying the shrapnel lying around us, I thought how silly it had been to lie on one's back presenting an unprotected face to what was coming down. Those pieces of hot metal falling out of the sky would have sliced right through bone and could have been fatal. It was strange that through all the training we had undertaken no one had ever mentioned that. Commonsense of course should would have prevailed, though it would have been a bit late if I had lost half my face. Next time I would put my steel helmet on, sit up and make myself the smallest target possible. If I had to look up I would do so under the rim of my tin hat; it was my first practical lesson.

A daylight raid mid-morning was driven off by the gunners. As the planes departed dozens of black men popped their heads out of the ground all around us. As with the ack-ack gun, I had not known of their presence. Investigating further, I found they were a pioneer battalion and had dug tunnels everywhere about a metre below the surface, deep enough to crawl through and lie in but not to stand up. They would give good protection against ground strafing but who wanted to be buried alive during a bombing raid? They did not appeal to me at all.

'Take the radio out of the truck and dig it in,' we were told. But everywhere we started to dig, up came empty beer bottles. What a boozers' retreat! It was finally decided to empty out an old dugout. The bottles! We dug all day, and the next, interrupted only by air raids and breaks to eat. We worked bare to the waist in the hot sun, glistening where we were not caked with dust. At the end of each day we would walk heavily down to the water's edge, there to remove our boots, drop shorts, stand for a moment in anticipated bliss, then plunge with closed eyes into cool, cool, water, the grime slipping off. This enveloping, soothing balm made it all almost worthwhile.

You could not get bored. There wasn't time.

'Get your radio back in the truck, we're moving out. Fill in your dugout.'

After all that work! There had been conferences going on ever since we had arrived. We had not seen Steve Weir since we had entered Mersa Matruh but here he was again. Freyberg had decided Matruh could not be successfully defended and was not going to have his men caught in a trap. Tobruk had fallen. That was difficult to credit. When the Aussies were there they had resisted all challenges. Tobruk possessed much stronger perimeters than Matruh. It had defences in depth yet it had been overwhelmed and thousands of South Africans captured. Yet the South Africans were reputed to be troops at their best when holding ground. Freyberg had decided we would go out and meet the Germans and Italians in the open on a place of our own choosing.

The NAAFI canteen was thrown open and we crammed our truck with canned apricots and beans so that every time in the next few days when we hit a bump, tins flew out. It was a pity we could not find the beer; there must have been tons of it somewhere. The night before I had run into an old friend from our group which had visited Jerusalem and we had gone to the NAAFI for a beer but had been informed it was closed. I could not think why, unless it was because of imminent attack and the enemy heading our way. Len had appeared to be unusually depressed, almost as if he had a premonition, and clearly was not looking forward to contact with Rommel's pursuing forces. I had butterflies in the stomach myself but had been expecting the worst for a long time — since first entering Trentham Camp, in fact. I was more or less resigned to the future although I would do my damnedest to survive because of the family back home.

Chapter 4

Black Smoke and Burning Sand

Minqar Qaim and beyond

It was dull and overcast as we left Matruh; this was unusual for the desert, and sitting alone in the back of the lurching truck I wished someone would just tell us what the hell was going on. We were still on wireless silence, no messages were coming through on the radio and in the headphones there was only static. The water sloshing around in the camel tank caught my attention and although it was absolutely forbidden to touch it, I unscrewed the cap to check how much had evaporated. I was not thirsty, there was water in my bottle and we still had plenty of those tinned apricots, but using a small narrow tin I dipped it in the tank until I had about one and a half inches of water in the tin. It tasted brackish and I felt slightly guilty but did not care. Drinking it was more a protest than anything else about this bloody army and the bloody situation I found myself in.

At dusk we were attacked by half a dozen planes concentrating on our particular little group, and although our fire forced them away, one nasty type turned back and had another go at us. If he had released a stick of bombs then it could have been curtains, but he kept on descending and boring in on us while the Bofors gun beside me hosed him with shells. They were passing over and under him and it was difficult to understand why the stream was not pouring through him, but in the end he suddenly gave up and turned away from the line of fire to rejoin his mates.

While this was going on the corporal had found an unoccupied slit trench but there was no room for me so I was stretched out on the surface along the edge of it, looking back and up over my left shoulder at the planes which were having us on.

'Keep your head down!' said the corporal from the safety of his trench. Of course I was keeping my head down. Did he think I was not scared of this persistent bugger overhead? We suffered casualties, losing one of our colonels, and as darkness fell there were groans and a kind of low screaming coming from a first aid truck parked nearby.

In the bright sunshine next morning we were joined by an artillery officer carrying a perspex-covered map board and a fist full of coloured pencils — a jaunty type.

'Rommel's broken through,' he cheerfully announced, 'and we're going to stop him.' Gawd! The Afrika Korps, and we were in its way!

To our left a gun crew was digging in a 25-pounder and setting up a Bren gun on a tripod against air attack. Stripped to their waists, they showed no sign of panic, no frantic hurry. They had done it all before many times, and that gun would fire if required until they ran out of ammunition or died, because that was the way the regiments operated. Immediately behind us the muzzle of another 25-pounder pointed directly at our radio set. Thinking it was too close for comfort, I asked the officer whether we should also dig in or whether we were moving on.

No, we were not staying. We soon moved a few yards away from under the muzzles to a couple of slit trenches dug close to Divisional Headquarters. Brigadier Weir was sitting on the ground with his feet in one so we parked the van alongside a signalman nearby who was lying on the sand surrounded by a single row of sandbags — he was manning a field telephone. We dug ourselves a joint L-shaped slit trench, perhaps a little deeper than usual, in between taking turns on the radio. The mood was serious here. It was clear that this was going to be no ordinary skirmish. The 8th Army was in full retreat behind us and we were going to take the shock of a whole advancing army by ourselves.

We did not have long to wait for action. With a crash the first 25-pounder opened up and the artillery song was on, the baritone roar rising and falling — a sound we were to hear all day. Then there was a different noise: the whistle, shriek, and 'crumph' of incoming shells, and not always in that order. It depended where they landed. There was big stuff too. Steve Weir's driver brought back on his shoulder a great hunk of one which had not fully disintegrated. It was about six to eight inches in diameter.

Heavy artillery fire numbs the mind, which is just as well, but I was interested in my reaction. If this was war, and it undoubtedly was, it seemed to be the most stupid, scary, crazy business I had ever been involved in. Here we were shelling hell out of people we could not see, and they were doing the same to us. Perhaps it made more sense to the infantry out front, because they could observe some of what was going on. It was this passive participation in hostilities which was going to get me in the end. An artilleryman or rifleman had the satisfaction, or the relief if you like, of hitting back and so to some extent became the hunter not the quarry. As a radio operator sitting high up in a soft-skinned vehicle with the headphones shutting out much of the battle noise, everybody else except the gunners lying below ground level, I used to feel terribly exposed and always the target.

Something had happened nearby, for Steve Weir was saying, 'Bad luck, I am sorry.' Our telephone line had also gone and the signalman could no longer use his phone. I became the runner to Divisional Headquarters, to find a single high-ranking officer sitting in a slit trench alongside the Divisional sign stuck in the ground. A telephone cradled in his lap, too busy to look up, he stretched out a free hand to take the messages as I brought them. As I passed the trench of one of the Defence Platoon dug in around him, looking down I met the terrified eyes of its occupant. He had placed his pack over his back and was crouching face downwards and had looked up at the sound of my footsteps in the sand. He was in worse shape than I was and actually I did not feel too bad. Not then, anyway.

Another crash, and God, there was our poor bloody annex over there, bloody being the operative word. So that is what all the hoo-ha in Syria had been about. It housed operators and radios connected by remotes to the signal office telephone exchange and had received almost a direct hit. I learned later that shell splinters passing through an open end had killed two men and wounded two. Two of our chaps were lying motionless, draped face down over the sand removed during the digging. Their backs were soaked with blood. I had known both of them quite well. The sergeant, grim faced, was removing their dog tags and pay books and putting them in his pocket. My friend Len, still sitting in the annex but looking white about the gills, pointed mutely to his ankle. His puttee had unravelled and was lying round his boot but he did not appear hurt. I could not stop and did not want to anyway. I had a 'better 'ole' and trotting and walking back to it under the screaming shells and flying metal was pretty awful, but not so bad as I had imagined it could be. Not so bad as having a screaming Jerry lunging for your guts with a naked bayonet, but I was not enjoying it, and neither was the telephone operator nor the corporal. It was not the first time for them.

'This is pretty bad, Jack,' said the telephone operator. I nodded, not knowing what to say. The corporal called for more rod aerial to be extended and it took a real act of will to climb up on to the roof of that truck and stand reaching up to take down the aerial then screw on more rods. I felt terribly naked since although the shelling was bad enough on the ground, occasional armour-piercing 88 millimetre shells striking the rock-hard ground would ricochet across; some at chest height, but others higher, just as flat stones can be made to skim across ponds. The incredible speed of them made my groin feel it was dissolving and I had visions of myself standing on the roof with a large hole drilled clean through my stomach and the wind blowing through.

Back to Headquarters again, looking down once more on the anxious faces of the Defence Platoon. They probably wondered how the hell I could walk around in it but the point was I had no option. I'd have been cringing in a trench too if I had been able. Shit! It was getting worse: black smoke, flame and burning sand! But walking back I was getting the hang of it, watching the grinning face of another operator on similar duties getting up from the ground. As the shells screamed in you dropped like a stone, getting up to walk on. This was apparently the form for moving about under fire. In actual fact it was probably a waste of time because you would never hear the one that got you, but the notion helped that you were dodging the horrors.

The corporal decided he had temporarily had enough although he still had a couple of hours to go on the set. The telephone line was back in working order and from now on we would work the radio hour on, hour off. He was the boss so I took over the set. It was rugged. Occasionally there would be a clang as a piece of shrapnel hit some part of the truck. Did I have to sit up there cold turkey? The gunnery officer was sitting in the cab. At least he had a little bit of steel around him, be it ever so thin. I had nothing but canvas. Another officer joined him, making a facetious remark but it sounded false — his voice was too high and too strained for it to be casual enough. I could hear the low hum of their conversation in the front.

My signals officer was nowhere to be seen. There was a set of headphones somewhere with a long lead. It was only a listening watch so why not plug them in and lie on the ground? I found them and joined the telephone operator at the back of the truck. He had sandbags but I felt a lot better lying down there. Surely if conditions were bad enough for a reputed fire-eater like Steve Weir to be sitting in a slit trench wearing a steel helmet then could I not stay this way providing I did my job?

It was the procedure that was troubling me. I did not know the form. Weir was eyeing me. The trouble was, you could not satisfactorily wear a steel helmet and the headphones at the same time and why some boffin had not thought of this earlier and provided a special helmet into which you could plug a wire I shall never know. Wearing the helmet and supported by my elbows, left hand holding an earphone to my ear, right hand clutching the radio call signs of the Artillery Regiments, I gazed back at the Brigadier from my belly-down position thinking — if I lower this headphone for one instant he'll do me. Still he looked my way. Trying to appear nonchalant, chatting to the telephone operator between calls, grinning inanely, consulting my little wireless diagram and occasionally getting back into the truck to answer check calls, I sensed the Brigadier was beginning to lose interest. Shortly he got up out of the trench and went somewhere in his jeep. Coming back he picked up the phone alongside. I heard him say, 'That was a very gallant action, I watched it through my glasses. Congratulate . . . . . ., it was a very fine piece of work.' Somebody at a crucial moment had taken a troop of our guns across the front and blasted Jerry back.

My hour came up. I handed over the long lead to the corporal who squatted on the ground against one of the rear wheels and headed for the L-shaped slit trench we had dug that morning to find one end occupied by our signals officer. As I stretched out he asked if I could move up a little and give him more room. What a bloody cheek! Slitties were personal things. You did not get into those belonging to other people. If he had

40

to be on tap for the Brigadier, why did he not sit with him as he had earlier? Be charitable, I thought, the corporal did not need it while on the set.

We must have been the only outfit where other ranks sat up unprotected while the officers sheltered in trenches. Not that I am casting aspersions — they did not operate the radios so there was no need for them to be above ground and it was just commonsense to take shelter in static positions. Nevertheless it was hard to rationalise it under heavy fire.

I listened to him trying to identify two of the enemy's heavier guns and speculating on their calibre. I had been unaware of any difference; it was all noise to me, but I could hear what he meant. Every minute above the noise there would be this heavier boom, boom; you would listen for a second, then over would come two shells. They must have been the heavies sending shot high in the air before coming down and I preferred them to the high-velocity 88s. Perhaps these were the guns from which that large hunk of shell had come, the piece Steve Weir had examined?

Bad news! I could hear it being reported from where I was lying — enemy tanks had broken our gun line. They were two hundred yards off and coming our way! I had been expecting this. One division cannot hold at bay a whole army. This was it! You could not fight tanks with rifles and bare hands once they pierced your gun ring. The story went that if you remained in your trench the tanks would crush you with their tracks for their own safety, because they did not want you dropping hand grenades into their turrets once they halted. But lying face downwards in the trench I had no thought of running. Where could you run to, anyway? Stand up when they come, do what the others do, watch Steve Weir and hope one can die with dignity. The dilemma left sickness in the stomach. The imminence of sudden death was accepted; it was inevitable. The decision once reached in some strange way afforded relief. No doubt we were all in a state of shock from the concussion; I just wanted it to end.

The rising crescendo and fury of our guns firing over open sights was incredible. They had been going for hours now and under this latest threat they moved from *forte* to *fortissimo*, somehow lifting the tempo. They were still holding, and holding, the tank thrust was slowing, stopping, turned! Relief flooded us. All those noble thoughts about dying . . . got carried away a bit there.

Several times during the day I had watched Don Section Signals' line truck going out to repair broken lines. They threaded the line through a kind of shepherd's crook fitted to the vehicle which enabled them to travel quite quickly, and here they were again making another run. Earlier I had admired one of the crew standing upright in the truck, his eyes on the line. That took guts. They were probably going out to repair lines cut by the tanks.

I thought the day would never end, but darkness comes swiftly in the desert and just as quickly as it started the battle finished. We could now compose ourselves and go to bed. Who wanted to eat, anyway? Food would have stuck in the throat. Fear always makes me dry. I took off my boots and dangled my feet in the trench. It felt marvellous. There wasn't a sound. I wondered what we did next.

Sitting there relaxing I did not know it had been a very close thing. More or less alone, we had just fought the battle of Minqar Qaim. Five separate Panzer attacks had been thrown back by the New Zealand gunners and infantrymen. What I also did not know was that Freyberg had been critically wounded, some of our guns were down to less than thirty rounds and that we were encircled by the Afrika Korps. Without ammunition it is absolutely certain the Division would not have survived another day and that it faced extinction, a disaster that could not be contemplated for people in a small country like New Zealand.

It was here that the superb leadership which the Division enjoyed asserted itself. Apparently, when asked how he would extricate his Division without ammunition, Freyberg from his sick-bed replied that he had ten thousand bayonets. The decision had been reached during the day that the Division would break out at night. Brigadier Inglis had taken over command from Freyberg and was faced with a very difficult task when you consider that the thousands of trucks and guns had no roads over which to travel and that the operation had to be accomplished under the cover of darkness. The plan was that a silent attack would be made by 4 Brigade to create a gap through which the Division would escape. Then 19 Battalion would attack through the centre, 20 Battalion on the left and 28 Maori Battalion on the right. As events proved, 19 Battalion did not encounter much opposition but 20 Battalion met stubborn resistance and were held up. The Maoris also had trouble but the breakthrough was successful.

Mind you, nobody had thought to put me in the picture and I was sitting bootless peering at an adjacent truck crammed with German prisoners when along came the Sergeant Major.

'Let's go, I'm driving,' he said, getting into the cab and starting up the engine. The corporal was already in the back manning the radio set. I picked up my boots and joined the Sergeant Major in the cab. All the trucks appeared to be lining up in columns so we got in behind. An hour passed, perhaps two. He hadn't uttered a bloody word and must surely have had something on his mind. Finally we moved off.

It was after midnight and it had been an exhausting day. I was slumped half asleep, my mood not objective, and if we were sneaking away from Jerry then that suited me. Nor was I greatly upset when an occasional burst of machine-gun fire came our way. One had to expect a bit of that I supposed, and the Bren gun carriers clattering alongside quickly silenced it each time.

We were grinding along in low gear when after another sporadic burst of automatic fire, a tank shell went screaming over our heads. Almost simultaneously, heavy fire erupted all along our front. Molten balls of flame began to whoosh just above us and down between the lines of vehicles; we were so close to the tanks which had us in their sights that we could see the gun flash and watch the white-hot shell go past at virtually the same moment. We were inside their range, and though their shells were lifting at the last moment to pass over us, their velocity constricted breathing.

We were about the fifth or sixth vehicle from the front, and seemed fortunate because the people behind us were getting it. As trucks burst into flames they illuminated the scene and an anti-tank portée came rapidly from the rear to stop and turn beside us. I had a grandstand view as its gun commenced rapid fire while still mounted on the portée. I had never seen anything like this at such close quarters in my life; it was immensely thrilling but also bloody terrifying.

A jeep from the front turned swiftly back, racing down our column, tracer just clearing the heads of its occupants. A few yards away was a slit trench dug during the day's fighting. How lucky can you be? Without bothering to put on my boots I took off in a flying dive. The trench was already occupied! The body beneath me was trembling, did not reply as I apologised and made no effort to shake me off. There we stayed for about a minute. Friend or foe? I didn't know.

Tracers were arcing over the top and I had the insane thought that if I lifted up a hand I could catch them. The jeep came back and I raised my eyes over the rim of the trench. The body beneath me was still shuddering. Somebody was standing up in a vehicle in front of us. It could have been Steve Weir or Colonel Gray, but was probably the latter, because I think Weir was in the jeep. We seemed to be all mixed up with Headquarters and 5 Brigade.

The figure standing up was waving an arm and shouting, 'Turn left! Turn left!'

Vehicles began to move. I was going to get left myself if I didn't do something. Using the body as a springboard I leaped from the trench. Our truck was advancing but I was still able to climb aboard. Perhaps this had taken five minutes? I just didn't know, it was so completely unreal. Whose trench had it been? We were so close, but surely not in their forward defence. Whoever he was, the shock of my silently landing on him in that noise must have been horrific.

Our truck took off on a great curving charge to the left, in what must be the wildest drive of my life. We left the red tracer fire and bedlam behind. We left everybody behind! The Sergeant Major was crouched over the steering wheel. He must have known this was coming up and could have told me, because who would want to take on Jerry in stockinged feet, but on the other hand he had probably saved me a couple of hours of anxiety. Ours was a V8 motor and we were going like the clappers, at times airborne as we hit the bumps, and I wondered how the corporal was making out in the back. He'd surely be spending most of his time in the air.

The BBC was later to report the Division's Balaclava-like charge but military pundits elsewhere pooh-poohed it, saying that such charges were not possible in modern warfare. What a lot of rot, I thought. In war anything is possible, and we charged for our lives because we had no alternative. Fortunately it came off.

Not everyone was lucky, and I had seen trucks burst into flames, a despatch rider fall from his bike, a first aid truck go up in smoke and also one of our quads. Good old Sergeant Major, even if he was a silent bastard. He had saved our bacon and we were alone with nobody in front, having outstripped them all.

Slowing down, we stopped in a hollow. Over the ridge behind us came pouring the rest of the Division, grinding gradually to a halt. We were just bedding down as the corporal joined us.

'What the hell was that! What happened?'

I don't think we even answered because it was surely self-explanatory. He probably didn't want an answer anyway, but was just relieving his feelings.

At first light everybody was up and moving on, but our faulty tyre had given up the ghost and was flat after the night's mad gallop. The Sergeant Major forsook us, boarding a more roadworthy vehicle, and the corporal undertook the wheel change while I walked dejectedly around, shouting after departing trucks to ask whether they had a spare tyre. Unsuccessful, I returned to the truck to find we were alone with the Germans presumably only yards away. The corporal had the spare on and we took off in the general direction the Division had taken, following their tracks where able to do so.

We were beginning to overtake a dust cloud rising ahead when another tyre went. This was serious; we had no spare. Jerry must be breathing down our necks by now and we could finish up in the bag. About two hundred yards on our flank a solitary New Zealand truck went by. They were singing and waved back when we gestured for help.

'Silly bastards,' said the corporal. 'I bet they are pissed on that Matruh beer.'

I thought about that. I could have done with a beer right then.

A large truck appeared coming from the opposite direction. Turning towards us, it came to a halt alongside. In it were two Tommies looking for their unit to deliver supplies, and as we explained our problem one produced tyre levers and set about removing the wheel while his companion proceeded to boil up some spuds over a primus. I hadn't seen potatoes for a long time and had not eaten any breakfast but in the circumstances felt not the slightest bit hungry. Our visitors were Army Service Corps and I suppose they spent their days mending punctures, but it was beautiful to watch; repairs to the tube were quickly completed, on went the tyre, a hose connected to the truck appeared and as the tyre swelled to its normal size our relief was enormous. While work was proceeding we tried to convince

44

our good samaritans that Jerry was only a couple of ridges away and that they should join us and get out mighty quick.

'Gotta find our unit,' they kept repeating.

We suggested that their unit was probably going lickety-split backwards like the rest of 8th Army, but it made no difference. Such loyalty was highly commendable even if it meant suicide, so we thanked them, handed them some tins of apricots and took off at high speed. As I looked back they were sitting down eating their spuds which were probably still warm when Jerry got to them.

We caught up with the Division in the Kaponga Box, a fortified eminence about half way between the sea and the Qattara Depression. Here we found the moonlight lit the place up like day and as the Box was easily identifiable we suffered persistent air raids carried out at low level. It was nerve-racking, but as usual we had a humorist in the vicinity and his stentorian roar, 'Why don't you bastards piss off and let me get some sleep?' brought laughs as the bombers almost on cue levelled off and disappeared over the lightening horizon.

The next few days, if not the most trying, were certainly the most confusing I ever spent in the Army. If we settled in one position we were immediately asked to move to another. I dug eleven slit trenches in three days in ground

A New Zealand truck on fire following heavy shelling at Minqar Qaim. 'It took an act of will to stand on the roof . . .' *Alexander Turnbull Library*

that was mainly rock; it wasn't soldiering but more like labouring on the roads. First, blisters appeared on the hands, then rubbed raw and bled, but it made no difference to our digging and it is surprising what a fit man can accomplish under duress. Although the wooden handles were slippery with blood we hammered that flinty ground until sparks flew from the pickaxes with every swing and we bent their ends as we clawed shallow graves in which to lie.

The situation continued to be fluid and Steve Weir spent time trying to locate what the enemy were doing while we toiled after him, repeatedly getting caught in soft sand patches. The truck which had valiantly carried us through at Minqar Qaim was not suitable for desert reconnaissances. We needed four-wheel drive and without it floundered hopelessly, having to dig tracks in front of the wheels, slide in the sand trays, put the handbrake on to control wheelspin, and with us at the rear pushing, slowly inch our way to firmer ground. As the truck cleared a patch and we fell flat on our faces there were times when I felt like continuing to lie there and let the bloody thing go to hell! We always arrived late to find the Brigadier gazing moodily through his binoculars at shapes on the horizon, ready to move off as soon as we reached him. With so many German aircraft about, reconnaissance never appealed to me because forever stuck in the sand we seemed so vulnerable.

There was a place somebody tagged 'Death Valley' where we were ordered to manhandle our truck into rough ground above the desert floor. It was a good idea. Stukas divebombed us all day and the people down on the flat got the worst of it. The planes never let up and with their banshee wails, exploding bombs and sand falling down upon us, it was pretty horrible and we suffered a number of casualties.

During a lull, the opportunity was taken to distribute mail. There was a letter from Claudia. Opening it, I spread the pages out on the floor of the trench a few inches from my face but had barely got to the end when there was another raid. It was not her usual style and she concluded by saying that things were going pretty well in her neck of the woods and trusted that I was finding it the same. As the ground shook once again the incongruity of my present position struck me; lying on my stomach with my face in her letter as more sand and stones came down on me, I almost wept. Calm, clear, remote beautiful New Zealand, oh to be there!

We moved on next day, all vehicles widely dispersed, under a sky filled with the angry buzz of enemy fighters. There were frequent stops, during which we ran fifty yards from our truck to squat down on the sand. It seemed the sensible thing to do as fighters strafed the vehicles ahead and behind us while their former occupants watched from the sideline as we were doing. Providing we did not move we were not easy to see; the greatest giveaway in the desert was shadow cast by guns and vehicles and our bleached shirts and boots and sand-covered faces camouflaged us.

Late in the afternoon, in an area filled with hollows, we took up a defensive position. After digging myself another slit trench, I sat and watched a troop of Royal Horse Medium Artillery blazing away at something out of sight, but at dusk we had to cut and run.

We were following a signals truck ahead of us when it stopped; apparently it had become separated from the main group. It was dark by then. This was a fine how-do-you-do; we were lost. It had never happened before but I suppose there has to be a first time. A signals Major was riding in the truck ahead so we just sat there and let him do the worrying — that's what he was paid for. Drawing his pistol, he commenced to stalk steadily on ahead of us on foot, peering at the ground for mines, while we gingerly followed the wheel tracks of the other vehicle. Red and green flares went up ahead on our left and automatic fire broke out. It was close but apparently not aimed at us. More flares and fire were answered by retaliatory bursts; it seemed a battle was going on, but who was who? For some odd reason we had a gunner in our little group and the 'mad Major', as we were now referring to him, ordered the gunner to bring his rifle and accompany him on a reconnaissance.

As they went off I mused on the Major's choice of a companion. Since we were signallers, perhaps he regarded us as non-combatants? Hell, I had done infantry training which I'm sure the gunner had not experienced. Not that I wanted to accompany the Major into trouble. Half an hour and they were back.

'Just a private war,' said the gunner, climbing back on the truck.

Off we went again, veering away from the fighting. The Major led us, but at the rumble and clank of tracked vehicles he hurriedly ordered us to stop and disperse. I grabbed my rifle and water bottle, picked up the signal codes, switched off the set and hurried off in the general direction of the others. Lying in the soft sand I scooped a shallow hole and buried the codes as two or three dark shapes ground past about thirty yards away. We gave them a few moments then uncovering the codes again, joined our vehicles and the trek continued.

The Major appeared to be on course, for low down on the ground a pale green light came up. It was shaded, and standing by it with his motorbike close by was a New Zealand provost. As we approached the solitary figure alone in the dark, waiting for stragglers like ourselves, or the Hun, I thought, you poor devil, that takes real guts to do what you are doing. He gave the Major a compass bearing and we were on our way again but now at normal speed. Half an hour's driving brought us to a New Zealand group with no sentries set, all dead to the world. They could have been quite easily too, for in their exhausted states it would have been no problem to slit their throats.

The Major's batman set out his boss's bedroll and in about sixty seconds there wasn't a single person awake except me. I had to stay on radio watch and it was times like this I silently railed against the inhumanity of the Divisional Signals system, which made no allowance for human frailty and the need for sleep. I'd had damn all sleep since we left Mersa Matruh and virtually none the night before; it was nearly daylight and there was to be no sleep for me this night, and no guarantee it would be any better tomorrow. The following afternoon, bleary eyed, we caught up with our unit.

They had something for us. The CRA was organising a 'Jock Column'. It was almost the last straw but what could one do? A Jock Column was composed of a mobile party of guns, anti-tank, carriers, and the odd tank, its aim being to find the enemy and engage him in action. They were popular with the 8th Army commanders but an anathema to Freyberg who considered they split units and reduced their effectiveness as a corporate body.

We trundled along in the usual fog of ignorance with me in the back wearing headphones when a shell burst immediately behind in the space we had occupied a split second earlier. I had not even heard it coming. As the black smoke cleared I could see another signals truck emerging from it. The corporal, head and shoulders projecting through the hatch in the cab roof, was actually grinning. I could not make up my mind whether this was at our near miss or whether he was actually enjoying the situation.

A battle was raging about us; shells were screaming one way and quads and their 25-pounders were galloping the other. There were no orders, but we hurriedly dug ourselves in. It was all very confusing; there was a constant cannonade but with the dust rising and the smoke I couldn't see a thing. That was the worst of being virtually a spectator; you never knew what the hell was going on. We were the radio link to the gun batteries and back to HQ, but it always seemed to be a question of fire at sight! In addition, our signals line sections were so quick at establishing telephone communications that the need for us was often over before we started. Where we did come into use was on the move.

It had been a bit like that at the battle of Minqar Qaim, of which the Official War History states that the part played by our signals section was 'neither spectacularly brilliant nor depressingly dull'. Brigadier Weir described it as follows: — '5 and 6 Field Regiments were connected to HQNZA by line and radio right throughout the battle and the fire of these two regiments was, in a crude way, directed on occasions from HQ New Zealand Artillery. Fourth Field Regiment was not connected by line but we were in touch by radio from time to time. Fourth Field Regiment were so far away that they virtually fought under command of 4 Infantry Brigade. However, in so far as actual battle was concerned, Minqar Qaim was the first operation in which HQNZA and its communications functioned under centralised control, and was the forerunner of the very highly efficient organisation which we built up at El Alamein.'

If our efforts at Minqar Qaim had been crude, on this occasion we appeared to have come along merely for the ride! I almost fell asleep lying in the slitty, attached to my long radio lead. The headphones shut out most of the noise erupting about me.

There was a lull as the shelling stopped and we moved a few chains and halted. I was sitting at the radio in the back of the vehicle, almost asleep again. Our truck was like today's utility with a canvas canopy at the rear. The back flap was down to keep out the dust. Encapsulated in a little world of my own, ears full of static, I was completely unaware of what was happening within yards of me, so that when the flap was abruptly dragged aside the sight of an enemy helmet above a bearded face inches from my own was heart-stopping.

I have always had good strong legs, and these acted like coiled springs to project me — headphones and all — in a manic reflex lunge straight at the apparition, knocking it backwards to the ground. I landed in a crouch on one knee, the black morse key still in my right hand instinctively pointing at him like a weapon. Sitting up, he raised both arms in surrender. If he was scared, I could hardly breathe as motioning him with the key to stay down, I climbed to my feet.

This was a fine how-do-you-do, because my rifle was standing in its bracket inside the cab. Thank God he was an Italian and not a German! As we watched each other he broke the impasse by pulling up a trouser leg to display a grazed leg, perhaps to convince me he was 'walking wounded', and as he now appeared no threat I exchanged the key for my rifle as quickly and as unobtrusively as I was able.

Gazing around I could see we were parked in a little hollow and were alone, except for a truck a few yards away from which projected two pairs of feet on stretchers. You could always identify corpses by the immobility of their boot soles; something I never got used to during the whole course of the war. Strapped to stretchers on jeeps or in carriers the hobnailed leathers always told their story. Where the hell was everybody? There was no sound, and I could not see over the rim of the depression we were in.

With some difficulty I gleaned from my captive that he had fallen from a motorbike while fleeing and had been motioned in my direction by my companions, who were apparently away looking for loot. Their total lack of responsibility made me furious and as one of them was an officer there was no excuse for it. Italians were not regarded highly as fighting men but on occasions they could fight very bravely when their heart was in it, and their gunners had a good reputation. All that Italian had to do was remove one of the loaded rifles from the cab, check whether anyone was in the back of the vehicle, put a bullet in him, roll him out, and take off in free transport. Not the slightest bit of risk existed and nobody in that area would have halted a British truck.

My companions on their return seemed to take the Italian's presence for granted. Still simmering, I kept my mouth shut in the presence of the officer. We retraced our route back to the rest of the Division where

49

our trophy evoked amused glances — a signals van with its own prisoner was perhaps a little unusual.

Apart from feeding him with some of our diminishing stores of tinned fruit and accidentally banging him on the head with a locker lid, little of note happened before an intelligence officer arrived to order him curtly into his jeep and take him away for interrogation. In our skirmish we had virtually destroyed a good part of the Italian Ariete Division and captured most of its guns; a highly creditable performance at a time when the 8th Army was in need of a boost in morale.

Chapter 5

Desert Days

The Alamein line

Since its return to Egypt, the New Zealand Division had been fully employed in helping to stem a rout and elsewhere South African, Indian and British troops were similarly engaged. In Cairo there were signs of panic; records were being destroyed, families moved across the Suez Canal. Even the evacuation of Egypt was being considered.

On 1 July the British fleet left Alexandria for safer waters. There was a curfew operating in Cairo and convoys were leaving for Palestine. It was extremely discouraging, because we knew we had more men and equipment than the enemy and it was humiliating to think that they were putting theirs to better use. There was nothing the matter with the British rank and file but they were confused and people were losing faith in the Higher Command. Some senior New Zealand officers were so disgusted that they were at the point of refusing to obey orders.

The thin Alamein line was still holding and the New Zealanders wanted to stand and fight. The South African Division was also becoming bloody-minded about the shambles. They were intact and did not want to run. Fifth Indian Division, a very soldierly unit composed of Indian and British troops, was now in the line, and 9 Australian Division was moving in. This was one of the best Divisions in the Middle East; the same troops who had held Tobruk. Good relations existed between our Divisions; I remember being overtaken by an Australian 25-pounder battery travelling parallel with us on the Desert Road. As one of their quads came abreast a beefy sergeant leaned out through the hatch, arms akimbo, and addressed our gunners, 'Moving up for the first time, mates?'

'Yeah,' said the gunners, 'we're new chums.'

The grinning Aussie, who had taken in every dent in the battered old quad, was having us on but nobody was rising to the bait.

Sanity must have prevailed in some quarters because no orders came through to carry out a retreat. By the middle of July the Alamein line began to firm up and the constant changing of positions ceased. We were directed to strip the truck, dig the radio in, and our transport was driven away. Minefields were laid ahead and behind, some of the anti-tank guns we had captured from the Ariete Division were placed about us and a new General named Montgomery advised in an order of the day that here we would stand and fight. At the same time, just to cheer us up, Jerry put down a curtain of artillery fire about a couple of hundred yards ahead of us; not a good introduction to our new position.

Now that the continual charging around the desert had ceased one might think that conditions would become a little easier but it was not to be so; the preceding weeks were beginning to take their toll. To maintain radio communications twenty-four hours a day, charge batteries, keep the vehicle mobile and chase after Steve Weir, feed ourselves while at the same time being bombed and shot at, was more than two people could endure for any length of time. Three was the minimum for that kind of caper but the corporal and I had been doing it for weeks. The corporal had all the responsibility and this coupled with fatigue made him like a bear with a sore head. My own dumb inexperience did not help matters. I had the feeling that flashpoint between us was not far away since I had suffered a gutsful of his sourness.

We changed shifts at 2 a.m. every morning and since the flies woke us at 5.30 we were averaging at the very most only about three hours sleep in twenty-four. I carried our only pencil thrust down my sock, and if there was anything guaranteed to inflame the corporal at two in the morning it was for me to forget and take it to bed still inside my sock.

As if this were not enough, we had a parachutist scare. It was rumoured that parachutists were going to breach the Alamein line so a strongpoint was dug in a few yards away from where we had established our radio set. I suppose I should have expected it, but it was with disbelief I learned that in addition to working the radio I was to sleep at the strongpoint, undertake a two-hour roving picket during the night, and stand to at dawn to repel the parachutists. The corporal was to take up any slack in the radio watch during my absence. Bloody hell! This cut us down to perhaps one hour's sleep in twenty-four, something I have never forgiven the Army to this day. I would dearly love to meet the person responsible for that timetable.

As I came off radio watch I reported late to the strongpoint, where obviously it was a case of first come, best served. A grinning group were fairly comfortably ensconced with Bren guns inside a circular dug-in position strongly protected by rows of sandbags. They made it clear there was no room at the inn for me or any other latecomers, so feeling very much an outsider I disconsolately dug myself a slit trench on their outskirts. They then added insult to injury by passing out a Boyes anti-tank gun and directing me to use it. From my experience in the infantry training battalion I knew there was only one way to fire these abominations, and that was on top of the ground while lying on your stomach and letting the recoil slide you backwards. I simply did not know how to handle one from a slit trench, where I could be in all sorts of trouble, so resolved that if light tanks were dropped from the air I would climb out of the trench and use it on the surface. They were useless weapons at the best of times and the thought of being so exposed was not a cheering one. As darkness fell I glumly covered myself with a blanket and stretching out in the trench without even bothering to remove my boots was asleep in two breaths.

In between the radio watches I undertook the roving pickets during the small hours and at first light stood to, peering up at the mackerel skies waiting for the bastards to come. As the sun rose higher we took time off to shave and as the days wore on an old man's face began to look back at me from my steel mirror. I was only twenty-four. When we had left Syria a few weeks earlier I had a full head of black hair. Now there were touches of grey at each ear and I looked to be under ten stone.

Sleep, or the thought of it, became a sick joke and the feeling was one of total despair. Exhaustion was making me dizzy and lightheaded. The situation was driving me into the ground; I could not stand much more and something was going to crack. But the corporal got there first. I came back from the strongpoint one day a somnambulist, to find the corporal had been evacuated to a field hospital; his kidneys had temporarily packed up. One of our signals captains was waiting with a sergeant to transport me back to Headquarters where he would arrange for a relief crew to take over.

Back at Headquarters no one mentioned parachutists but on the very first day I landed in trouble. All radio sets, the telephone exchange and administrative offices had been dug in and from the surface the area looked like a piece of ordinary desert with three or four vehicles very widely dispersed. I had commenced operating a radio immediately after breakfast. The set was in a little dug-out covered by a small camouflage net. Even its little rod aerial had been sandblasted and from a few yards away it was almost impossible to see it. I was working back to Corps Headquarters; the traffic inward was quite steady — all in five-letter cipher — and once I got used to the British operator's style I began to feel I was earning my keep.

About mid-morning and in answer to the call of nature, I took a spade and clambering out of the dug-out walked a few yards away and scraped a small hole. I had hardly resumed my position at the radio when distant shouting, growing louder, caused me to remove the headphones and listen. Somebody in a high voice was really going to town, shrieking in fact. I caught some of the words.

'Filthy beast! Disgusting! Sergeant, get that man's name!'

Good Lord! He was talking about me!

Apparently I was everything that's vile. What was he going on about? Even the Brigadier used a spade. I was about to stick my head up out of the dug-out when the raving was interrupted by the quiet voice of the sergeant.

'Sir, that signalman has just come in from the forward lines. That's the way they live out there, Sir, they don't have toilets.' Good, I thought that's telling the idiot.

'Well, tell him we have toilets here,' the voice screeched back, 'and make sure he uses them.'

Thinking how pathetic it all was, I listened to him receding, expecting the sergeant to poke his head down and admonish me, but he also walked away. He knew I had the message.

Conditions at Headquarters apart from that incident were infinitely better and health and morale improved. We even received a beer ration; the first for months. Unless one has experienced desert wartime conditions it would be difficult to understand what that beer meant to us. Water was rationed and we even had to forego some of our waterbottle supplies so that the cooks would have enough. The water was heavily chlorinated, tasted foul and made tea horrible to drink. Because of impurities and flying sand there usually remained about an inch of sludge in the dregs. Dust was a problem; even as we ate, a gossamer-thin skin of fine particles would settle in our pannikins and on windy days eating while squatting on one's hunkers was not easy. Cleaning utensils was also difficult and rubbing them with sand was a poor substitute for hot soapy water.

It was mandatory to shave and for this and cleaning my teeth I used a tablespoonful of water or perhaps a little less. Actually I used to fill the little lid in which I kept my toothpaste. Occasionally I enjoyed the luxury of a 'bath'. This consisted of filling my mug about a third full and using the shaving brush to dab water over my body. It was impossible to rinse off the soapy water so it was wiped off with the towel and this was the worst problem. The towels became sour and there was no way of washing them. I tried petrol but it did not improve matters, in fact after a short time the towel was in a worse condition than before. Water consumed for hygiene left less to drink, usually as tea or if you had been lucky enough to have received a food parcel, then cocoa.

The 8th Army began to improve its supply lines and we received clean darned socks, a pair of shorts and a shirt. Our rags were taken away and we were informed there would be regular changes. When we left Syria I wore a pair of shorts and a shirt and carried a change. In that climate we had no underwear, nor was it necessary. After six weeks I put on the change and wore them for seven weeks, then donned the first pair still unwashed. The strange thing was that I never smelled body odour on any desert soldier. Cynics may say this was for obvious reasons. But our liquid intake was small, the food very plain, and we did not perspire a great deal despite the heat. We also passed very little urine. Perhaps our bodies needed every drop of liquid? Each part of us was impregnated with white dust, our hair a caked mat impossible to comb. I received a bottle of hair oil in a food parcel once; I hate to think of the mess that brilliantine would have caused. The dust probably acted as a deodorant but I lean to the theory that if we do not wash, our own bacteria take over and clean us providing we do not upset their natural function.

We did have one inviolable rule, however, and it related to food parcels from New Zealand containing fruitcakes. These fruitcakes were deeply appreciated but the effect on our pauperised stomachs was nothing less than dramatic. No one, after eating fruitcake, was permitted to break wind inside a radio van but first must remove themselves to distant parts.

Everybody knows about the flies at El Alamein but there are flies and flies. Later I would walk through clouds of them in Italy but they never bothered us the way they did in the desert where they were crazy for moisture. Major battles had been fought about us and corpses left lying. About thirty yards away from where we slept was a large knocked-out armoured vehicle so badly damaged we could not identify it. Beneath its debris were the remains of bodies and from its ruins the flies came direct to us. It would have required a crane to lift and clear so there was nothing we could do but live with it. Desperate for moisture, they crawled over us like spiders, seeking eyes, lips and nostrils. We were always in a state of motion, brushing them off. I used to place my pannikin of food inside a little canvas bag, drawing its string tight and leaving only a small gap through which I would thrust my spoon. With the other hand I described circles round the spoon on its way to my mouth, attempting to get it there without flies. But it was all pretty futile. I picked fourteen struggling flies out of my mug of cocoa one day; I could not squander a mug of liquid because it made up a good deal of my day's ration.

Another problem was the condition of our skin. Perhaps it lacked sufficient moisture because it broke very easily. The slightest knock would cause a festering sore on fingers, arms, legs or just about anywhere. 'Desert sores' covered us. I had a lump in my armpit and a beautifully inflamed arm; nurturing it, I dreamed of being evacuated to hospital with blood poisoning, convalescing in Alexandria drinking cold beers.

There was no mental stimulation, nothing in the way of conversation, nothing to read except the odd letter from home. There was fear of course, but since this was as regular as our motions it did nothing for our brains. When I entered the Army I had been at an important period of my development. It was probably the same for most of us; those who became officers were obliged to use their initiative, but for the rest, blind obedience while living in a mental vacuum was quite disastrous. There was nothing but glare or grey bleakness; our eyes were starved for colour. Only the flash of a lizard would break the monotony. I had hoped to meet someone older than myself at whose feet, literally, I could sit and learn, a kind of guru, but sadly no such person ever eventuated.

We were all the same, thousands of us; dirty, gaunt faced, dessicated brown rats, clad only in bleached shirts and shorts, our boots rubbed white by the sand. With our uncut hair, swathed in grey bandages and little pieces of sticking plaster and surrounded by a halo of flies, we must have presented a weird sight to the plump, pink-faced, British infantry moving up through our lines. Fresh from the United Kingdom, legs and arms white as newspapers. How were they to know that the rags and plaster covered only desert sores and not wounds? They certainly stared, the poor dumb bastards. They had trained for years in the soft green English countryside and here they were in this strange lunar landscape inhabited by patched-up zombies. Bewilderment showed in their eyes as they plodded past. We felt sorry later; perhaps it was just another instance of bungling, but to put a new Division inexperienced in desert warfare into a night action so soon was difficult to understand. There is no cover in the desert, not one single blade of grass. They made a night attack, took their vehicles up too close and the highly efficient Jerry spotted them. In the illumination provided by burning transport the Germans cut them to pieces. The New Zealanders were obliged to go to their assistance and as a fighting unit it is possible they ceased to exist after that. The next day, and the day after, some came trickling back in twos and threes, carrying only their rifles and wondering what had happened to them. From our meagre supplies of water we brewed tea for them. It probably tasted horrible, but they were grateful and as they sat sipping, their humour reasserted itself; what they said about the effing war, the effing desert, and the effing High Command was extremely funny but quite unprintable. We watched them trudge away, hoping they would not blunder into minefields on their way out.

I was sitting in reflective mood one night on the Headquarters toilet seat enjoying the moonlight and stars and listening to a plane heading in our direction. We could usually identify the Luftwaffe because of the unsynchronised engine beat of their bombers; I thought this was one of ours and perhaps it was. It came on flying low and then there was an almighty 'crumph': they had let a bomb go and I was directly in the flight path. I threw myself on my face, hoping my bare white bottom would not act as a reflector in the moonlight and cringed waiting for the next bomb to fall. Talk about getting caught with your pants down!

The plane passed directly overhead and disappeared. One bomb out of nowhere was unusual because there was usually some sort of pattern in an attack. This particular bomb killed two chaps who had come in from a forward area, where their lives were probably at greater risk, to appear at an enquiry into a missing radio battery. I imagine after that the enquiry was not pursued.

The following evening I received a visit from the officer who on that first day had got so uptight about my lack of potty training. He was wearing his steel helmet and appeared agitated.

'Get your helmet on, the Germans are attacking.'

What was he going on about? To humour him I took off the headphones and put on my helmet, at which he went on his way. Surely he was not going around ordering people to put on their tin hats?

It was the night Rommel launched his attack to break through the Alamein

Signals operating a number 18 radio set at Baggush. *Alexander Turnbull Library*

line between Alam Halfa and the Qattara Depression, where his forces hampered by the heavy going in the soft sand were to get hammered by the artillery and nonstop bombing of the Desert Air Force. Earlier, I had stood up in the dug-out and looked out puzzled by the roar of the artillery behind us and the direction in which it was firing. From left to right and on our flank it was a sustained bombardment, the flashes of the guns lighting the skies like sheet lightning. I presumed the artillery knew what it was doing.

It was to be a peculiar night with little sleep for anyone. German planes began to drop bombs on us. First they dropped flares, at which a few people took pot-shots as they floated down illuminating the area. Then they commenced dive-bombing us, sometimes dropping bombs, sometimes just using their banshee wail. It went on and on, totally confusing and quite alarming but nobody seemed to be getting hurt. It was reminiscent of Guy Fawkes night in the suburbs when your street fills with smoke, rockets light the skies, and rocket sticks clatter on the roof. There were now strange glows in the direction in which our guns had been firing; a strong pungent smell of gunpowder in the yellow smoky haze which was forming.

It was all a little bit eerie. Finishing my shift, I went to get Ray. For some reason I wanted my gas mask which I had left in the dug-out by the radio. Had they been dropping gas instead of bombs in those dives? The air was certainly pretty thick. I ran after Ray, who heard my pattering bare feet in the sand and must have thought an anti-personnel bomb was rolling after him, for he stopped and did the most curious bunny hop high in the air.

A few days later I suffered quite a scare myself. Hurricane fighters were being used more and more for ground support and it became the practice, when jumped by the faster flying Messerschmitts, to use their smaller turning radius and come down low over our lines whereupon our Bofors anti-aircraft guns would put up carefully placed shots at the higher flying Germans. There was a ding-dong dogfight going on immediately overhead involving about fifteen planes and it was most interesting to watch. One of our chaps had lost a brother just a few days earlier, killed by a cannon shell in similar circumstances, but we always stood up to watch them. The nearest Bofors gun was taking opportunities to pump away single shots and to our delight they shot the tail clean off a Messerschmitt. The pilot immediately ejected, his parachute opening just in time to slow him down and the plane dropping like a stone, headed direct for my little dug-out. Shrinking down I pulled part of the radio frame, which was detached, over my head. As it was soft metal only a fraction of an inch thick I am not sure what exactly I had in mind, but the instinct for self-preservation is very strong.

There was a tremendous crash. I poked my nose over the rim of the dug-out to find the plane had landed the length of a swimming pool away and had burst into flames. One by one its cannon shells began to explode as the heat reached them and I had scarcely withdrawn my head when another crash virtually in or on my dug-out took me to my feet. Certainly some horrible things were falling out of the sky. Six inches from my chin and perched on the rim of the dug-out was a bomb almost three feet long and about a foot thick. Subsiding slowly at the knees I thought, 'I can't stay here.'

I arrived on the surface in a single bound, only to stop on realising it was not a bomb, or even half of one. It was merely a bomb container, used for dropping anti-personnel bombs. The containers opened in the air and down would come tumbling those little yellow horrors about the size of a fist. To each was attached a metal stick projection which on striking the ground caused the bomb to explode just above it, so that maximum blast was achieved. In the open and against sangars and shallow slit trenches they were lethal. I had not heard them exploding but in the racket that was going on it was not surprising.

The planes had moved away. The Messerschmitt was now a heap of smoking rubble in the blackened and burning sand. There had been enough excitement for one morning. I picked up the morse key and sent out a strength signal to inform anyone who had been calling me that the shop was open for business.

We were asked to vacate the dug-out we had been sleeping in because it was wanted for battery charging and as a workshop for radio maintenance. We took over one of the remaining signal vans a couple of hundred yards further up the slope. It was partially dug in to protect its wheels and tyres and covered with a camouflage net. Alongside was a gun pit in which an old Lewis gun was mounted on a tripod. Lewis guns were almost museum pieces but as they tended to spray their shot they were useful for ack-ack purposes.

One afternoon two or three of us were stretched out like lizards half asleep when small arms fire caused me to open my eyes. A very low-flying German bomber was about twenty feet above my head. There was black smoke pouring from it and I rolled over to see if I could spot the rear gunner in his little cupola at the tail, but could not see him. It appeared extremely doubtful whether the plane would reach the German lines and we watched the increasing plume of smoke as it disappeared over the ridge ahead.

In fact, we ended up in trouble over that particular incident. About a hundred or so yards to our right was the first aid post from which the doctor had watched the plane fly over. He reported our failure to man the gun and gratuitously added that we ran like rabbits every time there was an air raid. As a result we received a visit from one of our officers who demanded an explanation.

I had actually forgotten about the damned gun; that's what becoming a radio operator does to you. We should have manned it, but I am pretty certain there would not have been time. It all happened so quickly and that is exactly why the German pilot was holding the plane low — to avoid giving warning. In retrospect we could have raked the plane from end to end if we had been ready, and perhaps administered the *coup de grâce*. On the other hand any falling shot would have tickled up the gunners of the British medium battery higher up the slope. No training had been given on how to fire the gun, or whose responsibility it was to look after it. We were not the original occupants of the site; people were already there when we joined them and dug our own slit trenches. I had fired a Lewis gun as a school cadet but doubted whether the others had or were familiar with one. As for running like rabbits during air raids, it was not the German aircraft we worried about but our own anti-aircraft gunners. We were fairly high up the slope and during raids shrapnel used to fall quite heavily as the gunners below hosed the sky with their Bofors. We ran to put on our steel helmets. If we had been running from the bombs we'd have dived into our slit trenches; and if the doctor had bothered to walk over and talk to us instead of putting in his piddling report he would have found we had almost as many pieces of steel around us as there were stones.

I think the officer accepted the situation; with the flies and the stench from the corpses it was bad enough without the bloody doctor joining in. I speculated what would be his reaction if I put a burst from the Lewis gun next time up his rear end.

Someone passed a cablegram down to me in the dug-out: it was the first wartime one I had seen. It was from my girlfriend. It contained eight words; my best friend had been killed instructing a pupil in night flying and had been buried at Bournemouth in England. That was another one from the tennis club; there weren't many left.

Rumours of leave were in the air and they proved correct. This was tremendous news, because I was one of the early ones to go. Standing up in a truck rattling along the Desert Road, filled with exultation at the thought of three clear days in Cairo, I encountered in the party an old acquaintance from infantry days.

'What's it like out there?' I asked curiously.

'Bloody awful. You can only move after dark and that's when we get our rations. We all get up out of the trenches and walk around and stretch our legs. The heat during the day is terrible.'

I could quite believe it, and tried to envisage what it must be like pinned in a hot cramped little trench all day. Thank God I was out of that lot; at least we could move about on the surface most of the time, and walking to the distant cookhouse three times a day gave us plenty of exercise. These chaps would have their food brought up in hot boxes and would hardly move at all, except perhaps on night patrols.

Don had fallen silent; in fact he didn't have much to say at all. He was much quieter than he used to be. I studied him covertly and he appeared to have lost even more weight than I had. His poor weatherbeaten face was seared red on brown, there were deep ridges on his forehead, and sun wrinkles had cut their way down both sides of his nose. The poor beggar. It only confirmed we had done the right thing in getting out of the infantry. It was a short life and not even a merry one.

My old mate Len from Sig School was also in the truck. The last time I had seen him was when he was sitting in the annex at Minqar Qaim with his puttee lying round his ankle. We had plenty to talk about. A piece of the shell which he thought had killed five and wounded seven sliced through the tape which tied his puttee; you couldn't get anything closer than that and the experience appeared to have made him feel lucky because he was in excellent spirits.

The leave party was to be accommodated at the excellent New Zealand Club, and as we passed the pyramids with the green belt of the Nile and Cairo in sight, everyone's thoughts, after the hardships and austerity of the preceding months, were on the self-indulgence we were going to pursue amongst the city's fleshpots.

It was my intention to take a long hot bath first but the majority of our little group decided that shampoos and haircuts should be first on the agenda, so I went along with them. Will I ever forget watching the black stains as the barber soaped and rinsed my head over the basin!

'You been up the desert?'

I nodded, too embarrassed to speak. Then it was back to the Club for hot showers and clean gear. As darkness fell we entered a smart little restaurant, a new one to me; how wonderful to feel clean and sit on a chair at a table in the bright electric light. The waiter arrived with handles of cold dark beer, beaded with moisture. What ecstasy! We sipped our way through four apiece.

We ordered devilled kidneys underdone, with heaps of bacon. Finishing, we sat beaming at one another.

'Let's do it again.'

We were of one accord. Four more handles, and the kidney and bacon tasted as good as the first lot. Sated, we moved to a nightclub to sip slowly, sit with the hostesses, pay for their drinks and watch the belly dancers on the central stage. We had no energy for anything more.

The next two nights were probably repetitions of the first, because the only event which remains in my mind was disgustedly watching a South African soldier standing astride the door jamb of the main entrance of Groppies Nightclub, urinating profusely upon the pavement as passers-by took evasive action.

All too soon we were being driven slowly in convoy through the main streets of Alexandria. On the way down we had gone nowhere near the city and were obviously routed in this manner to give the impression that we were fresh reinforcements, and so raise civilian morale and spread alarm and despondency amongst fifth columnists. Who was to know we were the same old digs who had returned to Cairo via the pyramids and were now being 'recycled'?

On the Desert Road again, after leaving the city, it was clear that even in four or five days there had been an increase in activity. New equipment was everywhere. Tanks were being camouflaged to look like trucks and vice versa; dummy guns were being set up. There was also good news on arrival back at our unit; the Division was being pulled out of the line and was moving back to rest and refit.

We handed over to British troops and went onto an immediate radio silence. With nothing to do I was lounging in the back of the van when the bottom appeared to fall away, flinging me to the ceiling as the van crashed into a small shell or bomb crater. Picking myself up as we continued grinding on, I wondered if I had done myself any internal harm. I felt a little odd and had certainly received a terrible jolt. Actually something inside had ruptured, or perhaps been torn, because in our new position I passed blood for three days and on the advice of the sergeant reported it to the doctor. 'Bring a sample with you tomorrow in a bully beef tin,' was his reaction but it was just my luck: on the following morning my urine had returned to its normal colour, or at least normal for desert conditions, where it could vary considerably.

We were provided with new transport, and our old heaps were driven away. The new vehicles were infinitely better than what we were used to and the radio vans not only had all-metal bodies but they were four-wheel drive; no more canvas canopies sucking in the dust, no more grunting and pushing ourselves out of soft sand, or certainly much less. There were armoured cars and we were even provided with an armoured command vehicle. What a great beast it was. Inside were two of the larger No. 9 radio sets with swivel iron chairs for the operators, anchored to the floor. We had averaged only about four desert miles to the gallon in our vans. What would these monsters consume? None the less we were beginning to look like a pretty high class motorised Division.

I walked over to a little group who were passing around a German Luger pistol. The Luger was a neat weapon; a little touchy on the trigger, but it was everyone's ambition to get hold of one. There must have been about ten of us in a tight circle when an officer approached to see what was going on. He was a quiet chap, who at times had appeared to me to be a little out of his element and perhaps insecure in his relations with the rank and file. Just how insecure I was not to know. He held out his hand for the weapon which was passed to him; he put his finger on the trigger and the pistol discharged. Where that bullet went and what direction it took I'll never know. We were so close as to be touching, some looking over the shoulders of others. The barrel was pointing slightly downwards. Not a word was said as we melted away like snowflakes in the sun, leaving him holding the pistol.

There were great comings and goings of tanks, American Grants and Shermans, and plenty of aeroplanes flying around, most of them ours. Optimism was in the air. All too soon the Division was moving back into the Alamein line but some radio people were being left behind and I was one of them. Two of the old-type vans were being used to set up a radio deception scheme, and all day long and part of the night we sent off dummy messages to Corp Headquarters and received others in exchange. In the meantime the Division would maintain radio silence to disguise its presence in the line. Most of the radio operators, or at least a good number of them, were professionals trained either by the Post Office or Railways and capable of high-speed Morse of good calibre. Without any disrespect to other formations, I think perhaps it would have been fairly easy for the German intelligence to identify our radio network. Many British-trained Morse operators also had a distinctly different style of sending.

It was a bit of a lark being left to ourselves, just one officer and about half a dozen of us, and nice to feel detached from the war which was going on somewhere else. We certainly took it easy. Sitting up one dawn in my blanket I found myself studying the snail trails on the tumbleweed; the desert was surely a strange place to find small snails. You never saw them in the daytime. Where did they come from? Where did they go? I used half a pup tent to sleep under and keep off the dew. Other bundles around me were stirring and raising themselves up to rub sleep out of their eyes.

It was pleasant to sleep on top of the ground for a change instead of in a slitty.

The weather had been great but there was no way it was going to let us sit around nice and relaxed. It had a couple of surprises in store for us. Without warning and out of a clear blue sky, we were hit by a severe hailstorm which sent us scurrying for steel helmets. Most of the hail was as large as golf balls and one or two pieces almost the size of tennis balls. Fortunately it was soft, or getting soft, otherwise it would have inflicted injury. We went around after it was over, filling up our jerricans. Although it appeared white as it fell it was disappointing later to find only yellow muddy water in the cans and unusable at that.

The next *pièce de résistance* was a dust storm and a beauty it was too. I had heard of them, but this was my first experience. I was sitting in the radio van when suddenly it went dark. Looking through the window all I could see was a yellow opaqueness. The atmosphere became oppressively hot and visibility was down to six feet through the swirling dust, so that we dared not leave the van and remained virtually cut off from the occupants of the other truck only yards away for about two days. Small flies had arrived with the storm, and a bird about the size of a sparrow had joined us inside the van; goodness knows where he came from because he or it was the only bird I ever saw in the desert. He had beady eyes and was as perky as you like, quite prepared to share the van with us. There was no getting into your blankets, we just closed the door and sat inside the van.

When the storm cleared the bird was first out the door. What a changed scene it was outside; the whole landscape had been altered the way beaches change over the seasons when pounded by heavy seas. Where there had been flat ground were rising slopes; familiar depressions had disappeared, making way for new ones. It was just as well the Army operated by compass because the track by which we had come into this area had completely disappeared. We were obliged to dig the sand away from the vehicles, as it was now heaped above the tops of the wheels, and uncover various items of gear we had left strewn around when the storm hit us. It was an interesting experience but once was enough and it was good to get outside again and cook a meal.

We were still sitting around a greasy pan containing a hard old biscuit mixed with cheese, when an armoured car appeared; the first sign of life since the Division had disappeared over the horizon. It stopped a hundred yards away and a British officer stepped down and approached. He introduced himself to our officer who was sitting yarning with us, sat down, and proceeded to conduct a conversation with him. He was obviously fairly new to the desert. We were shortly joined by the driver of the car, who after a few minutes went back to it, returning with his rifle which he proceeded to clean. I cannot remember what he said, but as he cleaned and polished and oiled the barrel I thought, surely this was carrying naivety too far. After a while, his boss — who had not stopped talking — wandered over to the car himself and came back with an almost full bottle of whisky. Our faces must have been a study.

'Have one?' he said to our officer, but the offer was hurriedly declined.

'You don't mind if I do?'

'No, go ahead.'

For the next hour he sat there talking and scoffing the whisky while his driver industriously worked on the rifle. What a pair, and so well matched. I had never considered the possibility of anyone driving around the desert in an alcoholic haze. What about your reflexes if Jerry appeared? It might have been alright in England, darting into the local for a quickie, but not here. This joker was not going to last very long.

During those two hours that the one-pipper sat with us, not once in any way did he acknowledge our presence or address a single remark to us. I sat within eighteen inches of him, but for him I did not exist. Even my tatty old biscuit was consumed before they left, both unconscious of the irony.

A signal came ordering us to close down and rejoin the Division.

Chapter 6

The Advance Begins

Alamein to Tripoli

Bowling along the Desert Road there were two of us in the van. We had received a signal to close down and rejoin the Division. Losing the others in the heavy traffic, we were heading westwards looking for a South African Divisional sign, where we were to turn left off the road and follow a track.

We crested a ridge where there were signs and a couple of provosts directing traffic; I thought this must be the spot we were looking for, but the driver kept going so I sat back and relaxed. Shortly we passed through troops dug in on a forward slope, as we descended into a plain. They were bare from the waist up, tall, heavily muscled and brown as berries. Only Australians could look like that; they must be 9 Australian Division, which had recently joined us.

We were now on a dead straight stretch leading to higher ground. There was no sign of life to the left, right, or ahead. I felt extremely uneasy.

'Slow down!' the driver took his foot off the accelerator.

I had the distinct feeling of being watched. Those Australian troops back there, they were dug in on a forward slope, they were in their trenches and not walking around, and they were infantry. I don't recall what I shouted to the driver but he arrived at the same conclusion simultaneously. The van went round in a lurching, bucking U-turn without regard as to whether the edges of the road were mined or not. As we raced flat out back along the road I was expecting a shell up our backsides every moment.

Back through the Australians we roared, not stopping until we reached the ridge where I had seen the provosts. There was the South African Divisional sign; this was the place. We had nearly presented Jerry with a perfectly good truck and a radio set in operating order, and finished up in the bag ourselves. The alternative could have been to blow ourselves up on one of our own mines.

There was tension and excitement at Headquarters. The date was 23 October 1942 and that night the 8th Army was going to make an attack along the whole front. Somebody said we had 900 guns ahead of us, almost wheel to wheel, and there was going to be the biggest gun barrage ever heard in the Middle East. Bofors anti-aircraft guns would also be used, firing tracer to mark the lines of advance.

We also learned that 4 Brigade had gone back to Cairo to be trained and reorganised into an armoured brigade, and that the Division had been strengthened by the addition of 4 Light Armoured Brigade and 9 Armoured Brigade. These British units had joined us while we were engaged in our deception scheme. The plan was for us to operate with 1 and 7 Armoured Divisions as a pursuit force under 10 Corps. Nothing was planned for our little group, however, and uncertain of my role I sat with others on the roof of a cab, like spectators at a Chinese fireworks display before the show starts.

We were waiting for the moon to rise. In Montgomery's words, this was where we were to 'hit the enemy for six right out of Africa.' What a different feeling from those earlier months when we danced to Rommel's tune!

The first flash came, and then a ripple of fire along the whole front. Uneven to start with, soon the flashes synchronised to a growing drum beat. It went on and on and on. By early morning the New Zealanders had advanced 6000 yards and captured Miteiriya Ridge, but the enemy was offering stubborn resistance and the attack gradually ground to a halt.

Early exultation was disappearing, to be replaced by concern; 9 Armoured after initial success were unable to breach the enemy's gun line and were taking a lot of casualties. Their determination and gallantry, however, were to do a great deal to alleviate the bitterness many New Zealanders felt towards the British armoured formations after the disastrous New Zealand casualties suffered at Ruweisat and Mrier where the expected armoured support was not given by the British when requested.

Something had to break the stalemate and it was the Australians who

Messerschmitt fighter shot down by a Hurricane burns outside Sollum.
Alexander Turnbull Library

did it. Ninth Australian Division out on the coast, the troops we had driven through, made a spectacular advance in their sector which created a serious bulge in the enemy's defences which Montgomery was quick to exploit. It was the beginning of the end. After eleven days of heavy fighting, 10 Corp finally broke through and leaving the Italians to their own devices, Rommel endeavoured to withdraw his forces as quickly as possible to avoid annihilation. The chase was on.

I had been teamed up with another corporal and we set off in a brand-new radio van to rendezvous at the El Alamein Railway Station with a divisional ammunition company for whom we were to provide radio communication. Like all things in the desert, the station was not easy to find; in fact I have not seen it to this day. We had some difficulty skirting minefields but linked up with the ammo company in due course. Jack was driving and I was sitting in the cab with him, wearing the headphones, the radio behind me within reaching distance. What an improvement it was on the old 'bread vans' and 'pick-ups', and how marvellous it was to be advancing instead of running backwards in retreat.

Another operator, very close to our frequency, was pumping out immaculate Morse even although he was on the move like us; I knew it was Tubby because I recognised his distinctive style. He was one of our 'professionals' and 'rolled' his Morse as did several ex-Post Office telegraphists in our company; that is, while still sending perfect signals, they could impart to their morse a rhythmic roll which was pleasant to listen to and, despite its high speed, easy to receive and take down. Tubby's sending was in tune with our engine note and it was good to be all going forward together.

The actual passage through the minefields and enemy defences the first night was very confusing. It was dark and we could not tell friend from foe as we moved in column, keeping an eye on the white tapes which marked the route. This was a stop-start business with infantry still dug in on either side. To our left was a hovering aircraft which was attracting a good deal of small-arms fire but it was impossible to tell who was doing the shooting and what the forces in the dark around us were engaged in. At one stage one of our chaps was hit in the foot by a bullet, but we finally got clear and shortly after dawn were hard on the heels of the fleeing forces.

Abandoned equipment and demolished vehicles were strewn everywhere, some still smoking. Near Fuka we crossed a piece of road where it was clear that the Desert Air Force had had a go at enemy transport and the scene was grim. It was all becoming a bit of a mad gallop when short of Matruh down came heavy rain, the first I had encountered in North Africa. This occurred on 7 November and could not have happened at a worse time for the Allied forces. The effect was devastating, turning the desert into a muddy bog through which it was almost impossible to make progress. Jack and I were on the extreme left flank, and as the going got worse we found ourselves skirting a minefield and drawing further away from the rest of the transport on our right. It was a case of everyone for himself; if we had been using our old pick-up we would not have advanced a yard.

For some time we had been digging great ruts with the mud almost up to the floor, but with the four-wheel drive were able to reverse back through the ruts then charge down them again, engine racing, to gain a few more yards. Progress was slow and heavy on petrol but we appeared to have found a base down to which the rain had not yet penetrated. We were rather enjoying the unique method of progressing when we were motioned to stop. It was our first chance to look around and as far as the eye could see were hundreds of vehicles completely immobilised. This was serious. The Germans, retiring along the Desert Road, would not be affected to the same extent and would in all probability escape.

We were only a few yards away from Colonel Crump's staff car as we were to find out next morning, when, fed up with standing in a puddle every time I got in and out of the car, I endeavoured to move it a yard only to be halted by Crump's stentorian roar. (At that time he commanded the NZ Army Service Corps.)

Perhaps a day later, as the ground dried out and became reasonably firm, we moved towards Halfaya Pass on the coast where traffic congestion built up as desert formations reduced to single columns. We were halted half way up the pass, actually a steep bare escarpment, when a shout stopped a Bren carrier overtaking us.

'Don't you know this bloody pass is mined!'

It was interesting to see how quickly the crew quit that carrier to join us, stepping delicately as if walking on eggs. The driver remained in his seat; the motor was ticking over and so were his thoughts. One false move and he could be blown sky-high, perhaps taking us with him.

'Straight back, now, nice and slow,' an officer cautioned him quietly.

The driver's chest rose as he sucked in air, engaged gear, then slowly moved back, none of us breathing, until the carrier regained the track and stopped behind us.

We had only just relaxed when there was an air raid and bombs began to explode at the foot of the pass. As huge palls of smoke rose and more planes came in we looked around for cover but dared not leave the track. Being so high up with no vegetation we were ridiculously exposed but we were lucky; in single file we offered nothing like the targets congested below and the planes ignored us.

We moved to the top of the pass where engineers were prodding the ground with bayonets looking for mines. One came over to us.

'We're going to set off a few mines, so you'd better take cover.'

Thinking that there was never a dull moment, I stretched out on the ground behind one of our rear wheels and the mines went off barely feet away, several of them at once.

A 6 Field Regiment quad and gun climbing Halfaya Pass. *Alexander Turnbull Library*

We stayed with the Ammo Coy until the Division halted at Menastir near Bardia, where we went into bivouac. We had been buzzed by the odd two or three aircraft and heard gunfire ahead, passed knocked-out tanks but never ourselves caught up with the action in front. At Menastir we rejoined Divisional Signals. I was sorry to leave the Ammo Coy because their cooks operated with panache; daily while on the move their cook truck would range alongside and toss us tins of rations. As their 'guests' I think we received a few extras which were much appreciated. I remember eating a tin of diced beetroot; it was so juicy and such a treat in the dry desert the memory of it stayed with me for months.

Normally the food we consumed gave us no pleasure and was simply fuel to keep us going; mainly bully beef and rice, soya links which tasted like sawdust, occasionally bread and margarine which resembled white axle grease — the stuff they use as a water repellant and lubricant on outboard motors and trailer wheel bearings. Later we would enjoy tinned meat and vegetables even when not warmed up but they were yet to come.

At the end of each day, if not doing a shift on the radio, we wrapped ourselves in a blanket, lowered ourselves into a slitty and, hoping the bloody bombers wouldn't come, went to sleep. We had been doing this for months and dialogue had diminished. There was nothing to read and yarns had long ago stopped being recounted. Sexual desire had disappeared. We were becoming ascetics, almost like monks who had taken the vow of silence. The desert produced far-sighted vision, eyes permanently focussed across aridness to the distance horizon; seamen and pilots will know what I mean. We had also developed other senses; we could detect the presence of enemy planes minutes before they appeared on the horizon. On one occasion I even had time to dig a slit trench before they arrived.

It was good therefore in the bivouac area to see the goal posts go up and to play rugby again. An early casualty on the rock-hard ground, I watched our 'selector', Harry Jones. Clad in a pair of binoculars, faded khaki shorts, boots and no socks he still contrived with his fair hair to look like a distinguished man of the world striding up and down the sideline exhorting better efforts.

I took a ride into Bardia one day; what a dump. It apparently consisted of a single street on a high promontory with a few buildings down below on the waterfront. A place on the map, that's about all, the small harbour the reason for its existence. A cameraman was filming 'The Capture of Bardia', using British troops in a carrier. What a fake it all was. There were several re-takes because the occupants of the carrier persisted in looking sheepish instead of warrior bold, as plenty of advice, most of it ribald, was volunteered from those on the sidewalk.

At Bardia I encountered one of those disgusting spectacles which cropped up from time to time. It stopped me in my tracks as I came out of a doorway into a large square: for a moment I had some difficulty in accepting that what I was looking at was a monumental public toilet. At my feet were thousands of neat little piles of drying human excrement; the concept of civilised human beings publicly participating in such unsavouriness was revolting.

There is no doubt elements of chance affect soldiers' lives. Standing in the sun gossiping for once, we dropped automatically at the shriek of an incoming shell — a tank shell, because of its velocity and the fact that it did not explode. A figure some yards away did not get up with the rest of us. The enemy were miles away, so where the hell did the shell come from?

Later we heard that two soldiers had stopped to fiddle with a knocked-out tank. A shot was up the spout, but perhaps they didn't know. Anyway, the gun fired and registered our casualty.

We experienced another khamseen, which I endured in a pup tent panting and bathed in gritty sweat. It was like night outside the tent and nothing moved. Sunk in a sea of black depression, thoughts crawled. It was an hiatus in living.

Soon we had put Bardia behind us, grinding along in low gear, never quite getting up with the action. Not that we wanted to — the Germans were only using delaying tactics involving our Divisional Cavalry and the units attached. One day was like another: swallow the soya bean links, start up the motor, stay in desert formation, keep your distance from the vehicle in front, brew up a cup of tea if the opportunity presented itself. Perhaps there would be a couple of air raids from fighter bombers during the day to liven things up. Then there was the same routine each night: heat a couple of cans of meat and vegetable, run out the 'Enfed' aerial, hoping its post would not get knocked down during the night, dig a slitty to sleep in, connect the spare batteries to the petrol-driven battery charger and get it going, do a shift on the radio or get into your slitty under a blanket and hope there would be no night raids. There usually were. Even if not always in one's immediate vicinity, they were close enough to make one sleep fitfully.

Winter was coming quickly so battledress was issued to replace our shorts. The jacket they gave me was passable but the trousers were threadbare with both knees neatly darned. It was said that women in the armed services back home received an issue of two. I had never envisaged going to war in patched pants and mused bleakly that if the ladies could have two pairs, surely troops in the field were entitled to one that was warm and decent.

I still believe that on this particular part of the advance we passed through Derna, Barce, and Benghazi, but the official war histories show 2 New Zealand Division's route from Bardia to Wadi Matratin as passing from Bir Hacheim to Msus, and at El Haseiat doing the left hook round the El Agheila defences between Marsa Brega and Sidi Tabet. I must be confusing it with our route back to Egypt at the end of the campaign, but it is still puzzling.

We saw very little action from Bardia to the commencement of the left

Clearing mines from route of 8th Army to Tripoli. After extracting the teller mine, the engineer digs deeper for a possible second mine; a common trick of the enemy. *Alexander Turnbull Library*

hook, except for air activity, but it was exhausting and the going hard. The van was overloaded with leaking petrol tins and lighting the primus within its reeking confines was risky. Risks in war are relative; how can you compare blowing yourself up with your own primus with being blown up by the enemy? I did cause an explosion one night when I struck a match and held it over the battery apertures to inspect the level of the electrolyte. The exploding gas was frightening as was the acid sprayed· in my face and hastily upending the water bottle over my eyes I was lucky not to suffer permanent eye damage. It was a stupid thing to do but could be attributed to senses dulled through fatigue.

There was a good deal of tension on this part of the journey because of hit-and-run attacks by enemy aircraft. I remember five fighter bombers in the last phase of their low-level dive and the bombs in the air accompanying them when a shell from a Bofors flipped one completely upside down thirty feet over our heads, sending us scurrying madly to get from beneath it before it crashed. On one knee I gained some satisfaction watching one of our officers trip over his own feet and go 'arse over kite' trying to dodge another bomb. But I must admit to being prejudiced; he was our local rich boy back home.

Rugby Championships, Tripoli, between Maoris and Divisional Signals.
Alexander Turnbull Library

The intention of the left hook had been to get behind the El Agheila defences, cut the coast road and stand firm to await the arrival of the Afrika Korps and block their retreat. By catching them between our force and the pursuing 8th Army it was hoped to annihilate them. We dug ourselves in, thinking that with only rifles on our little sector it would be pretty hairy if we were overrun by tanks, armoured cars and transport during the night; it made deciding which way to align one's trench a little difficult.

Behind us, the crew on the cook truck were displaying their ingenuity by digging a long curving trench and straddling it with the truck. I had to grin; they looked damned silly crouching in their trench regarding me seriously from under their helmets and holding rifles poking over the top — to date I had always seen them on the other end of a ladle. An officer checking our 'defences' said some men could sleep and then left. I must have dozed off, waking at dawn to gunfire. Enemy transport were visible but thank God they were veering to the left. Perhaps I haven't got the killer instinct but it was with relief I watched them escape through a gap. We were spread too thinly, had too much ground to cover, and in the hurry and darkness of the previous night some of our formations had not properly located the positions they were supposed to hold. Only 4 Field Regiment really became involved in any action.

We moved off in pursuit and as we neared Nofilia shelling from our right flank made me veer instinctively to the left. I had to use quite a bit of 'right hand down' to bring the van back in line with the vehicle ahead. About a thousand yards away, perhaps less, fleeing enemy transport was clearly visible, going like the clappers. Shells were bursting around them and our gunners were working hard but light was failing and we did not appear to be having any great success in knocking out vehicles.

We stopped in the Nofilia area on learning that the coast road was heavily mined and that Nofilia itself was extensively booby-trapped; our engineers suffered several casualties clearing the obstacles. We had also reached the end of our immediate objectives. Other units would continue the pursuit, and while the outflanking move had not been overly successful it had helped the enemy decide to pull out of the El Agheila line. So it was up again with the rugby goalposts and get ready for the Christmas of 1942.

A lot of people had put in a good deal of effort to make sure we had a decent time, and as was the custom the meal was served by our officers. Tiny Freyberg, in a very genial mood, said a few words to mark the occasion. Afterwards, feeling bloated by the unaccustomed beer and good food, I sat on a jerrican watching British troops moving up to take over. They may not even have been aware it was Christmas Day and we must have presented a weird sight. There we were in no-man's-land with football posts stuck up, a couple of keen types taking drop kicks, and the rest of us, although not exactly smoking cigars and into the port, looking more relaxed than any soldier has the right to be on active service. We were also elated at having passed El Agheila, the furthermost limit of any previous

8th Army advance, and at the prospect of a possible end to this interminable Desert War.

We left Nofilia about 3 January, passing through Wadi Zemzem. Here I lost a workmate during a bombing raid. I recalled a conversation with Ron when he first caught up with me at Maadi; he was a fast bowler representing Wellington in Plunket Shield cricket and a noisy, cheerful extrovert. He had sucked air through his teeth with a hissing sound and jocularly announced, 'I don't like this war stuff, it's bloody dangerous!'

He was right; another friend gone.

Ahead of us the Scots Greys and the Divisional Cavalry were keeping Jerry on the move; there were no set battle pieces. As we neared Tripoli, Freyberg who was right up front as usual got shot up and was lucky to escape injury. Here I caught my first sight of grass in many months and at the first opportunity flung myself face down in it to sniff its fragrance. What a relief to drive upon a proper road!

Tripoli fell as we got there and fighting was over for us for a time. We turned off a road into cultivated land and parked under trees. There were no houses but the olives were in full blossom and I drove our vehicle right into them. Entranced, I remained at the steering wheel staring at the profusion of pink and white blossom pressed against the windscreen and side windows. After so many months in the desert it was unbelievably beautiful.

That night it rained heavily; a unique experience for us. My mate and I decided that if we were going to expect rain we had better get ourselves organised and dig the pup tent in properly: a rectangle about two feet deep, a trench down the middle for our feet, a couple of tent flies to sit on and lean against, round the edges a row of sandbags to keep out the water and on top of it all the tent. A few personal bits and pieces and we had the best accommodation 8th Army could provide.

Some found wine but it was purple, incredibly dry and tasted vile. Less than half a mug was all I could stomach. Proper 'plonk', later known as 'purple death'. I filled a steel can but when the bottom fell out decided it was not for me. Others took more convincing; my mate went to a 'party', stumbling into the dug-out in the small hours muttering, 'God, I'm crook.' After taking one look at the sunlight next morning he retired to his bed for two days.

Harry, who was older than the rest of us, arrived to do a shift on the radio bringing with him a can of the ghastly stuff. He seemed for all the world an alcoholic. Perhaps he was in civilian life. I helped him into the van, obtained his solemn assurance that not another drop would so much as touch his lips, and closed the door on him.

Discipline in the field was of a high standard and we needed no supervision because we all depended on one another for survival. Accordingly, once out of the line we were left pretty much to our own devices, our officers needing a break just as much as ourselves. The Division was in bivouac,

Long Range Desert Group, the desert scouts and route finders for our 'left hooks'. *Alexander Turnbull Library*

there was no traffic and I did not know why we had not closed the radio down. But if one of our officers decided to pay one of their rare visits he was in for a shock because I was certain that after a couple more nips, Harry would be flaked out, snoring his head off.

We were looking forward to leave in Tripoli because it would be the first city we had seen since leaving Alexandria, months ago. My battledress was now fairly dilapidated, particularly my trousers which had both knees out and a hole in the seat, so I did my best with black cotton to cobble up the rents and make myself respectable. There was plenty of water, so bathed and shaved to perfection I fell in with the leave party to await inspection. Chin up, shoulders back, as the inspecting officer came slowly down the line. He stopped in front of me, eyes travelling up from my boots to the top of my head.

'Some of you are not fit to go on leave,' he observed and moved on.

Coming down behind us I knew he had halted; there was a touch on my shoulder, his voice in my ear, 'Two paces forward soldier, march!'

I stepped forward, heart sinking. He was telling others to fall out, and returning to the front delivered a brief homily on what a disreputable bunch we were and the bad impression we would create in Tripoli with the local population. Well, what did he expect? We were wearing the only clothes we had and second-hand ones at that. We had advanced fifteen hundred miles across desert, slept in them in the dirt, been desperately short of water. There were no laundries or steam irons. It is doubtful whether a clothes brush existed within the whole Division.

'Sergeant Major,' he said, pointing to me. 'At least this man has tried to make himself presentable.' (Thank goodness for those hurried stitches.) Get the Quartermaster to issue him with a pair of trousers. I'll hold the leave party.' He motioned me away.

It was unbelievable. I had a pair of trousers in no time flat from the grinning Quartermaster, although the sod had assured me more than once that he carried no spares. The survivors of the leave party, now half their original number, hauled me over the tailboard of their truck and off we rattled through the bluegums into town.

Tripoli possessed an imposing facade of waterfront buildings, gardens, and towering palms. Outside the Citadel on the waterfront, 51 Highland Division in dark kilts was on parade to skirling pipes. It was wonderful simply to stand by the sea in the warm sunshine and study passing representatives of the illustrious 8th Army. They were a rum-looking lot apart from the Highlanders, and the prize for the most unsoldierly, most disreputable weirdos must surely have gone to the LRDGs (Long Range Desert Group), many of whom were New Zealanders. Their fame was legendary but they were rarely seen. These were the first I had laid eyes on. Half a dozen individuals, each alone. Still in summer gear consisting of shirt, baggy Bombay bloomers hacked off at the knee, no socks or puttees just bare calves and boots and tatty faded Bedouin head-dress. Some were bearded, and what a piratical looking bunch they were.

These were the desert scouts, the hit-and-run merchants, the adventurers who suddenly appeared hundreds of miles behind the enemy lines to shoot up aerodromes and other suitable targets before disappearing to go to ground at first light as enemy aircraft and reconnaissance units sought them out to exact retribution. These were the people who found the routes for our desert marches and it was a New Zealand patrol of the LRDG which carried out a reconnaissance in January to find a passage through the Matmata Hills which would enable us later to undertake the left hook round the Mareth Line between the north-western end and the impassable Djebel Tebaga.

Away from the waterfront, Tripoli was disappointing. The buildings were shoddy and virtually all the shops were closed or boarded up. There were very few civilians visible, nothing to do, and one trip was enough.

We were quite happy to get back to the olive groves and play or watch rugby on the Castel Benito aerodrome where the finals of the competition were played out between Divisional Signals and the Maori Battalion, the latter winning. We were close to the aerodrome and sometimes I walked over to the end of the runway towards dusk to watch with trepidation as the heavily laden bombers, off to bomb Europe, lumbered down, engines screaming, to lift at the last moment and clear the trees.

The Kiwi Concert Party put on a concert in Tripoli and one day there I also saw Greer Garson in the film *Mrs Miniver*; it was an odd experience watching it while being in the middle of a war oneself. The big event, however, during our stay there was the full Divisional parade for the Army Commander and the British Prime Minister, Winston Churchill, whose belligerent bullfrog voice had put heart into us in the dark days. He was dressed in uniform and his white, pudgy face stood out like dough in that lean, tanned throng, and once again we were stirred to our boot soles by his words.

I met Len after the parade, still doing my old job and cracking hearty; it was the last time I was to see his long, droll face.

Chapter 7

Winners and Losers

Medenine — Tebaga Gap — Gabes — Takrouna — Cairo

About a week after we arrived in Tripoli, forward elements of the 8th Army crossed the frontier into Tunisia where Rommel had retired behind the Mareth Line; this was very strongly fortified and had been constructed before the war by the French to guard against any possible threat from the Italians in Tripolitania. Capturing this fortress by frontal assault would be extremely difficult and would involve heavy casualties.

After attacking American formations in the 1st Army which had landed some time previously in North Africa, Rommel turned back to Mareth to prepare for the 8th Army's coming attack, and then set up a counterattack himself. His intentions were known at the time and the New Zealand Division was obliged at fairly short notice to pack up and advance to Medenine, a distance of 190 miles. The move to Medenine was made at night and proved one of our roughest yet. At Tripoli we had received some long-overdue reinforcements and there were extra bodies on our vehicles. On this occasion I was travelling in one of the old soft-skinned ex-command vehicles, and lying on a table when we went over what must have been a four-foot drop. Heavy iron chairs, miscellaneous gear and radio operators all hit the roof but we kept going, nursing bruised ankles and grazed elbows.

The Medenine battle commenced on 6 March and as predicted, the enemy tanks ran straight into the 8th Army gun line, losing about fifty of their number. Our artillery and anti-tank guns, although not heavily engaged, were well sited and my old form master 'Gussy' Glasgow, commanding one of the regiments, won his DSO that day. Divisional Headquarters received some heavy shells early on, and those of us who had been left somewhat in the rear across the road from a Field Ambulance company were congratulating ourselves at being out of it when, at about five o'clock, we were jumped by a low-flying formation of fourteen Me 109s. They were within fifty yards, strafing everything in sight, when I took off in a flying dive towards my slit trench. The guns on these fighters could fire sideways and down at an angle of about forty-five degrees, and as the heavy-calibre bullets stitched their way towards me and hammered into the sand and rock alongside my neck and spine, the muscles of my neck and back were

Long Range Desert Group truck with anti-tank gun mounted at rear.
Alexander Turnbull Library

braced for impact and never had I felt so defenceless. Two members of the ambulance unit including a doctor were killed, but even bad occasions have their lighter moments; I could hear a familiar voice roaring after them, 'You bloody bastards, I've just spent two bloody days fixing this bloody engine, and you bloody had to go and put bloody bullets through the bloody thing.'

The unexpectedness of the attack caught me off balance. It was my closest shave for a time and for the next couple of days at about five I found myself looking into the setting sun just in case the performance was repeated while we remained there.

On 12 March we moved back to Ben Gardane, leaving the command of 30 Corps to become the New Zealand Corps. This included additional units comprising the Kings Dragoon Guards, regiments of Royal Artillery, anti-tank guns, 8 Armoured Brigade, General Le Clerc's French from Chad, and a Free French Group. This was the first stage of our left hook around Mareth and was to be the most eventful since the fighting at Alamein.

We found the coastal areas of Tunisia green and cultivated and the hillsides carpeted with gold and red wild flowers, but the mosquitoes were bad. The Luftwaffe were also about and one day amongst low hills we were jumped once again by fighters. As we tried to put as much room between ourselves and our vehicles, the sergeant, cool as always, was admonishing, 'Walk! Don't Run.'

We did as he said. Stretched motionless face down in the grass I slowly lifted my head over the tips of the grass blades. There were a few stunted trees in the area and behind one a bizarre piece of action caused me to laugh. Hearing this, my companions raised their heads to join in. What was happening only a short distance away was desperately serious but absurdly funny too.

One of our chaps had taken shelter behind a slim trunk but had been observed by a German fighter pilot who was making low-level runs at him with blazing guns. As the plane shot past almost touching the top of the little tree, the victim would dodge to the other side of the trunk as banking high it would come down for another run. This went on four or five times and the German pilot must have been almost wetting his pants laughing, when the roar of engines low over our heads, perhaps also heading for the tree, caused us to bury our faces again in the grass. When I looked up again there was no longer a figure standing behind the tree and the planes had departed.

Towards dusk one evening we reduced from desert formation to single column to pass through 'Wilder Gap', discovered by the LRDG. As I trundled along beside rising escarpments I became aware that although about a hundred vehicles were following me there was nobody in front. I stopped and walked back to the truck behind, which stopped too.

'D'you know where we are going?'

I was answered by an obviously British voice, 'No, don't you? I'm following you.'

Hell's bells! There was nothing for it but an 180–degree turn. I felt slightly lightheaded watching this huge column which had been following me driving soberly up and turning at the point where I did, still in line behind us.

We came to a halt at a line of vehicles stationary across our front and jumping down I ran towards them.

'Do you know where the New Zealanders are?' I asked anxiously.

No one replied but heads turned, and they looked at me curiously. Good God, it was Don Section signals, but in the half-dark and without their New Zealand shoulder flashes I had mistaken them for British troops.

There was a gap behind a jeep, and pleased at being able to shed my long tail I tucked our van in behind. What a relief! I could have led that convoy all the way back to Medenine, perhaps even given away our left hook.

The jeep moved off and our column began to pass between white tapes. We were used to these through minefields or where the bulldozers produced a pass through difficult terrain. As the dust rose we bumped into the jeep. We proceded more cautiously but we did it again, and again. I started to get a fit of the giggles as indignant protests rose from the jeep in front. Another bump was followed by threats on the night air to 'do' us. I climbed out and sat on a front mudguard, directing the driver with hand signals.

No more bumps, thank goodness. I couldn't see the jeep but the dark canopy of a truck ahead was faintly discernible and somewhere in between beneath the dust I made allowance for the jeep.

Next day we got into real desert with long sandy slopes; we were entering the Sahara. Absolute secrecy was essential; no dust clouds were wanted now. We put the camouflage nets over ourselves at every stop and faced north to provide as little shadow as possible, moving only at night. These measures must have been successful because we encountered no aircraft.

We were approaching Tebaga Gap when a flight of American fighters attacked H Section, killing one of our signalmen. It wasn't the first time they had done this and we were a bit anti-American at this time. H Section seemed an unlucky unit for signalmen.

The Germans apparently were now aware of us because an artillery duel broke out. Because of the little hills around us we could not see our own 25-pounders but alongside was a troop of captured 88 millimetre guns we were using, known as Mac troop. They suddenly became the target for an air raid out of the sun. I was standing at the back of our van talking to one of our officers and watching a Major from Administration transmitting a radio message with the assistance of one of our new reinforcements. At the whistle of a bomb coming in our direction I collided in mid-air with the officer in a joint dive for my slit trench, but I was underneath. The reinforcement witnessing our performance flung himself out the back of the van, his headphones tearing themselves from their socket, and as the shrapnel from the exploding bomb screamed over us the Major, also wearing headphones, fell legs in the air out the back also. Dusting himself down, furious at his temporary loss of dignity, he angrily wanted to know what the hell was going on. I could not have cared less, because in a dive-bomb attack it was every man for himself. What did he expect? Should we have said, 'Excuse me, Sir . . .?'

The action was certainly hotting up. The guns were blazing, and long before sunset we gazed open-mouthed as a formation of large German bombers slowly circled us for a bomb run on the 25-pounders. This was most unusual and the Germans must have been getting desperate at our flanking move. Attacks by Stukas and fighter bombers coming from a great height out of the sun were difficult to counter because of the surprise factor and the speed at which they came in their almost vertical dives, but to lay on a level stately procession in broad daylight over a gun group such as ours was asking for trouble. We would cut them up for dog's meat. All around, our anti-aircraft guns and automatic fire opened up. One plane crashed immediately. I had time to watch only one other lumbering towards us on fire. A parachute blossomed, then another appeared but tangled on opening. As the poor devil, apparently on fire, hurtled earthwards and thumped into the ground to burst near us, we all cheered, and cheered again as the bomber with the rest of the crew inside also hit the ground, exploded into flame and in a single 'whoosh' incinerated the crew. Through the black smoke and burning sand the rest of the flight were just smoking plumes disappearing behind the hill. We were not ghouls because we laughed and cheered; we had been on the receiving end from the Luftwaffe for a very long time.

H Section had got it again. This time it was Len, hit in the chest from an airburst while standing beside the artillery command vehicle. Apparently they had got too close to Jerry and amid some mild panic hurriedly withdrew, the command vehicle dragging its camouflage net behind but leaving Len lying there. He died without regaining consciousness, and although I was never able to get the full details one or two of our chaps thought it a pretty bad show. I just felt sick. It was 21 March, the day before my birthday.

It seemed to be just one damned thing after another. At about 10 p.m. and nearing the end of my first shift, I heard the sound of a low-flying fighter coming our way. The moon was not yet up and it was as black as pitch. I was just getting out the back door of the van when he let go an horrendous burst right at me. Startled out of my wits, I fell rolling down into the little wadi on whose lip we were parked. It was totally unexpected and I could see no reason for it unless he had been following the line of the wadi and giving it a burst occasionally. Then again, we were parked a little close to a British signal van in the wadi; perhaps they had shown a light or he had a direction finder in the plane and picked up their signals?

As the moon came out and lit the desert up we were visited by a bomber which decided to stay around. It flew low-level runs directly over the armoured command vehicle, backwards and forwards, always the same height, each run the same length. On my back, looking up at the big belly, I could have raked it from end to end with a tommy gun but orders not to retaliate at night did not permit this.

We believed that the Germans were equipped with radio direction finders, something denied by the official war histories, but they did seem to seek signals out. The armoured command vehicle carried two transmitters and also showed a small blue light under a flat disc on a pole above it, but surely this could not be seen from the air? Or could it, if you flew low enough? What the hell was he doing as we watched him, heads tucked into our shoulders? Then we heard them coming; small anti-personnel bombs exploding all along the flight path. There were shouts for a stretcher and the bomber kept going.

The point of half these night attacks was difficult to determine because the cost, time and effort for what they accomplished — apart from making our nights miserable — was not justified. In this instance we suffered a single casualty; one of our reinforcements, a quiet, likeable little guy who had been with us only five minutes. An anti-personnel bomb landed on his legs in his slitty and he died of the wounds it inflicted. It was 27 March, 1943.

Next day I was ordered to rejoin H Section to take Len's place. On the way I recalled his despondency that evening at Mersa Matruh when we had wandered around looking for beer, wondering what the next day had in store for us; his white face in that bloody annex at Minqar Qaim; our leave together for a couple of days from Alamein in Cairo; and him getting into the truck after the parade at Tripoli. It was a curious turn of events; he had taken my place and been killed doing my old job and now from a couple of hundred signallers I was being slotted in to take his.

H Section had not improved much. Sleep was still a problem. At some stage of the night we would stop and the Intelligence Officer travelling with us in the ACV would open up his camp stretcher, climb into it as he was and instantly fall asleep. The other radio operator and I would sit in front of our transmitters, arms folded, hunched in our seats with our feet up on the batteries with just two little pilot lights relieving the gloom. We never spoke during these periods and were never relieved; I suppose he catnapped the way I did. We were using radio telephony, otherwise it would have been impossible.

In the break through Tebaga Gap and the battle of El Hamma for the first time we had in support tank-buster Hurricanes and as we put up yellow smoke for markers they closed in. There was a lot of juddering cannon fire but once the dust began to rise and mix with the smoke we saw virtually nothing. It was clear however from the jubilation of senior officers that things were going well; the battle of El Hamma and Montgomery's decision to reinforce the New Zealand Corps with 1 Armoured Division to break through to Gabes was a brilliant success.

General view of the feature of Takrouna. *Alexander Turnbull Library*

Moving towards the coast we came upon cultivation again and green cactus; towards dusk we parked the armoured car in which I was now riding in a quaint little gully. I found an old trench and sitting with my feet in it watched a trail of ants, wondering whether to ignore them. The rocks and mounds seemed to have a pattern. Good Lord! I was sitting in an old cemetery. This was not a slit trench but an old grave. Perhaps it once held a corpse? Many times digging slitties their similarity to graves· was only too obvious but I drew the line at sleeping in a real one and sharing it with the ants proceeding from another. That night I slept on the surface and enjoyed what seemed the longest sleep of my life, but then that's what cemeteries are for.

Gabes came up, then Sousse; small battered towns with a few civilians but they were just passing shades. We were travelling fast in a great flood through green fields, salmon-coloured earth, palms and cactus hedges emerging into open country.

It must have been about here that Alan Moorehead, the Australian war correspondent, met us, because in his book *African Trilogy* he wrote:

> At last we cut around a field of cactus and joined the main road north of Sousse. With the main road we hit the New Zealand Division coming head on towards us — in the way the enemy would see it coming. They

Nearing the end of the 2000 mile journey back to Cairo. *Alexander Turnbull Library*

rolled by with their tanks and their guns and armoured cars, the finest troops of their kind in the world, the outflanking experts, the men who had fought the Germans in the desert for two years, the victors of half a dozen pitched battles. They were too gaunt and lean to be handsome, too hard and sinewy to be graceful, too youthful and physical to be complete. But if ever you wished to see the most resilient and practised fighter of the Anglo-Saxon armies this was he. This wonderful division took a good deal of its fighting morale from its English General, Freyberg, the VC who through two wars had probably been more critically wounded more often than any other living man.

After Freyberg had defended Crete and carried his gospel of the bayonet through half a dozen campaigns in the Middle East, the Germans very nearly killed him at Mersa Matruh. By continuing to conduct the battle with a wound through the back of his neck, the General practically threw away his chance of survival, but somehow he had been patched up. And now the old gentleman himself rode up the road standing in the open turret of a tank, and he looked a good deal younger and tougher than I had ever seen him before.

High praise indeed, from an Australian.

In the late afternoon we fanned out to stop and laager, with us on the periphery. Perhaps we were getting careless because dispersal was not good and our desert yellow showed out against the greenness surrounding us. Because of the variable weather we had recently adopted the practice of pitching pup tents at night over shallow depressions we scooped out of the soft earth, and had hardly finished putting up our 'canvas town' when the Battery Major emerging from the ACV and confronted by our tents practically turned purple shouting, 'What the bloody hell do you think you're doing? Get those bloody tents away from here.'

I repitched my tent in the far end of a little dried river bed and was walking back to the ACV when a roar in the sky and the bark of a Bofors gun made me look up over my left shoulder. Diving at us from out of the sun was a formation of enemy planes. One solitary pup tent remained and it was within feet of me; hoping it was slightly dug in I took off in a crouching run to fling myself headlong through the flap to lie alongside its occupant, Lloyd. The roar of the engines and the whistle of the bombs were in our ears as Lloyd quickly said, 'Have some of this,' passing part of his blanket over me. A blanket would not stop metal but it could give some protection against burns and bomb blast. We had heard so many bombs: first the whistle, then the shriek tapering off, and then the crumph of the explosion simultaneous with the blast, and the ground shaking; but these bombs were for us. The whistle held this time right down into my spine, there was a rush of wings, distant explosions and the Bofors stopped.

I couldn't believe it; I was intact. What happened? Emerging from the tent my eyes fell upon the black tailfin of an unexploded bomb, perhaps ten yards away. That was close, and others had gone off around us, but I thought the bomb had been closer than that because it had sounded as if it were joining us in the pup tent. We crouched behind the ACV while an engineering officer had several goes at blowing it up but without success. Telling us to give it a wide berth, he left in his jeep.

Now that the excitement was over I felt the need to urinate. I walked back to the little tent in which I had sought sanctuary and passing it unbuttoning my fly, I stopped in my tracks. At my feet was the tailfin of another unexploded bomb, buried deeper than the first. We had missed finding it. If that bomb had exploded it would have been curtains for Lloyd and me, there was no possible doubt of that; it had almost joined us in the tent.

I reported the find to the Battery Major.

'Leave it,' brusquely, 'we're moving in a few minutes.'

I ran to tear down my tent and clamber into the car, and as we slowly rounded the bomb the engineer had tinkered with, a lugubriousness filled me as I thought about how I must just have used up about eight of my nine lives.

I was standing by the ACV a few days later when, startled by the most tremendous boom, I struck my head against its steel door; a huge gun had just fired a shell somewhere in the direction of Tunis. The long barrel was still descending behind an adjacent hedge.

Recovering, I heard one of our artillery officers mutter, 'Bloody hell! That bastard's going to wake them up, this'd be a good place to be out of.'

The Battery Major appeared through the door and indicated he was of the same mind. Who could blame him? Who would want to be next door neighbour to the biggest gun on the Allied side? We moved away, albeit forward, but with a feeling of relief; those chaps manning that gun were welcome to all its nastiness, both going and coming.

The coastal plain rose into the foothills of a mountain range and to our left ahead, a prominent feature called Takrouna dominated the area. It appeared to stand by itself and had steep dark sides with a few buildings discernible near the top. Our people were giving it a good deal of attention because it was occupied by the enemy who could watch our every move. It was surprising therefore when we received a most peculiar signal from Headquarters to commence practising semaphore signalling with flags. It could have been a spoof but seemed official enough. If so, it must have emanated from someone far in the rear, perhaps at Maadi Camp over a thousand miles away, someone completely unaware that we were clearly visible to the enemy up on Takrouna.

This was even more unbelievable than the time at Alamein when we queried having to replace our faded old camouflage net which matched the sand around us with a brand new one of brilliant green. Some flatly announced that whoever gave the order must be out of his small mind, and as our officer agreed and with the Battery Major, not wanting anyone waving flags around his headquarters, probably adding his weight, we heard no more about it. I am certain also if we had used our white flags for semaphore we'd have had the enemy thinking we were surrendering, and coming to round us up.

There was fierce and bloody fighting on Takrouna above us and close to our infantry on the plain we could see them being mortared, the bomb flashes showing amidst their trenches. We heard later that Takrouna had been taken after desperate hand-to-hand struggles in which men had been forced over cliffs, and then we had to watch the survivors being hammered by enemy artillery. In and around Takrouna, casualties to officers and NCOs were unusually high. I recall the driver of one of our open armoured scout cars which had been spotting for the guns telling me of the rough time they had had trying to skirt the foot of Takrouna.

'The armour-piercing shells were coming so close and mixed up with small arms fire I decided to get out and crawl under the car and could actually see the anti-tank shells as dark shapes before they whooshed overhead. It was wild, man, it was wild!'

We occupied a little oasis fenced by cactus, a pleasant spot amid olive trees, a large fig tree, and a big stone well. It was rapidly becoming obvious, however, that these mountains ahead of us were not something we could gallop easily around, and that desert-type advances were coming to an end. Although Tunis had always been our goal, there was a strong possibility the 1st Army would get there before us, even although we were so close and had covered so many miles. In fact it was possible we might never see Tunis.

There was a growing feeling of disappointment that the campaign would not finish on a high note, but I cannot honestly say that we were fired up about it; we were not accustomed to victory parades and never would be. Even in Italy in the battles to come, our Cinderella role would continue, sometimes even for political purposes. When we hammered Florence for three days, for example, and the Germans fled, in marched the South Africans while we continued pursuit round the outskirts of the city.

Some of us were given a break and told to take a truck to the beach at Monastir a short distance away. It was sheer delight to be let loose in such picturesque surroundings; light brown earth, low stone walls, little square stone houses painted white, grills on the windows, and Wedgwood blue doors. Green grass, hedges, palm trees, dazzling white sand and sparkling blue sea. Cheerful native fishermen in white calf-length shirts, sandals, blue and red head scarves, flashing white teeth contrasting with the brown skins as they laughed and chattered under the palms fringing the beach. A small boy called Hadji, sharing his fried pieces of fish with us; we had little with which to reciprocate but did our best. This was the old Barbary Coast where, in ancient times, women lit lights on rocks lying off the beach to lure ships ashore. The beauty and the relaxation were working wonders when after three days we were recalled to the well.

I was beneath the fig tree leaning against the wall of the well when the VIP arrived accompanied by top brass. It was Fred Jones, the New Zealand Minister of Defence; it must have been an experience for him to visit us and know he was within range of enemy fire but it did not show. What pale faces civilians had! To our eyes they appeared ill. Jones gazed in my direction a couple of times so I stared back. Excusing himself, he came over, shook hands and chatted, saying he would tell my mother when he got back that I was looking well. He was a quiet man, a nice man in the truest sense, and once again I could not help reflecting what an egalitarian society New Zealanders possessed in 1943.

Speculating whether Jones had come to discuss our return home to fight the Japanese, I moved to sit in the shade of the cactus, legs stretched out, leaning back on my hands. A flicker of movement turned my head and eighteen inches from my right hand were two flat-looking little snakes, forked tongues flicking in and out. Thinking of Cleopatra's asp I did my fourth levitation of the war, but they disappeared equally quickly. I would have liked a closer look because although they possessed two tiny front legs there were none at the rear, and they were not lizards or geckos. They were not seen again, leaving me feeling I had almost dreamed the experience but they were alive, there was no doubt about that.

Mr Jones departed and for the next couple of days the only real activity was a steady stream of shells coming in on our right flank towards Enfidaville, but most of them were not exploding and one had a very strong feeling that the enemy was not so much concerned with shelling us as getting rid of his live ammunition. Somebody said the war was over and we received confirmation from our officer but there was no jumping up and down, no celebrating. It made no difference. You cannot turn off a war like turning off a tap, and although the mind kept saying it was over, the body refused to listen. We remained taut, still half-watching the sky and the horizon, still identifying every sound and remaining uneasy when some of the lights in North Africa began to come on again.

It was 13 May 1943 and the war in Africa was over. Alan Moorehead best describes it:

> . . . In the southern sector the New Zealanders and the German Ninetieth Light Division broke off their fighting at last. These two divisions were the élite of the British and German armies. For two years they had mauled one another across the desert. We had killed two of the Ninetieth Light's commanders. The Ninetieth Light had almost killed Freyberg. They had charged up to the gates of Egypt in the previous summer, and it was the New Zealanders who broke the German division's heart outside Mersa Matruh. There is hardly a major battlefield in the desert where you will not find the intermingled graves of the New Zealanders and the men

of the Ninetieth Light. And now at last it was all over.

Eight minutes to eight o'clock on May 12th is the official time given for the cessation of all organised enemy resistance in Africa. [We made it the 13th.]

No special incident marked that moment. This tragedy of three years and three acts simply ended with all the actors crowding on to the stage too exhausted to be exultant or defiant or humiliated or resentful. At the end the battlefield fell to pieces and lost all pattern and design, and those who had fought hardest on both sides found they had nothing to say, nothing to feel beyond an enveloping sense of gratitude and rest. The anger subsided at the surrender, and for the first time the German and Allied soldiers stood together looking at one another with listless and passionless curiosity.

The struggle had gone on so long. It had been so bitter. There were so many dead. There was nothing more to say.

The last of the German generals came down to the landing field and was flown off to captivity. The last of many thousand enemy soldiers trudged into the internment camps.

And in our ranks the soldiers stripped off their uniforms, washed, and fell asleep in the sunshine.

All Africa was ours.

End of North African Campaign showing our welcome party of two street urchins. *Alexander Turnbull Library*

Next day we lost one of our most popular sergeants; killed when he tossed a box of enemy pistols into the back of a jeep. We also learned that we would not be making a landing in Sicily, which we had surmised would be our next task. Instead, we were going to motor back along 1800 miles of North African coastline, to Cairo and a film unit would accompany us and show films to our various groups.

As we set off in convoy it was a strange sensation requiring a good deal of mental adjustment. The war was far from being ended or won. Yet here we were, operating in what was no longer a war zone. We still carried weapons, the radio transmitter before which we had spent so many hours remained in the armoured car, but there was no watch to keep, no war to fight. There was just the driver and I and a skinny pie dog — a couple of temporary civilians with a dog which we lost after a couple of days. I was not sorry to see him disappear because he had piddled in my lap and my enthusiasm for him had declined appreciably.

Since we were moving every day we were back to rationing water but following the coast we swam as often as we could and felt reasonably clean and fresh. At night we watched the films in the open, taking perhaps a little while to overcome our reluctance to showing lights. The first film was June Allyson in *Three Smart Girls* and the actresses looked so shiningly clean and beautiful, and the interiors of the houses so grand, that surely it was life on another planet.

One night as we relaxed in front of the screen, sitting on boxes gathered up in the darkness and arranged along the slope, the film disappeared off the screen and in the sudden dark a voice announced, 'Gentlemen, I wonder if you are aware that many of you are sitting on Italian box mines which are extremely dangerous and could explode at any moment?'

A sort of sigh ran around the audience.

'Would you please, very carefully, restack them where you found them.'

We had hardly returned from putting them all back when rapid movement and unidentifiable thudding sounds lifted us all about a foot in the air; some wag had found a heavy iron tank wheel and let it go from the top of the slope. I suppose we got back to the theme of the film again, but it was difficult as the bizarre side of the night's entertainment drew occasional guffaws completely unconnected with what was appearing on the screen.

Back through Marble Arch, Benghazi, Tobruk, Halfaya Pass, Sollum, Matruh and El Alamein, names which even after forty years bring back vestiges of depression, and there in front of us were the pyramids, and beyond them the green belt of the Nile.

On the outskirts of Cairo we felt we were coming home and straightened our backs because we were a victorious army. We had accomplished mighty feats of arms, rolled back the barbarians, made one of the greatest advances in military history; but the locals couldn't have cared less. A couple of street urchins grinned and gave us the victory sign with their fingers and that was it, except for a single jeep with two New Zealand girls and a

Journey's end: New Zealand base camp at Maadi after nearly a year's continuous campaigning. *Alexander Turnbull Library*

Kiwi waiting for us at the end of a long straight. I do not know how they felt, but their enthusiastic waving brought a lump to my throat and probably to many others. Although diminished in numbers we were in our thousands and our welcome party, the people who cared — two girls and a guy!

At Maadi Camp mail was handed out just before lunch. There were three from my girlfriend; one of normal size and two slim ones. I placed them in date order and opened the bulky one first. Although there were about thirty of us in the hut everybody was absorbed in their mail and the only sound was the rustle of paper. One always read letters two or three times before putting them down; they were our only link with sanity. I finished the first and started on the second. Some of the chaps were getting up to go to lunch. I had a slight sense of foreboding at the opening words but was utterly unprepared for what came next. It wasn't true!

'I am getting engaged to John.'

I tore open the next letter and this was even worse! She was marrying John on 22 June. That was tomorrow!

Who the hell was John? I reached for the first letter. He didn't exist then; the letter was completely normal.

'Are you coming to lunch?'

I found I was standing, with my mate on the next bed looking up at me pannikins in his hand. We were the only two left in the hut.

'What the hell's the matter with you, you look as if you've seen a ghost.'

I tried to reply but could only croak like a hooked gurnard, 'My girl is getting married.'

'Is that all?' he said, and off he went to lunch.

Alone in the empty hut I felt like screaming. If only I could do something, smash something, meet this John. Even plead. As the numbness diminished I don't think I had ever felt so frustrated in my life. In my pocket was one Egyptian pound. Bludger's Hill, that's where the cable office was. They took my pound. It was just enough. Three words. 'How could you?'

In retrospect, I really had no claim. On final leave she had said quickly one night as we left a tram, 'Do you mind if I go out with other boys while you are away?'

Of course I minded, but what justification was there for exacting any kind of promise? I strongly doubted my chances of survival in an infantry battalion and anyway, engagements or marriages by servicemen immediately prior to departure had always seemed to me to be slightly unfair. All I had ever given her was my busted signet ring, broken through lifting weights at the gymnasium; now it seemed appropriate.

I washed dishes in the Sergeants' Mess where they were entertaining Americans. Bloody Yanks! I bet that John was a Yank. I chewed it over at the sink. I had a drink, and another; I was the best damned dishwasher in the Middle East. Christ, I was getting maudlin! At midnight a friendly American sergeant was assuring me I sure could throw those dishes around. They carted me off to bed, arms over their shoulders, tipsy as an Irish pedlar, the only time I've been in that condition in my life.

Hung over next morning, I went to Cairo and standing on the top balcony of a brothel watched four South African soldiers two floors below us urinating down on to the heads of native Egyptians in the street.

'Dirty buggers,' said Joe, spitting down on their heads.

'Let's get out of here quickly,' said somebody else. We stood politely aside on the stairway as four burly South Africans passed us on vengeance bent.

We sat round a table in a café garden all afternoon. I counted the empties but still felt sober as a judge. At camp I couldn't keep still and returned to Cairo the following day without a leave pass. I was entering a service club in Esbekiah Gardens, when the glass doors burst open as a soldier, a gallon of beer gushing from his opened throat, turned around and rushed inside again, presumably to top up. Disgusted, I changed my mind and walked over to the swimming pool. I swam twenty-nine lengths but it made no difference.

Returning late in the truck to camp that night there was a sudden crash and then oblivion. The truck was empty when I came to. I eased myself over the end but could put only one foot to the ground and had difficulty in standing up. Where was everybody? There had been twenty or thirty of us in the truck, some standing, some sitting. I had been in a group on the floor at the rear.

There was a shout in the darkness from a small pick-up truck, 'Are you all right, do you want a lift?'

I hobbled over and they helped me aboard and asked where I wanted to be dropped off.

They put me down at the Signal School lines as requested and I limped over to my hut. The moon had come out and it was as bright as day. The buildings were clearly outlined and everybody was asleep. But I couldn't find my hut! It was ridiculous. I had spent six months here, off and on, and I was lost in my own backyard. I sat down against the wall of the nearest hut and as the effect of concussion wore off, my own hut came into focus directly opposite. With some difficulty I hobbled there to collapse on my blanket and fall asleep fully dressed.

It was hopeless in the morning; I could not put foot to ground. They carried me to the doctor and from there to the Camp Hospital. No permanent damage had been done but my ankle was a mess. A small metal case carried in my pocket had been flattened almost beyond recognition into wafer thinness, so I must have been airborne in the accident.

My only visitor was a Provost Sergeant with a notebook. His first question was whether I had been in possession of a leave pass. What could I tell him about the accident? But I could not remember anything. He said we had knocked down an Egyptian and collided with a tree and that others had been injured. I must have been lying unconscious, overlooked in the pitch darkness.

I heard nothing more about not having a leave pass, and lying between sheets in the comfortable hospital bed, eventually regained my balance and my peace of mind.

Chapter 8

A Change of Scene

North Africa to Europe

The usual practice when patients were discharged from hospital was for them to be passed through convalescent depots, where they would remain for a few days depending upon their state of health. Most depots were desolate places. The particular one in which I found myself was no exception, comprising wind-swept tents in which one slept on bare ground. There was a toilet and ablution block, and a mess room in which food was dished out haphazardly on to trestle tables. Daily inspections were undertaken by an officer and a sergeant, and we were glumly surveying the kumara-like sweet potatoes on our plates when the officer appeared. These particular potatoes were not only large and lumpy but also looked as if the soil had not been washed off them, and when one member at an adjoining table stood up and indignantly informed the inspecting officer that the food was not fit for pigs to eat, we listened with interest. Generally speaking, the Army attended to legitimate complaints, but to our disgust this jack-in-office merely replied, 'Well perhaps you'd like to do better,' and placed the complainant on cookhouse fatigues for the following day; needless to say there was no improvement.

We undertook all fatigues necessary to run the camp and carried out night patrols within the camp precincts. These roving patrols, which were maintained in pairs, may on occasion have been diligently performed but since the only enemy in the area would have been petty thieves, this would have been unlikely. Most of us would not have cared if they had walked away with the camp. We usually sought some sheltered spot to sit down and quietly yarn away the two-hour stint until shouts from nearby tents to clear off and let them get some sleep would set us wandering again. Since we all yelled when the guards stopped outside to gossip, we felt like robbers' dogs when patrolling.

I had a long conversation one night with Dick, who came from Invercargill and was serving in the infantry. He was telling me that perhaps because he was a relatively new chum, he always seemed to be given the Bren gun to carry during attacks. Half humorously, he described how one day in broad daylight while he was crawling up a slope pushing the Bren in front of him, he was almost shocked out of his mind when arriving at

GERMANY

SWITZERLAND

AUSTRIA

HUNGARY

TRIESTE

MILAN

VENICE

PO RIVER

YUGOSLAVIA

BOLOGNA

FAENZA

FORLI

RIMINI

FLORENCE

ANCONA

ARNO RIVER

CORSICA

ORSOGNA

SANGRO
RIVER

ADRIATIC
SEA

ROME

ALBANIA

ANZIO

CASSINO

BARI

SARDINIA

NAPLES

BRINDISI

TARANTO

TYRRHENIAN
SEA

SICILY

IONIAN
SEA

TUNIS

MEDITERRANEAN
SEA

N

TUNISIA

TRIPOLI

TRIPOLITANIA

the lip of a little hollow, he found himself peering down on the head and shoulders of a German tank commander standing up in the open turret of his vehicle. As Dick said, 'You read about not shooting until you see the whites of their eyes, but I could see the fine hairs on the back of his neck. He was just so close, and it was so personal, I didn't know whether to fire the bloody Bren or tap him on the head with it. Where the hell was the rest of the platoon or somebody with experience? Perhaps I cocked the Bren, I dunno, but the Jerry suddenly dropped like a stone and the hatch was slammed shut.'

As the tank engine revved to life, Dick flung himself backwards down the slope. The tank emerged from where it had been hiding and did a half circle round him, Dick on his knees covering it with the Bren but withholding his fire. He was immensely relieved to see it turn away and drive off. Apparently they had not spotted him through their aperture slits, but were suspicious nonetheless.

It was a crazy business this war, and quite different in many ways from what one expected. Sometimes it was even funny, but it could be chilling when sand burst into flame and gouts of blood and lumps of flesh flew; when whole vertebrae with gristle attached, or thigh and shin bone, were flung to swing obscenely on the barrel of the turret gun. These were scenes to maim your mind. A tank battle at night put the fear of God in you if it was coming your way; like metal monsters out there, they humped and snarled, guttural like gigantic grunting pigs. There was tracer and the sudden red glow as tanks received direct hits and brewed up. Armour-piercing shells would penetrate four inches of thick armour on the front of turrets, to emerge through another four inches in the rear; or failing that would become a whirling horror, ricochetting round inside the tank, discing the crew into bloody lumps, barons of beef before they roasted. Surviving tanks stopped alongside us to unload their dead and dying: uniforms in tatters bearing terrible stains, bloodless lips, ashen faces where not burned or blackened, and shock so palpable you recoiled from it. And those poor bloody tank commanders had to turn their tanks around and go on firing.

We could not make up our minds which was the worse; to be in tanks or in the infantry. I think the infantry won by a short margin, in the desert anyway. That night I spent the whole patrol telling Dick he had no long-term future in the infantry, and to get out of it if he could into some other unit. He said he would think about it, but we both knew we were talking through holes in the tops of our heads, because there was no way he could do it; neither of us realised, however, that the conversation was to prove prophetic.

On return to Maadi Camp where, because of my foot, I was probably just another nuisance, I was included in a party bound for a seaside resort a few miles up the coast from Alexandria. It proved a delightful spot, where before the war the well-to-do of Egypt lived part of their time in large beach houses amid the palms and flowering shrubs. On arrival we were greeted by a burly New Zealand Major who welcomed us, mentioned a few standing orders, and said that he would provide a wet canteen before dinner every night if we behaved ourselves.

'And if you don't,' he added, 'I'll personally pin the bloody ears back of any of you who misbehave.'

'Let him just bloody try,' muttered someone alongside me, but there was no trouble and the canteen remained open.

I liked the Major. He looked after us, we knew where we stood, and he placed not the slightest restriction upon us. We could even select our own villas, and half a dozen of us occupied a low, single-storey house with paved floors. Next day, exploring, I found a magnificent three-storey place and saying nothing to the others moved out and commandeered it for myself. There was an open, airy room right on the very top of the flat roof with no door or glass in the windows, but it had a bed, and from the room the breakers were visible less than forty yards away over the tops of the palms. It was superb. All day and every day the sun shone down on the whitest of sand and the blue, blue sea. There was no wind, and gentle breakers rolled quietly in at about waist height, so regular they were perfect for body surfing, every wave carrying a swimmer fifty yards into the beach. The temperature of the water was ideal and we spent hours in and out of the sea, until the white portions of our bodies, were tanned to match the rest of us. Before dinner we downed cool beers. Life was idyllic, except that there was no feminine company or entertainment of any kind.

One could visit Alexandria every day in one of the trucks provided and we took the opportunity a few times, but there was a limit to our funds. After the rigours of the desert it certainly was a sybarite's existence but the evening left an awful amount of time to fill, unless you played cards, which I did but rarely. It was easy however to sit musing on my roof, watching the sea as darkness fell, and lapse into moronic vacuity; the solitude was balm and with the sea air, all the swimming, and a languor introduced by the beer, lying watching the moonlight it was easy to fall asleep early and wake in the morning to a glittering new day. Rising, I would step through the open doorway, bare as the day I was born, suck lungfuls of ozone and gaze down on the blue Mediterranean spread before me.

I liked Alexandria, perhaps because it was more European than Cairo, situated by the seaside and certainly cleaner. There were beautiful beaches were one could bathe like a civilian, and good Services Clubs. I remember one which had a wooden dance floor in the garden where I danced with a Greek girl; a pleasant change from one of the hard-faced hostesses in a booze hall. Dark-haired and attractive, her name was Paola but she spoke no English and it was difficult to converse in halting French. She came with a younger sister and we met again on a second visit, but she was absent the final time I visited the club just to see her.

Relationships with women in Egypt for other ranks were rare, fleeting, and confusing, because we were never invited into homes, and had no real contact with the Tuis in the New Zealand clubs or the nursing staff. This left only the hostesses in the beer halls. I met an Israeli girl at a garden party in a palace we blundered into one night on the outskirts of Cairo. She worked in the Army barracks and sharing a taxi back into town sang sad, Russian-sounding songs. I had an awful job contacting her later to take her out but what with one thing and another it never eventuated; a pity, because it could have broken the cycle of cinema, booze, food, more booze and belly dancers.

Our status with people outside the Services appeared to be on a level with the fellaheen, the illiterate peasants who slept under thatched hovels by their patches of cultivation along the Nile. So where did people like Paola and her sister fit in? Alexandria may have had a different set of values from Cairo because of its long association with the British Navy, and our soldiers had also endeavoured to save Greece. Perhaps the Greek community in Alexandria were grateful and allowed their daughters to attend the Services Club, but it was very much a garden party atmosphere and this was presumably as far as it went.

It was a much nicer place than Cairo, however, where at times I used to feel ashamed. On Maadi Railway Station waiting civilians stood back while we poured into carriages through doors and windows like locusts, leaving them stranded there as the now overburdened train continued its journey. Along with our darker skins we had learned a smattering of Egyptian epithets which protected us from shoeshine boys, the pimps and the beggars and the gully gully men. We had learned not to consume large amounts of alcohol early in the day, confining ourselves to a cold beer and a salad, spending the afternoons in air-conditioned cinemas or open-air swimming pools. We might walk through the bazaars, a mosque or a museum, or visit the brothel area just to look. While discouraging, the latter experience could be colourful and sometimes educational. I even took part in a yacht race on the Nile. In the streets one almost got to like the smell of dung, Turkish cigarettes and coffee.

Sometimes we were barred at the doors of the dancehalls. A haggle would develop over the price of admission, pressure in the queue would grow, and then finally the doorman would be swept aside by sheer weight of numbers as we entered for nothing. We had our 'regular' hostesses who would welcome us with smiles and sit and dance with us so long as we continued to pay for their 'whisky', which was actually cold tea. We knew, and they knew that we knew, but we all went along with the pantomime. Sometimes there were fights, but once chairs began to fly the Kiwis, most of them without leave passes, would melt away before the provosts arrived. Generally, however, it was all good-natured roistering and one day a week of this was thoroughly recommended if you wanted to retain your mental equilibrium.

I remember a night at the Globe dancing with a giggling little bundle who thought she would liven things up. We were the only couple on the raised floor when she started doing bumps and grinds against me, holding on so tightly I could not free myself. The crowd, catching on, began to shout encouragement and urge her to greater frenzy. If it had been a little more private I might not have been averse to it continuing but I was not going to put on a floorshow and provide eroticism for a couple of hundred shouting soldiers. Unable to wrestle free I struggled off the floor with her clinging like a limpet, arms and legs wrapped around me, to fall across our table where she collapsed, laughing her head off.

The same type of beer halls probably existed in Alexandria but on my visits there from the beach resort I did not encounter any, and confined myself to cafés and clubs. There were sordid scenes outside these, too. To get to the Services Club I used to pass the YWCA where one day I found a ragged Arab urchin lying outside the gate exposing himself and masturbating as girls entering or leaving the club stepped over him. In Maadi Camp I had witnessed an Egyptian teenager helping in the cookhouse quietly doing the same thing out by the rubbish tins, until the sergeant catching him had fired him on the spot. But could you blame these pathetic people? God knows, they had little to entertain them or to look forward to.

I watched two New Zealand girls ostensibly gazing at a fishing boat but their eyes were riveted on the naked Arab standing at the bow just twenty feet from the promenade. He had pulled his shirt over his head prior to diving to free something caught under the boat, but it had not been necessary. He stood like a proud black statue as they remained, presumably unable to drag themselves away, taking no notice of loud comments from passing Kiwis. Where was the difference?

I could have easily spent the rest of the war as a beach bum at that resort but the Army had work for us so it was back to Maadi Camp and Cairo.

It was four months since we had returned from the Tunisian campaign, during which time about 6000 of the furlough draft had left for New Zealand, taking with them a good deal of experience and expertise. Reorganisation was under way and 4 Infantry Brigade had come back to us as an armoured brigade with 150 Sherman tanks, and various units had been re-equipped with new and more powerful weapons. The anti-tank companies now possessed not only six-pounder anti-tank guns, which at Alamein had replaced the two-pounders, but also seventeen-pounders which with their long barrels packed a lot of wallop. The Divisional Cavalry had received massive armoured cars called Staghounds and these were bigger than some earlier tanks. That old abomination, the Boyes anti-tank rifle, had been replaced by the Piat gun. The letters tood for Projector, Infantry, Anti-tank. The Piat fired a powerful and very effective rocket, and as it could be handled like a tommy gun and virtually fired from the hip, it was a big improvement in infantry defence. Heavier mortars and the introduction of a light No.38 wireless set brought a new dimension in coordinating firepower, making the Division a most formidable war machine and apparently the equivalent of two German divisions. If you added to that the usual quota of miscellaneous British units, such as the medium artillery we always had in support, and about 4500 vehicles, we were something which would take a lot of stopping. I couldn't see all this equipment being shipped off to fight in some Pacific jungle. Because of the furlough scheme, the addition of an armoured brigade and the type of training we were undergoing, it looked as if we could say goodbye to returning to New Zealand in the near future.

What we did not know was that the New Zealand Government, after a good deal of soul-searching and perhaps inspired by Winston Churchill's rhetoric, had decided not to recall us but to let us continue our Middle East role into Europe. There had been rumours flying for some time that we were going to Italy and they eventually proved correct.

The British 8th Army and the American 7th Army had invaded Sicily in July. The campaign was short-lived, being over in thirty-eight days. At a very early stage it became obvious that the Italians had no heart for the war — if they ever did — and that the possibility of their seeking a separate peace was definitely there. This eventuated when a separate armistice was signed in Sicily with Alexander, and in early September the 5th Army landed at Salerno. The Germans, however, were determined to hold Italy and poured divisions of troops in from the north. We expected to join the 8th Army, which had crossed over from Sicily and were now slogging it out somewhere around the airfields of Foggia, and on confirmation we received orders to remove all distinguishing badges, tabs and the signs on our vehicles.

The physical side of training was stepped up and it was impressed upon us that the fighting ahead was going to be very tough indeed. We would be facing German divisions and experience to date of winkling them out of strongly defended and solidly constructed stone houses showed it to be a very painful process. Because of the nature of the terrain, all transport, guns and tanks were virtually confined to the roads; there were not only gullies, gorges and rivers, demolitions and mines, but every mile or so blown bridges had to be overcome. It was definitely a type of warfare different from the one to which we were accustomed, with plenty of natural cover and protection for defending forces. There would be no more fluid rushes, in-or-go-round stuff; no more left hooks and tally-ho gallops, just hard slogging and set battle pieces with the inevitable heavier casualties.

Because our transport was to travel separately, we were loaded with everything but the proverbial kitchen sink. Entry to our particular troop ship for some reason was made through the lower compartments of tall wharf cranes, up narrow steep ladders. The doorways of the cranes had not been designed to accept the passage of troops laden with packs, bedrolls, tents, tent poles, shovels, pick axes, gas masks, gas capes, water bottles, one gallon water cans, rifles, ammunition, steel helmets and axes. It was hilarious and sweaty, with members of the crew pushing us from the rear, others pulling from the front, while we remained wedged and with our arms full unable to free ourselves. First a steel helmet slung over one shoulder would become caught in some projection; this would be freed but in the interim the pick axe had become wedged between our legs and the rungs of the ladders. It was a wonder the crew did not collapse from exhaustion; whoever decided upon this manner of embarkation must surely have gazed bemused upon the chaos for which he was responsible.

It was like old times being on a troopship and easy to let oneself imagine we were on our way home, but the green hilly country on the port bow was Sicily, and wasn't that Mount Aetna poking up?

We left in two groups, the first sailing on 6 October and arriving on 9 October, the second on 18 October, getting there on 22 October. We had air cover and escorts of destroyers which at dusk each day rushed busily about our sterns, belching great clouds of black smoke to hang low over the water and screen us from U-boats. The short trip was uneventful and we woke one morning to hear the engines stopped and find we were at anchor half a mile offshore at Taranto. The sun was lending opalescence to the smooth blue sea, and Italy that morning looked everything I had ever dreamed it to be: the pastel blues, pinks and ochres of distant buildings, a smudge of dark smoke which had risen high to taper motionless in the sky, the warmth, the atmosphere, the delicate hues and tints reflected again in the water, these were for all the world a replica of the work of some old master. But troops were already descending into lighters alongside and soon jam-packed, eager as crickets, we were ferried ashore where reality proved somewhat different from the magical seaward view.

There were dilapidated buildings with paint flaking off, and rubble in the streets, but Italy had been fought over and it was too soon to start passing judgments. A woman came down the street; perhaps the chief harlot, with hennaed hair, face painted, powdered and rouged, chest thrusting forward like one of Nelson's ships of line, skimpy skirt, mincing on high platform soles. What a sight she was, and clearly one known to the locals.

Two British soldiers came out of the doorway to watch our crocodile procession from the wharves.

'Don't know who they are, chum, but by God they're a fine-looking lot!' was clearly audible on the morning air.

Of course we were a fine-looking lot! Were we not Tiny's forty thousand thieves? We were 8th Army and had been fighting the Germans for years, not like some other outfits around with five minutes of war behind them. Arrogant? Perhaps, but not consciously so. In time we would become like any other soldiers in the Allied Army wearing battledress and mud, but on that morning we perhaps presented a physical splendour not repeated again. Some had shed their shirts and were down to shorts, lean, beautifully muscled, incredibly bronzed. Before leaving Egypt we had been issued with soft brown leather jerkins with Robin Hood green linings. Designed to be worn over battledress and greatcoats they were too full to be worn buttoned over shirts or bare chests, so we had opened the fronts and folded them neatly back to show about six inches of green on either side. Wearing them was the easiest way of carrying them. They came below the waist and worn over bare skin and shorts, coupled with the accoutrements gathered over a couple of years in the desert, resulted in something of a cross between Robin's Sherwood Foresters and the hordes of Aga Khan. It was easy to understand the Tommy's comments. No troops in the United Kingdom ever looked like these, so who were these soldiers in burnished gold? Where had they come from, to help in this war?

We walked for miles, a good deal of it uphill; it was just as well we were fit because there was no transport. Recently we had walked a hundred odd miles from Cairo to Alexandria, spread over about four or five evenings, and although route marches were usually regarded as a challenge, that continuing desert trek had proved unbelievably boring; like marching inside a tunnel. On the coast where we had spent a few days before embarkation, our officer had made us don packs and leading us himself, put us through the most ferocious high-speed marches I had ever endured up the steepest slopes he could find. I recall ascending the sides of a steep wadi under blazing sun with jets of perspiration from my forward-tilted face sweeping clear the dust and soaking the tops of my boots. Unless you had witnessed it you would never comprehend the velocity at which under certain conditions perspiration can be extruded from overworked pores. So walking through pleasant new countryside on a fine sunny morning was indeed enjoyable. We finally stopped adjacent to an Italian artillery fortification which commanded a view of the port and sea.

We set up pup tents, purchased luscious grapes from the gathering children and looked around. Over the low stone walls and through copses of trees a few chains away I encountered my first castle; a novel experience for anyone from a young country like New Zealand. At first light it was run a mile along the road and back before breakfast. I've seen this recommended in physical recreation manuals and many people do it, and although a bit of a nut myself on fitness at one time, if there was anything guaranteed to make me feel listless all day it was this kind of caper. I'm certain it does not agree with everybody until they have eaten and their bodies have warmed up slowly; until they are, how would you put it, going concerns.

Next day down came the rain, the first experienced in five months, and for a couple of days we remained crouched in the two-man tents playing cribbage. A few vehicles had arrived so we bludged a ride to Taranto. It was hair-raising because the truck had no sides; there was standing room only and nothing to hang on to. The only people who had a grip on anything were those immediately behind the cab, and as we went round bends at over forty miles an hour all we could do was to flex at the knees to maintain our balance and pray. Half way there I wished to goodness I'd never boarded the truck, but we made it safely.

Taranto as a new experience was interesting, but there was poverty all about and one visit was enough. Next day we walked northwards to a small village. Here we found that the only café had little wine and outside in the street again frequent showers began to make things a bit dismal. Our brown skins and jerkins were arousing curiosity, but it was with relief we accepted an invitation from a jolly-looking woman on her doorstep to come inside. This was the first house we had entered since leaving New Zealand and it was strange to look around at family possessions. The living room was large but cluttered with furniture and the family stood around us, all smiles and fingering our jerkins with lots of 'multi benes'; one got the impression that soft leather was a commodity in short supply and much prized. Momma plied us with wine, and later sent out for food. We ate small tasty pieces of meat; unused to the wine I developed a stinking headache, at which Momma became most solicitous, insisting I lie down on the long sofa while she bound my head tightly with a red cotton scarf.

The others were obviously enjoying themselves and it had become almost a party with neighbours crowding the room, when I decided I needed to go to the toilet. Momma, comprehending, beckoned me into another large room crammed with beds. Were there only two rooms in this house? Reaching under one bed Momma triumphantly produced a large china chamberpot. We all used it as Momma, giggling, retreated to the other room. Somehow and much later we got home, but I've never forgotten that woman's hospitality.

As soon as all the transport had arrived we were on our way, this time attached to an artillery field regiment and travelling in a White armoured scout car. The duties involved working back to H Section at Divisional Artillery Headquarters, forward to the three batteries of guns which made up the regiment of 25-pounders, and undertaking reconnaissances carried out by the Colonel. In the event he found our car too restrictive for viewing enemy positions, so used his two feet and a stout stick, or took a jeep with a radio fitted in the back. This was my first time in a signals section under the direct command of a signals officer, and a new experience because in the desert I had never stayed long enough in any one unit to really get to know people.

The section consisted of telephone operators, drivers, Morse operators, despatch riders and linesmen. At our first game of rugby in Italy we had lost our signals officer, injured in a tackle; this was bad news because his replacement was going to make my life as miserable as he possibly could. He was well over six foot but the Colonel of the regiment was even taller. Somewhat saturnine, the Colonel was a product of Duntroon; later he would rise to great heights in the military hierarchy. Even then he was held in high regard by the regiment because of his expertise and fairness, but my

God he was aloof; I think he addressed two words to me the whole time I served under him. He was also very mature, and at the time I had no conception that he was the same age as myself. He would perhaps have been the youngest Colonel in the Division. Ah well, I had cut my teeth with no lesser person than the Commander of Artillery, Steve Weir. With these types it was essential to do one's job efficiently and maintain a low profile.

It rained off and on as we rumbled miles in convoy through bleak wintry conditions; as we began to near the front the old sinking feeling in the stomach began to reassert itself. I hadn't felt it since North Africa, months earlier. I had also left my dog tags hanging over a bush back near Taranto. If I copped it, how would they ever identify me?

We were on our usual wireless silence when moving up, not that this made much difference, because fifth columnists must have identified us. In this connection I had an experience one night which left me disconcerted; at dusk I stood on a kerb watching some of our chaps milling around in a little village square.

'You're New Zealanders, aren't you?'

I glanced at the speaker; a tall, dark-haired British soldier alongside, hands thrust in the pockets of his greatcoat.

'Yeah,' I replied.

We stood observing a bit of shiacking going on in front of us.

'You're not 2 New Zealand Division?'

'Yeah, the same old mob.'

'But I thought you had all gone home?'

'No, only some of us.'

'You are the best damned allies we have got.'

That really did it. I had been growing restive at the questions and the formality of that last statement set the alarm bells ringing. No 'chum' would surely use a term like 'allies'. Good Lord, we did not consider ourselves allies of the British. We *were* British! I tried to look him over unobtrusively. No unit patches showed on the greatcoat and I couldn't see a badge on his hat. For that matter his was the only greatcoat in the square and he certainly didn't speak like a chum. Every British soldier I had met to date had an accent of some kind. This chap was well spoken and accentless. He saw me looking at him, said goodnight and marched off. British soldiers don't terminate street conversations with a polite 'goodnight'; they either say 'cheerio' or mutter a casual obscenity. He left me feeling I could kick myself, sure that he was not what he purported to be. If I had put my foot in it, it was too late now to do anything about it. He had mentioned at one stage he was at Corps Headquarters but if he was at Corps, surely he must know we were 2 New Zealand Division? I put the incident out of my mind.

We took over in the dark hills from an Indian regiment which was firing at almost the extreme range of 12 000 yards; our unit moved in closer to the enemy and I am pretty sure the Colonel pushed the guns up to within 3000 yards. We camped on a wet hill slope in bleak, steep country alongside a single small stone house. It was dark and gloomy with patches of mist. Behind us on a backward slope were slit trenches and whoever had occupied them must have had a rough time because they were surrounded by craters left by 25-pounder shells.

Sleeping in a slit trench in this country was going to pose problems, because the ones we had seen were full of water. Our armoured car was equipped with a folding canopy and rolled up against its side was a canvas awning we called the penthouse. Each night when we stopped, the Colonel's batman would extend and set it up with our help. Next, he unwrapped a camp stretcher and put the Colonel's sleeping bag on it, set out his canvas folding washstand, and then hung a mirror and a picture of the Colonel's lady on the bracket which supported our aerial. His last chore would be to dig the Colonel's slit trench and in view of the latter's height this was some undertaking. These and a few other jobs completed, he could then start on sleeping arrangements for himself. Although quite a busy lad at times, he did not work radio shifts as he was a gunner; if conditions were good he could sleep all night, more or less.

Since we were on wireless silence the driver and I decided to sleep in the armoured car because it was pretty late and we had not had a chance to forage around and get the lie of the land. With this wet weather, war in Italy was already beginning to look like an experience unlike any we had met before. One of our batteries down the hill was already in action and as we opened out our blankets their gun flashes were lighting the sky. Hoping there would be no retaliation I fell asleep, but during the night a shell landed right in our lines sending shrapnel screaming low over our heads and down the rocky slope.

The Colonel heard it too, and I listened to his stretcher creaking as he turned over. He was sleeping in the lee of the car, but he was welcome to his penthouse and stretcher. I much preferred my position stretched out across the seat surrounded by ⅜-inch armour; it would not stop a direct hit but would keep out most of those smaller pieces of white-hot metal unless they started firing airbursts, which would send me under the car, perhaps even the Colonel's stretcher. That was an unlikely situation and I tried to imagine it. Airbursts were lethal and I had never understood why they were not used more extensively in the desert, because they seemed more effective against people sheltering in slitties than ordinary shelling. It was an airburst which had got Len.

No more shells came in but we had a funny conversation with Smithy in the morning. He had pitched his pup tent alongside a track which meandered up the steep rugged slope.

'You know,' he said, 'some jokers came right down past me last night whispering in some foreign lingo. I took a dekko but it was as black as hell, couldn't see a damn thing.'

Lucky for him and perhaps for us. We heard later in the morning a German patrol had tried to blow up the bridge behind us during the night, but had been driven off by members of the division we were taking over from.

One can only speculate as to whether he heard the patrol, and whether they knew we were there and ignored us in pursuit of their objective. A few stick grenades would have quickly put paid to the Colonel and the rest of us. But it had been a particularly dark night and possibly we were not observed; they would certainly not be expecting to find anyone there because we had just moved in.

When you think about it, it was curious the way we used to doss down in new positions without setting sentries, always in the sublime belief that our infantry were out in front protecting us. We rarely ever set guards and had got away with it to date but might have to change our style. I hoped not, because those roving patrols at Alamein and the stands-to at dawn coupled with the radio shifts had been a bit much.

We were now operational, so there was no more sleeping in the scout car. Incoming shells were beginning to whine steadily overhead so I looked around for alternative accommodation. Once Jerry shortened his range we could get plastered. I found that most of the others had moved into adjacent caves; it was really one cave but had several entrances. It had also been used for many years as a lavatory, and when I began to shift rubble to create a level space for my blankets the stench became so foul that there were immediate howls of protest from earlier occupants in their various nooks and crannies and I had to desist.

Higher up the slope there was a much better cave but it was occupied by a British infantry section under the command of a corporal. The floor was covered with straw, it had a high ceiling and a decent sort of entrance which let in the light. I was standing at the entrance sheltering under the overhang from the rain and weighing up the prospects of getting a comfortable billet in the cave when I was joined by one of our new reinforcements. The German artillery was still trying to get the bridge, which was vital to us, and you could hear the boom of the guns before the shells roared over to crash and explode in the ravine below us. There may have been only one gun but the fire was steady and they were keeping it up.

'I didn't know you had all that time to hear shells coming,' said the reinforcement.

I felt obliged to enlighten him.

'Listen, mate, you'd better get it straight. That gun is not firing at us. It's having a go at that bridge they tried to blow up last night. The trajectory of those shells is high above us and to the right. If they were coming our way they would arrive together with the explosion. If they were 88s, you wouldn't hear a thing.'

Having put him straight I entered the cave; talking about shells had only made me more eager to get settled in somewhere. One of our blokes was already ensconced there so I sat down with him on his bed-roll and looked around. The British soldiers were talking quietly and sounded cynical, bitter and depressed. I gradually got the drift of their complaints. There was no bloody officer, no sergeant, just the corporal and his little section with orders to undertake a patrol every night, and they were just about ready to get up and go out on another one. As the corporal rose from his blanket, shouldering the sling of his rifle, the others stood up and I asked whether he minded if I shared their cave with them.

'Suit yourself, mate, after tonight we may not even need it,' was the wry reply as he led them away in single file up the dark wet slope.

It was almost dusk and watching their bent figures I thought, you poor bastards, fancy having to do that every night. What, exactly, were they expected to accomplish? Why didn't your bloody officer or sergeant take a turn with them? Outside it was now as black as the inside of a cow.

They did not come back in the morning and their blanket rolls lying there really affected me next day. As I went about my chores the rain and the sadness of it all brought black depression.

Chapter 9

The Doves of War

Sangro River — Orsogna — Casalbordino — Volturno Valley

Most of us had never heard of the Sangro River, but it was to be our next objective. We moved down from the hills and took over a railway station in the valley where we set up our signal office. There was a small cluster of brick houses around the station, a few interspersed amongst trees, and a single street — or more correctly, road. In this largely rural area there were many open fields.

The Colonel installed himself in a two-storey matchbox house a hundred yards up the road. The Sergeant Major and the officers' cooks occupied the ground floor, the Colonel and the Adjutant the upper floor. A dark attic with no windows was ours; a signalman and the Colonel's batman. As thin tiles covering the rafters were the only thing between us and incoming shells, I decided it was not for me and elected to sleep by the staircase just inside the front door. An uncovered window prevented me from using a light so my evenings were spent sitting on the floor in the dark.

It was pretty quiet that first night so I walked down the road and called in at a little stone house which housed a few of our signalmen. They were sitting round a roaring fire, toasting their feet and quietly yarning. I took off my boots and as the heat soaked into my feet thought, this beats desert warfare. It was like being a civilian. The desert was a stark existence when you looked back on it and compared it with this. Mud and rain were outside and the occasional muffled thud of a gun not far away, but you could almost forget you were at war, or at least the kind of war with which we were familiar.

There were patrols out in front but the infantry were still moving in and next night I stood by the gate in the darkness as a whole battalion went by. Dark shadowy shapes under helmets and gas capes, all in step but not consciously so, the left foot going down in that almost lazy style, each man with his own thoughts. For many perhaps it was the first time, as they speculated upon the menace waiting in the darkness ahead.

One of our Majors joined us at the gate, bringing with him a storm lantern lighting up pale countenances beneath dripping helmets.

'Don't you think you should put the light out?' asked the Adjutant.

'Do you think so?' replied the Major. Bloody hell! How is it that some people can presumably be good at their job and yet be such utter twits? The Major was nice enough, perhaps a little donnish, but not really on the ball when it came to practicalities.

To our relief he doused the light, so we remained at the gate. As the companies went by I listened to the creak of rifle slings, the soft rubbing of water bottles on hips, and the rain falling on the gas capes; old familiar sounds which made me feel again like a deserter.

In the morning the Colonel went walking carrying a stick as a staff; he seemed to find it amusing. Next he'll be riding a horse, I thought sourly. Instead, he took our great lumbering armoured car forward where we stopped behind a hill. He left us in the grounds of a large church while he went off to make his reconnaissance. The church was a substantial edifice with residential quarters and on the Colonel's return we moved in upstairs. Good heavens! We were going to sleep in a double bedroom, lace curtains and all. It was unbelieveable and I wondered if we were violating any conventions, sleeping in a church or monastery. There was even electric light, a great iron bed and mattress, a counterpane, chairs and drawers. A charcoal brazier sat on the floor.

Through the curtained windows we could see a priest down below in the garden, swinging a similar brazier slowly round and round his head until it began to glow into a nice warm spot of colour in the growing dusk. We thought we would do the same. You have never seen anything like it. The room filled with smoke, as did the church. There was smoke everywhere, and pungent stuff at that. Coughing and spluttering we had tears running down our cheeks. The priest, also in tears, was wringing his hands, entreating us to take the brazier outside. 'Basta, basta,' he kept repeating and the message was clear.

We had to oblige or we would have passed out. We brought the brazier back upstairs again with its nice red glow, but then things got slightly out of hand. Perhaps it was the lace curtains, perhaps the double bed or the smoke, but a pillow fight developed. Two fully grown men jumped on the bed as if it were a trampoline, thumping hell out of each other with pillows until the bed collapsed. I'd remonstrated earlier, but this was the last straw. As corporal, I thought it time to pull my rank, but they just sat amidst the ruins of the bed giggling hysterically. We finally put the bed together again, with reservations as to whether it would ever be the same. Still on wireless silence we spread three bed-rolls over the big bed and went to sleep like lambs; the first proper bed we had been on in three years, if you excluded our trip to Jerusalem.

Next day by myself I got down to the river where the engineers were operating a bulldozer, endeavouring to put a Bailey bridge across. The bulldozer was making a great deal of noise and noticing the trees and bushes slashed by artillery fire I thought it not a good place to linger. Walking back to the church I found the Colonel ready to return to the regiment and we followed him back to the railway station where it was reasonably quiet.

Because of the trees and hedges our gun batteries were not visible from the station, but they were close by nonetheless and we had run telephone lines to them. The guns were engaging targets as directed but wireless silence was still in force and our radio was closed down, so for the first time I found myself working a telephone exchange. Earlier, the lines corporal had asked me not to put any calls through to the Colonel without letting him know, because he was outside working on the 'snake'; the junction through which all wires led into the exchange.

I was busy answering calls when he burst in shouting, 'What the bloody hell do you think you're doing? I told you not to ring the Colonel.'

When one cranked the generator handle on the exchange to ring a number, a strong electric impulse travelled through the snake and the corporal crouching outside on the wet ground had just received a nasty electrical shock. I denied ringing the number but obviously was not believed. Muttering, he went outside.

Five minutes later he was frothing at the door.

'You bloody bastard,' he advanced towards me, 'You threw me twenty feet.'

Pale with fury, and perhaps shock, he showed every sign of dragging me from the switchboard. One electric shock was bad enough but two on a dark wet night were too much for his generally even temperament. Fortunately support came from an unexpected quarter; since the first outburst the sergeant had been keeping tabs on me and now he intervened. There was actually a short which we found on one of the other lines to the Colonel and this was causing the trouble.

Apart from this altercation it was a quiet night; Jerry was leaving us alone. It rained a bit, the guns fired a bit, and there was no retaliation from enemy artillery.

At one stage a largish officer, perhaps a little older than the average but with a bright cheerful face, breezed in through the door of the signal office. He did not appear to want anybody and although I knew it was cold outside, high-ranking officers as this one obviously was did not normally pay social calls to people like us. Easing his rump on to a table he started to chat and took out a packet of cigarettes. They were a vastly superior brand to Army issue and he passed them around.

'Give one to the corporal,' he said, but I had my hands busy at the exchange.

'Stick it behind his ear.'

I nodded my thanks. Although not a smoker at the time, I appreciated the gesture. The officer left shortly afterwards, saying goodnight to the others. As he went through the doorway he waved to me and with a 'goodnight, Corp' disappeared into the darkness.

In a free moment, I asked 'Who was that chap, he was pretty friendly?'

The bridge the enemy tried to blow up on our first night in action in Italy. The truck crossing the bridge is under direct enemy observation. A shell killed a New Zealand officer just off the bridge. *Alexander Turnbull Library*

'Don't you know him? That was "Whisky Bill", he's a good bloke.'

I had noticed the gentleman's fresh complexion and that he was above the rank of major, but had not realised he was at the top of the tree and had commanded the New Zealand Division at the battle of Minqar Qaim after Freyberg was wounded. It was Brigadier Inglis, and he had behaved like one of the boys, completely natural, yarning and laughing with them; he had made me feel a person for a moment, not a bloody NCO. In fact, in that short space of time I received more from him than from my own colonel over a period of months. Could you imagine it in the British Army, or any other army for that matter? No wonder people like him and another of the same calibre, Brigadier Kippenberger, elicited such loyalty.

Our cookhouse truck was parked outside the railway station and three times a day I walked down the road to the station for meals. It was lunchtime

111

and I had just rinsed my pannikin in a dixie of steaming hot water, when there was the most awful crash, black smoke and screaming pieces of metal, followed by the boom of a gun. Out of the blue, the first shot had nearly cleaned up the cookhouse. In front of me was a flimsy little pagoda; it was the first time I had noticed it and I plunged inside to find half a dozen chaps lying on straw looking up at me. This must be where some of the signal office staff slept. As I stood there looking down on them nobody spoke, and I was surprised to see some faces whitening as blood receded from their cheeks. It was the first time I had observed this phenomenon in soldiers. There was another thunderous crash, and a whistle, as a shell, nearly taking the roof off, exploded just behind us. Then came the boom of a gun and shouts; somebody outside had copped it.

'Help! Help! Come out you bastards, come out and give me some help!'

It was Buff's voice; one of our linesmen. For a moment I remained in the doorway, looking down. Nobody moved. It was only half a second but thoughts were coursing through my mind. There were a couple of our hard cases in that group, noisy extroverts, and there had been times in the past when I had wondered about their bloody cheerfulness. They were not looking so good now and were showing no signs of moving. I used to worry at times about survival, and had wondered whether they lacked imagination. Normally under some degree of tension when within enemy range, I found that direct enemy action always in some strange way afforded me relief. As we came under fire, adrenalin would begin to flow into my system, dispersing some of the tension.

Reluctant as I was to leave the hut and afraid of what I might find, my conscience wouldn't let me remain. I rushed outside to help as another shell crashed in, shying like a frightened horse as I nearly stepped on a short-cropped hairy thing lying in my path. Oh Jesus, it was the back of somebody's neck and I recognised the scalp! The second shell had landed right alongside the 'snake', blowing two chaps into oblivion, wounding others and hurling one of our corporals back through the door of the railway station.

Somebody appeared with a stretcher; it could have been Bob, the driver of our water tanker. Buff was on his knees in the middle of the human wreckage, helping as best he could.

I felt absolutely useless because I did not even know how to put on let alone hold a tourniquet. Like all of us, I had carried the standard field dressing in my pocket since arrival in Egypt, but didn't even know what was inside it. They trained us to fight and kill, and then they trained us to become radio operators and good ones too, but not once in all these years had they trained us how to help the wounded or how to save lives. What do you do when your mates disintegrate into bloody lumps and those awful stains appear on their uniforms? Do you pull out your pitiful little field dressing or do you bellow 'stretchers'?

I did not have to do anything. Standing there I watched the broken bodies lifted on to the stretchers and as they carried them at a crouching run into the house where the first aid post was located, I followed them to the door.

The poor doctor. The medical orderlies went quickly into action but the doctor appeared to be trying to make up his mind where to start. Another whoosh and earsplitting crack, and the ground around me burst into flame. Then another, accompanied by falling masonry or was it bricks? Better get out of here, I thought, or inside somewhere, leave it to the Doc and the orderlies. The bastards really have us taped. Another vicious blast and I ran through the smoke thinking, I must get under cover, this is stupid out here with the shells landing right on us.

I set off up the road intending to get back to the Colonel's house, but approaching the shells as they screamed in and half way there in the face of them I hesitated, spotting the little stone house where I had warmed my feet in front of the fire. I bolted for the doorway. As I rushed in, somebody else rushed out. It was empty inside, not a stick of furniture remained; had they burned everything to keep the fire going? I stood in the middle of the room on the bare stone floor assessing the situation as more shells came in, too close for comfort. Then there was a great walloping clang and black smoke came in through the open doorway. Had the house been hit?

25 pounder firing on the Sangro River front, Italy. *Alexander Turnbull Library*

The petrol tank of the truck parked across the doorway certainly had because petrol was gushing out and flowing across the floor towards my feet. I dashed outside again. Heads were poking out of the ground from a deep dry ditch in a paddock across the road; it ran at right angles to the line of fire and you couldn't have found anything better in which to shelter.

Haring across the road I jumped into the ditch just as two more soldiers came running down the road carrying an empty stretcher, nearly tripping themselves up as they went past. They were laughing but it had a pretty hollow ring to it. Both looked pale and the situation hardly called for guffaws. We all ducked as another shell screamed in but the fire was regular now and we could time it; duck, stand up, duck. A British jeep came hell-for-leather up the road and foolishly stopped. In it were two other ranks and an officer. Standing up in the jeep he asked what was going on then jumped out and joined me in the ditch. The two soldiers remained sitting in the jeep with its engine running. Bloody hell! Were they waiting for orders to take shelter? I'll never understand those British sitting there like turkeys.

I cannot recall what the officer asked us but I suggested he would be much better off if he kept going, adding that where we were was currently a disaster area and there was no point in staying if he did not have to. It must have made sense because he got back into the jeep and they roared away.

The fire shifted to the trees behind and to the right of the railway station. Perhaps they were going to do over our gun batteries? My God! If that shell put the snake out of commission they could be without telephone communications, and the Adjutant may be wanting to take counter-battery action and looking for me to break the radio silence and come up on the air!

If I had been scared of the shelling I was even more scared of what the Colonel might say about my not being on the spot. I was out of that ditch and up the road once more like a hare.

The Colonel was standing in the shelter of the house at a side door, and turned his head as I came pounding in through the gate to stutter to a hob-nailed stop alongside the Sergeant Major, leaning with his back against the wall. Beyond them our armoured car was visible out in the open; it was not manned but a large piece of turf had been flung from somewhere to lie upon its bonnet. Nobody seemed greatly concerned; mind you most of the shells must have gone over their heads to land around us at the station.

The Colonel turned his attention back to the grape vines and trees in front of him, and as another shell whooshed over fairly close he shouted, 'Mind yourself, sig.'

'It's all right, Sir, I've got to fix these lines.'

Good Lord, it was Buff, up a bloody tree mending the breaks caused by flying splinters. What a mad bastard; the last time I saw him was by the snake back at the station. He won the Military Medal that day. Some said later that he was lucky because he was doing his stuff in front of the Colonel whereas the other corporal was doing an equally good job out of sight in the trees, repairing the lines to the guns. But Buff earned his medal, because I had been with him by the snake and now watching him there was no doubt of his courage.

I took stock of myself. One must keep priorities in mind despite the numbing effect of shellfire. I had not simply run around in diminishing circles because the old brain had been ticking over and I had given that officer in the jeep sound advice when nobody else had answered him. But until the shells started falling near our guns the penny had not dropped. In looking after my own skin I had not remembered my reason for being there. There was of course the excuse that the radios had not operated for months, since the war finished in North Africa, and there was still a wireless silence, but I should have considered the possibility of counter-battery fire being required and returned immediately to the Colonel's house instead of stopping off in the ditch on the way. In the event, the Adjutant kept his counter-battery fire to later when the lines were patched up and he had a target, so I was never on the hook but it was a lesson.

We had noticed that the top half of the railway station facing the enemy had been painted black, and thought it looked odd because it stood out; later we learned to avoid areas adjacent to buildings decorated in this manner because it was the work of the Germans. They marked buildings so that they could use them for artillery ranging purposes. No wonder that first shell landed right on target, and no wonder that fire was so accurate it chased us round the buildings and me up the road — it was calibrated to do so!

The Division was pushing patrols over the river and the infantry were obliged to wade across streams of varying depth amid mud and shingle banks. Planned attacks would later be put off because the heavy rain raised the level of the river.

On 25 November the skies started to clear and on the 28th we attacked. We shifted the armoured car to behind a haystack for added protection, switched on the radio and broke our wireless silence by calling up all the sets on our link; they came in loud and clear. As we sat there in the semi-darkness with the glowing dials and the old familiar shaded light, the crackle of static in our headphones, shades of North Africa returned. We waited for the first crash of the guns crouched around us, muzzles raised to the dark sky. To date there had been only what one might term desultory shelling from individual batteries, but this was to be an attack by the whole Division to cross the Sangro River and force the Germans out of their defences on the other side. To support the infantry a full-scale divisional artillery barrage was required, our first in Italy.

As the sky lit up with lightning flashes and the deafening drum beat rolled back from the hills around us, it was like old times. I hated war, but one could not fail to thrill to and be inspired by the thunderous roar of our guns firing in unison. This was New Zealand at war! Give them hell, the bastards! Give them hell! One sometimes felt like that when all revved up. We were a small but intensely proud nation and we knew the country was right behind us; every man, woman, child and dog. We were its spearhead, and although we moaned, cursed and got drunk occasionally, we wore its shoulder tabs with honour, a little like our All Black rugby teams, proud to be its representatives.

Out there on the cold flowing river were the infantry. We wondered how they were getting on. Were they pinned down by fire in icy water up to their chests? Had the engineers succeeded with the Bailey bridge? Go on guns, give it to them, give it to them! Howling cacophony ripping the night apart!

In actual fact almost all our objectives were taken with light casualties. The engineers succeeded with the bridge, and tanks and supporting arms were across the river and consolidating. German retaliation in our area seemed to be confined to a few shellbursts. By day the Luftwaffe was nowhere to be seen and we had complete command of the air with fighter bombers flying overhead looking for targets. What a change from the desert, and what a relief to be able to forget about enemy aircraft. How life improves when you're on the other end of things and on the winning side, moving forward aware you have superiority in men and equipment, and that the enemy are taking a beating. On 2 December we heard that the main German winter line on the Castelfrentano ridge had been broken and that it was expected we would shortly advance our guns across the Sangro.

When we did move it was to find the road choked with traffic. There were masses of equipment channelled on to the only route available and one could not but perceive that whereas we might have cut a mighty swathe with it in North Africa, its effectiveness in this type of country was severely reduced by weather, mud and terrain. There were already reports filtering back that our tanks were being halted by mines on the only access roads and coming under fire from cleverly sited anti-tank guns and tanks. The Germans were also letting our Sherman tanks equipped with the original smaller gun to come through, then picking off those which had the new larger gun. Tanks were also slithering off the roads, getting stuck in the mud and sheltering behind farm houses, frustrated because of the difficulty in determining exactly what to shoot at. Their spearhead, however, had penetrated the German's flank between his 26 Panzer Divison and 65 Division and forced a withdrawal.

Packed into our scout car it was not far down to the river, but darkness had fallen as we ground forward and it was impossible to see more than a few yards. There was the sound of creaking timbers and the murmur of the river; we were crossing the bridge. There was a metallic clang and we jerked to a stop.

A gun crew at the Sangro River. *Alexander Turnbull Library*

'Hell! We've broken an axle,' said the driver. 'What a place to happen, right in the middle of the bloody bridge!'

I was thinking this could have dire consequences for us, sitting in the middle of the only bridge across the Sangro. What a lovely target! I hoped we could be towed off. Left sitting by the river bank by the towing vehicle, we watched as the rest of the regiment moved on. All through that cold night I listened to the gurgle of the river wondering what the dawn would bring and feeling horribly exposed. We were sure to get the crap shelled out of us in the morning.

At first light they came back and towed us a few yards to obscurity at the foot of a steep bluff and maintenance people got to work on the car. Late in the day we ground forward again to halt below a farmhouse on the far side of a village. The village was deserted and occupied only by troops. Across the road just a few yards away a battery of 25-pounders was already dug in under camouflage nets.

Where to sleep? The armoured car was operational, so that was out. Looking around we found as usual that the Adjutant and Colonel had secured the best accommodation in the farm house and why not? They were doing the picking. We were invited to sleep in the signal office, but it was crowded and stuck up like a pimple on the upper floor. I had noticed most of our guns were behind us in gullies down the slope and ahead of us was a ridge. If Jerry decided to go after them with his 88s I could visualise shells clipping the signal office roof on their way down. The telephone exchange would also be manned twenty-four hours a day and that did not appeal, so two of us decided to dig in on a steep slope behind a large haystack.

The stack was already occupied by two gunners who had burrowed into it. We found the ground awfully wet and as we dug, water oozed into the hole. This was a problem but at some stage I found a large wooden door which we lowered into the wide trench on to three or four bricks, and placed the pup tent over it. Wrapped in our cocoon-like bedrolls there was just room for us on the door providing we did not thrash around.

The sides of the trench glistened wet inches from my face as moisture ran down to form a pool beneath the door; lying still watching it, one could only speculate what friends back home would make of this accommodation. It was hardly five-star. Because of the steep slope we had been obliged to build up the entrance with sandbags and this was preventing the water from getting away. A large empty jam tin brought in to use as a chamber pot proved handy, and as the water crept to within a couple of inches of the door one of us would sit up and bale out over the tops of the sandbags.

The seepage was permanent whether it rained or not, but we stayed dry although there were times when I felt like a water baby sleeping on a lily pond. It was also awfully cold, but we were better off than the two steaming inside the haystack. They were plagued by field mice and sundry other pests, and frequently there were shouts, curses, hilarity and furious rustlings from inside the stack. It would be interesting to consider the effect of an 88-millimetre armour-piercing shell upon the stack but my mind refused to entertain the thought.

It is amazing what the human frame can stand when necessity demands, and what circumstances one can sleep through. About fifty yards down the slope behind us we looked straight into the muzzles of our guns. That first evening at twilight as we crawled into bed they opened fire. Even if you have stood to the side, or behind, an artillery piece when it is fired you will not have experienced anything like the ear-splitting blast which reaches you directly in front. As I said, we were virtually looking down the muzzles.

'Let's hope they don't have any prematures,' said my mate.

Premature explosions happened occasionally and in this position we could buy it.

118

Going to bed meant removing our boots and climbing into the blankets; by eight o'clock we were reaching that slightly dazed state that constant concussion brings. No civilian in a million would sleep through that din but we did. The constant roar obliterated everything and numbed the mind.

One can usually sleep through barrages but never during harassing fire, raising the question of just who is being harassed. A single gunshot every fifteen minutes could almost drive one insane, particularly if the enemy answered back. It seemed so pointless yet could go on for hours and nobody ever got much sleep on nights when it took place.

The cookhouse truck was situated just off the road in bare ground further down the village street. On the road itself by the truck were the severed remains of two or three Germans; legs encased in trousers and jackboots, the odd arm or two, pieces of jacket, indescribable lumps, stick bombs and a couple of coal-scuttle steel helmets. As we queued at the tailboard of the truck a single shell whooshed over our heads to land in front of the bonnet, but all the blast, smoke and metal went forward down the slope without injuring anybody. We waited for the next one, sure we were observed, but none came. This kind of thing was not exactly good for one's appetite, but one has to eat.

As we sat there munching, someone eyed the gruesome remains on the road and asked, 'I wonder what the hell happened to them?'

'The tankies were telling me,' said another. 'They were watching two chaps walking up the road when they met another two coming down the road and they stopped to talk, so they let them have one.'

We sat there thinking of the impact of a 75-millimetre shell on four guys. What a mess it was. Nobody did anything about it for two or three days, despite its proximity to the cookhouse, until the padre ordered the remains carried across the road and covered with earth with a wooden cross placed on it. Later, the cookhouse was placed on a more permanent footing across the road by the mound, and on another occasion when we were having lunch, a grave registration unit stopped and began to dig into the mound until howls that it contained only pieces of Jerry made them desist — at least while we ate our lunch.

Christmas Day 1944 brought with it memories of the last one at Nofilia in North Africa. We were all geared up again in a queue with delicious food being spooned out into our pannikins when Jerry let go with a Merry Christmas. I'm sure he had our cookhouse fairly well taped because right on time he put five shells around us. One went so close to an artillery officer that he dropped even although it did not explode; we heard later that the shell had passed over his left shoulder close to his neck and that he had fainted from shock. Wouldn't you?

From the amount of artillery fire we were putting down we knew the Division was pushing hard, and early on there had been high hopes that we again had the Germans on the run. But now they were dug in at a town called Orsogna and it was proving a pretty tough nut to crack. On high ground in rugged country, because of the mud and greasy conditions Orsogna was proving virtually impossible to approach with heavy weapons and tanks. There were reports of infantry attacks and counter-attacks, of capturing houses and being chased out of them again. Of one fellow rushing up out of a doorway with his Piat gun and letting a tank have it and knocking it out. Of a horse's ghostly hoofbeats, heard only at night. It was all a bit confusing because we did not know the battle plan and got no opportunity to look at maps, but it was clear the Germans were dug in on a strong winter line and determined to hold it.

Up ahead of us were the crossroads where you could see Orsogna on the next ridge. At the crossroads was a large empty brickworks where one road forked back on our right flank, rising high to the village of Castelfrentano. Every yard between the brickworks and Castelfrentano was under enemy observation, and nobody wasted any time going up or down it. Jerry spent a good deal of time shelling transport using the road and having a go at the brickworks. We used to watch the shellbursts following vehicles and while I don't think I ever saw one receive a direct hit, it must have been nervewracking for the drivers forced to use the road regularly. Needless to say it earned the sobriquet of the 'mad mile'. Over the years we had experienced one or two of these and this may have been the best, perhaps even better than Route 6 yet to come at Cassino.

The days dragged and the guns kept firing — not only our 25-pounders but British 3.7 ack-ack guns and 5.5s towards the rear of the village. The 3.7s, which were being used as field artillery, were high-velocity jobs similar to the German 88s and they possessed a most vicious blast which thrown back from adjacent buildings produced a double whipcrack easily identifiable above the roar of the 25-pounders. It was fascinating to stand and listen to the shells in flight overhead, winging their way towards the German lines. I had never experienced it previously but suppose it was because we were ahead and directly above our guns. Strange whirring noises were made by the driving bands on the shells, some sounding as if they were in level flight, others going lazily end over end. One or two would halt us in our tracks, sounding as if they were not going to clear the hill but land and explode in our laps. This was an illusion, and we knew that New Zealand gunnery was of an exceptionally high standard.

The expertise of the gunners had been developed by Steve Weir to a state never previously reached in history; areas of land on the Divisional front were surveyed, mapped, divided up into pockets, given code names and our guns calibrated on to these spots. We could fire various forms of saturation known as 'Stonks' and 'Murders' and any troops inside those target areas could suffer hellish concentrations of exploding shells. As we advanced up the length of Italy we found the fields carpeted with small shell-holes from our 25-pounders, black on green, sometimes as close as five yards apart. The cost in ammunition must have been enormous, and one had to admire the Germans for being able to take it. We got hammered at times but in no way could it compare with being pulverised by almost a hundred guns at the one time. Jerry usually contented himself with tickling us up with a few 88s, one or two heavies, the odd mortar, self-propelled or tank guns, and one or two miscellaneous pieces.

Notwithstanding our high standards there were accidents when our own troops were shelled, usually on start lines for attack when a gun was out of calibration. We had one now and spent a day firing every gun singly until the culprit was identified. Then there were the prematures, but with these it was usually the gunners themselves who suffered.

Matters were getting a bit tense in our forward lines and early one evening the signals officer approached me in serious mood as I sat in the armoured car on radio watch. 'I want you to keep on your toes tonight because we are expecting a counter-attack on 21 and 23 Battalions' fronts.'

He stood considering the matter, with me pondering the unusualness of it all.

'I'll give you a runner. If you hear the call "Fire Dove", send him to the Adjutant immediately. Have you got that? Dove! Make no mistake, now watch it.' And he left. I sat thinking, Fire Dove; that has funny connotations for a fire order. Perhaps for the code they gave each area the name of a bird?

A few minutes later the runner arrived, grumbling at being inconvenienced

New Zealand artillerymen manhandling guns in heavy mud on the Sangro.
Alexander Turnbull Library

and carrying his bed-roll. Good Lord, he was going to spend the watch sleeping! He was one of those crack-hearty types who had stayed on the straw watching me when we were shelled back at the railway station. Stretched out across the wide front seat he was soon asleep.

It was icy cold with no heating in the car, and black as pitch outside. The hours dragged, midnight passed and the guns were silent. Then it came! 'Hullo K Z L, Hullo K Z L, Fire DOVE, Fire DOVE. Out.'

Sharp staccato words, then silence. I nearly pushed my finger clean through the microphone switch.

'Wilco out.'

I shook the runner awake, shouting, 'It's come, it's come! Dove! Dove! Tell the Adjutant!'

He started to get out of his blankets. Again came the call: 'DOVE! DOVE! Fire DOVE!' The voice was not quite so matter-of-fact as the first call, the omission of the call sign indicating urgency.

'Hurry up, get a bloody move on.'

'Got to get my bloody boots tied, running up there in the dark.'

Fuming, I could have hit him. I nearly threw down the microphone and was on the point of rushing up the hill when he opened the door and took off. I sat there willing him to hurry.

There was movement across the road, commands, the clank of a breech being closed. My word that was quick, the gunners must have been almost sitting at their guns. Fire orders rang clear on the night air and then the first crash of a 25-pounder. It was on! Rapid fire, with the shells whooshing away into the night. The Adjutant had obviously used the field telephone to activate the batteries.

The air in my headphones suddenly came alive; the radio operator back at Divisional Artillery Headquarters was shouting, 'Fire DOVE! Fire DOVE!' Calling up all sets on the link, he continued, 'Fire DOVE! Fire DOVE!' It had become Divisional as seventy-two guns took up the challenge. This was a 'Murder'; the shells were screaming over in rafts and the gun flashes were lighting up the inside of the car. Our guns had momentarily stopped after completing the first fire orders but were pounding away again. Tense, breathing quickly, I listened to the cannonade; there was nothing like a bit of excitement to set the old adrenalin going. Finally it stopped. We must have held them, otherwise the guns would still be going. There was just blackness and silence out there, not even a flash.

In the bright sunlight of the following morning we heard more about it from the Adjutant and over the BBC news. An officer from one of the battalions had come back to thank us.

'It was black magic,' he says. 'The Jerries were massed out in front of us, hundreds of them, I was trying to fire two tommy-guns at once as they came at us. Then out of the sky your guns. The shells landed right amongst them. Dead on. It was incredible. Cut them to pieces. It was marvellous!' He was exuberant.

18 Regiment at Guardiagrele. *Alexander Turnbull Library*

So was the Adjutant.

'Division rang and said, "Fire DOVE". Told them I already had, but happy to oblige them again.'

The BBC reported that a heavy counter-attack by the Germans on the Orsogna Front had been repulsed by elements of the 8th Army with the Germans suffering heavy casualties. The figure of five hundred was mentioned.

Afterwards, I thought, as one does, about my part in it all in intercepting that first signal. How many people was I directly responsible for killing or maiming in those first shots we fired before it became Divisional? It was sad, but I was only a link in a chain and there were no regrets.

It was a case of 'them or us'. If I had missed the intercept how many of our people may have bought it? Thirty years later, by some strange coincidence I was to meet one of the officers involved in 'Fire DOVE' and hear him use it as an analogy during a church service in Auckland.

I heard later that the Adjutant was on the warpath, but not against Sigs. Apparently one of our batteries had not fired the first time, and he was investigating the breakdown in communications. Only sixteen of our guns had answered the call instead of twenty-four; a line was out, so why did they not come up on my radio link? I never did hear the outcome.

It was strange how we were not subjected to counter-battery fire. Perhaps it was because our guns were cunningly sited; perhaps the Germans could not see their smoke. But surely they were able to observe the flashes? Maybe the terrain and the way the village dropped away behind the ridge prevented them laying their 88s on us. We were out of mortar range and what they needed perhaps were howitzers, not high-velocity guns with their flat trajectories. They shelled the brickworks at the crossroads incessantly, they chased every vehicle up and down the 'mad mile' and were forever shelling the British 162 (25-pounder) Regiment just ahead and, to the left, immediately behind the ridge. But by and large they left us alone. This was quite incredible when you considered the mauling we were giving them, but we were not complaining.

Apart from a few odd shells the only retaliation was a single fighter bomber. I was sunning myself against the wall of the farm house one morning when the sound of an aeroplane made me look up into the clear blue sky. It was coming high and fast and I wasn't wholly certain it was not one of ours — the German Air Force was virtually non-existent — but it was dipping and as it went into its dive the largest bomb I had ever seen released by a fighter bomber detached itself from the plane. Instinctively I took off and without quite realising it found myself heading a rush into the Adjutant's office. Startled by us galloping rudely into his command post without invitation, he tersely wanted to know what the hell was going on. He had heard the plane but not the whistle and there had been no explosion. Sheepishly, we retreated from his presence. That plane had come so fast not one of our ack-ack guns had time to get away a single shot, and it showed us we were no longer the gun group we had been in North Africa where the sky would have been filled with air bursts before it even got overhead.

That pilot was dead unlucky. He placed his big bomb right in the middle of the village, three feet from the left wheel of a British 5.5 gun, and it had failed to explode. Landing on the road it would have blown half the village to kingdom come. God was on our side; what a fatuous thought. I walked down the road to view the unexploded bomb. Certainly it was a big one, and it had drilled a neat cylindrical hole. Twelve feet down in the soft damp earth I could see its ugly black tailfin. The British gunners were looking a little serious, which was not surprising. Close ones like that scared hell out of you, and they still had to shift their gun. Operating a heavy field piece twelve feet above a large unexploded bomb was just not on. Also, for all we knew there could be a timing device set to blow. With this in mind I did not envy them.

Perhaps the Adjutant had a talk with the Signals Officer, I don't know. Perhaps he didn't like his peace disturbed by soldiers with time on their hands rushing into his command post, because when I arrived back at the farm house they had a job for me. I was to go up to the brickworks and give radio lectures and demonstrations to the Regimental Signallers, taking with me one of our more powerful radio transmitters and its batteries in the back of a jeep. This project was almost in the same class as the flag-waving semaphore practice we were asked to undertake in full view of the enemy at Takrouna in North Africa. We would not be under direct observation, but in the words of my late friend Ron, killed at Wadi Zem

124

Zem, it was 'bloody dangerous' up there and the order was hard to fathom. The gunners thought the same, because never more than four of them were ever visible at the same time. However, they carried in the batteries and the radio before they disappeared. I set up the radio, connected the batteries, and joined a couple of gunners by a window after a thumping crash as more bricks fell down.

Every pane of glass in the building had long since disappeared and it was open and airy. We had a strong sense of being exposed, and gunners kept arriving and then disappearing, giving running commentaries on every shot striking the building or landing on the mad mile of which we had an excellent view. Accepting the futility of rounding them up to deliver my lecture, I became a spectator myself. Late in the day at what I considered a reasonable hour I returned down the road to Regimental Headquarters, the gunners again obligingly helping to reload the jeep. If they were thinking I was an eccentric, one could hardly blame them. What a fatuous proposition it had been, endeavouring to lecture them under those conditions.

'How did it go?' said the officer.

'Good,' I said.

The brickworks was a very substantial building, dry and a great place for observation. That is probably why Jerry shelled it. If the silly bastards wanted to send me up there every day to lecture and the gunners had other ideas I did not mind. It had been nerve-racking but once you sorted out a sheltered spot it was not too bad, and as a place to see what was going on it was superb; certainly better than crouched on your hunkers behind a wet haystack bored out of your mind. Unfortunately — or perhaps not — the lecture at the brickworks was a oncer.

The nights were getting colder and hunched up in a greatcoat in front of the radio I felt my hands grow numb but one couldn't leave the set and stomp around outside to warm up. I had recently become friendly with the gunner-driver and Johnny proved a real pal sitting with me in the scout car at night to cook hot suppers over a charcoal brazier he had procured from somewhere. He would light the brazier outside the car and one night we must have lit the primus as well. Snugged up inside, the baked beans on the brazier and the tea water boiling on the primus I dazedly became aware that I had the most ferocious headache and Johnny was beginning to swim before my eyes.

'Don't feel too good,' I mumbled.

'Me either,' said Johnny and we both looked at the brazier because we had used primuses hundreds of times with no ill-effects.

'Open the car up, put the brazier outside.'

We stood outside in the cold night air, steadying ourselves against its steel sides as our heads slowly cleared. Johnny went off to his hole in the ground or wherever he slept, and wrapping myself up, I huddled against the slight warmth of the radio. There was a stink in the car of cold charcoal, spaghetti and baked beans.

The mule train Orsogna. Tired, cold, wet, and muddy, on Christmas morning December 1943, F. Hore (Cent. Otago) and C. Hoey (Whangarei). *Alexander Turnbull Library*

A warning notice appeared in standing orders a couple of days later: 'On no account should charcoal braziers be lit in tanks, vehicles or other confined spaces because they emit poisonous fumes.' So others had experienced similar trouble! I am certain Johnny and I were close to passing out that night.

The hole where we slept was getting too dank and so were our blankets, so my tentmate and I thought about moving into the stable on the ground floor of the farm house. It was occupied by cows and the brick floor was wet with manure and urine but the smell of cows is not bad and we thought that if we placed our door on the floor and haltered the cows to their feed boxes to stop them treading or licking us we might be better off than in the slimy hole we were occupying. It was a funny old world with animals inside and us outside in the depths of winter.

Fortunately two spare bunks became available in the farm house as people moved out. They were rough, but it was absolute luxury to be able to stand erect and sleep within dry walls. We got inside just in time because snow began falling heavily and many of our infantry and gunners had to be dug out after their tents collapsed on top of them. Some suffered from exposure and it was clear with the arrival of the snow the campaign must come to a halt. There was no alternative but to get troops inside under cover and convert the solid farm houses into strongpoints as the Germans had already done.

We entered a new phase and white camouflage suits were issued to the infantry similar to those used by the enemy. Now was the time for sentries to shiver in pits dug short distances from the farm houses and for ghostly patrols to stalk at night when the moon lit the white landscape like day.

Johnny disappeared for a couple of days.

When he returned, I asked, 'Where the hell have you been?'

'You wouldn't read about it. I've been on patrol.'

'Balls, where have you been?'

'No really, I have been out on patrol, it was not my idea.'

He told me about it. Johnny had driven one of our observation officers up to an infantry position and spent a couple of days there. One night as the men were getting dressed to go out on patrol the officer suggested Johnny should join them. He was horrified because he was a gunner and completely inexperienced in infantry work.

It is difficult to understand that officer's mentality. Johnny was scared and he could have put that whole patrol at risk. Why didn't the officer volunteer himself? However as Johnny graphically described the patrol I had to laugh.

Grimly clutching a rifle, he had attached himself as last man in the patrol, but there was a new reinforcement also there. At every opportunity he got behind Johnny, who spent most of the time watching his shadow instead of looking out for the enemy. He found the experience 'quite spooky' and did not want any repeat performances.

With all the need to get people inside there was considerable congestion, so some of the folk further down the village were asked to close up and I was shifted to the first aid post. There they had a stove and I was allocated a spot alongside. There was also better conversation. This was no disrespect to Johnny who was also a good conversationalist but there weren't many like him. Perhaps a couple of the first aid people were slightly effeminate but they were a vocal, light-hearted bunch and definitely more witty than Post Office signalmen like myself. The arrival of winter underwear had them parading in their woollies round the stove 'showing a leg'; the effect was hilarious.

Outside it was a different story. The snow brought down our telephone lines and we were involved in helping our linesmen repair the faults, floundering in wet soft snow up to our armpits.

The word went around that we were being pulled out of the line. We were due for a spell and I was sitting in the car working when a gun across the road fired its last shots. There were only two rounds to go when a 'premature' occurred right in front of the muzzle. From the shouts I knew somebody had copped it; several gunners were injured and one killed.

An hour later at one o'clock a sergeant brought a letter up from 'B' echelon a couple of miles back. They had been clearing out a truck prior to the move and found the letter in a security box. It had been there for a long time; since before we left Egypt. The contents were devastating;

the letter granted compassionate leave to the gunner who had just been killed. How unlucky can you be? That bloke should have been in New Zealand when the gun was fired.

The move was hush-hush so once again the shoulder flashes and badges came off. We painted out the silver ferns on the vehicles; 'white feathers', the Poms called them. We were relieved by 4 Indian Division on 11 January and moved to San Severo where it was understood the Division would rest and train for about four weeks. The move was accompanied by a great deal of secrecy even to the extent of providing a patrol of Spitfires to discourage interest by enemy planes. We travelled by night about thirty miles to stop at Casalbordino but next morning were heading for the front on the Mediterranean side to join the 5th Army. The convoy passed through the Apennine Divide into the plains to Cancello, about twenty miles from Naples, and the final leg took us into the Volturno Valley.

I recalled our first visit to one of the towns in which we stopped; we had camped in the village square and our latrines had only low scrim walls. The houses were two stories high, which made using the latrine quite embarrassing. But there had been a worse occasion; I had been sitting on an open seat one morning when a woman came out of a nearby house and commenced hanging washing on a line which passed over my head. There was nothing to do but brazen it out, trousers round my ankles.

'Buon giorno,' she said.

'Buon giorno,' I replied and remained motionless on the seat until she had emptied the basket and returned indoors.

I remembered also how I played a lot of chess in that village with 'Doc', the boy from Karamea, a gentle giant and a Christian. He had the type of face depicted by earlier painters of Jesus Christ and if there was anything unpleasant involved, was always first to volunteer. In Tripoli we talked him into playing rugby for the first time. Powerfully built, he turned out to be a natural driving forward and would tear into rucks scattering the opposition like chaff. If only we had been able to convince him that it was not necessary to apologise and pick people up he would have been All Black material.

I was sitting playing chess with Doc one night when a rifle shot immediately outside the awning brought us to our feet and we rushed outside to find one of our sentries lying dead beside his rifle. We all took turns at sentry duty to protect our equipment from light-fingered gentry who might be in the vicinity; this was another anomaly, because we rarely set guards when close to the enemy. The poor chap had clearly committed suicide and as we hardly knew him we left him to the first aid orderlies and continued the game, speculating on what had made him do it. Such cases were relatively rare and were usually put down to marital troubles. This chap, when we thought about it, was only a little bloke, very quiet, and had kept very much to himself.

Next morning I had a look to see what they had done with him. There he was, all neatly stitched up in one of our grey army blankets, lying on a stretcher under a little tent they had erected over him. Later a pick-up truck arrived to take him to a cemetery we had started down the road; he would be the number two occupant. The orderlies had trouble fitting the stretcher into the back of the truck and at one stage it slipped and the body rolled off to the accompaniment of 'oohs' from some children who had gathered around. We waved them away, and finally got the stretcher wedged so that it could not slip again. One of us got up in the truck to sit with it on its short journey. There is little dignity in such a death and we did not want to make it worse.

Chapter 10

Scenes from the Underworld

Monte Cassino

Although still winter, it seemed almost autumn in the Volturno Valley after the snows of Orsogna. We bivouaced in a pleasant spot with lots of trees near Alife, and from an upstairs window of a better class farm house it was easy to imagine one was looking out on a pastoral scene back home in Otago. We cleared a rugby field, played a few games and I got carted off once again; this time it was Johnny's shoulder in a delicate place as two players tackled me simultaneously. It was to be our last game for a while, and it came as a surprise to learn that there was to be a ceremonial parade on the field and adjoining paddocks. Surely we had not lifted all the rocks for that — there was a very bloody war going on not far away. There must have been supreme confidence in Allied air superiority because we would have made a beautiful target and I still do not understand why it was held.

We tidied ourselves up a bit and in half a dozen or so columns advanced on the field. With our quads, guns, and armoured cars with their pennants proudly waving, the regiment made a fine sight and I felt proud standing up at salute; it was the only victory parade I was ever to take part in, although it was perhaps a bit premature in view of the horrors to come.

Our armoured car was on the extreme right nearest the saluting dais and as we approached my eye was caught by the unexpected sight of a large contingent of New Zealand nurses on parade alongside the dais. Thus distracted, it was like an electric shock to be suddenly confronted by the searchlike glare emanating from the General himself as we drew abreast of him. Good Lord, I had forgotten all about him and there he was, stiffly drawn up in salute and drilling me with his gaze.

On our way into the Volturno Valley we had made our first contact with American troops in their unfamiliar green combat jackets and differently shaped steel helmets. They probably thought we were 'Limeys' and took little notice, but they were closely scrutinised by us. If we were well equipped for fighting, they certainly out-did us in amenities. It was absolutely marvellous to go through their large outdoor showers enjoying loads of hot water, soap and towels, emerging through a canvas corridor into a marquee to don new underwear. Something else which fascinated us were their communication wires. We had never seen anything which even remotely resembled them; the roads were festooned with military telephone wires on a scale never previously experienced, and the Yanks must be great talkers. There were smart white-helmeted military police brusquely waving us this way and that, a whole new milieu and mood completely alien to our old informal 8th Army routine. There also appeared to be a lot more devastation than we had been leaving in our wake in Italy to date.

We learned that 4 Indian Division, which had relieved us at Orsogna, was itself being relieved and on its way to join the 5th Army. The Indians, who were trained in mountain warfare, would operate north of Route 6 and the New Zealand Division in the Liri Valley. After some reorganisation which involved moving to another scout car the regiment started advancing towards the front. The hills closing in on us were dark and the mountains ahead bleak and depressing. It was clear the country had been fought over; there were shell holes, bomb craters — some quite big — tree stumps and blackened trees raising scratchy outlines. We had plenty of time to look around because congestion on the only road to the front caused many stops and starts. There was time to sit and think; to become aware of the old, cold, gut feeling.

On the left the bare slopes of an elongated mount rose about six hundred feet and ahead in the distance a huge massif with a snowy crest seemingly touched the sky. Near the summit could be seen a white building which looked like a monastery so spectacularly sited it must possess one of the most wonderful views in the world. Mount Cairo, they said, and that high ground on the left was Mount Trocchio, a name to become as familiar to us as Tobruk. We had a long halt at a crossroads where half-demolished buildings reminded one of pictures of the Western Front in the First World War. Here we proceeded left to halt a few chains up the hill. The sun came out and we sat in the car enjoying it, in that blank frame of mind common in tedious convoy if no immediate danger is apparent.

'Up here!' shouted our officer from a bank above us.

The armoured car jerked forward, turning as the wheels failed to get purchase in the heavy ground. It slid back and then stalled. Restarting the engine, the driver had another go with the same result. A third attempt with us pushing also failed which was not surprising because the vehicle weighed tons and was not designed to climb banks. A loud roar came from above.

'Corporal Blythe! Why hasn't that car got chains? I'll put you on charge!'

Fortunately we made it on the next attempt but what was the idiot shouting about? Chains? I had seen them on vehicles in Otago as a boy, but never on an Army vehicle. In any case vehicles were the responsibility of the drivers and if we were entering country where chains were required why hadn't somebody issued a warning order? I had never seen any chains in our unit but I knew their value; although we were experienced in desert warfare we had a lot to learn about operating in snow and mud and on roads again. During our trek across from the Adriatic I had observed more than one quad and gun carriage overturned where drivers had fallen asleep and run off the road. In the desert it had required only a hearty thump to wake a sleepy driver when there was no road to stay on; it did not matter if one temporarily kipped out, but Italy was a different story and we would have to adapt. Even walking was different in this country where mud and twigs built great birdnests round one's feet until, under their own weight, these accumulations would detach themselves and fall to the ground. Obviously chains would have been an advantage, but why do one's scone about it? He was certainly living up to his nickname.

We followed his instruction to park the armoured car up at the farm house and left him marshalling the rest of the vehicles. After a matter of yards we were halted by one of the more solid trees amidst the grape vines. Perhaps the chains incident had upset the driver, because he chose this moment to get down from the car, muttering sullenly that he couldn't go any bloody further, and seated himself on the ground with his back against the front bumper. The rest of the crew sat in the car like mutes. A shell came screaming in to explode just a few yards away, then another, the black smoke drifting towards us. What a situation; that screaming bastard down on the road and a prima donna for a driver. Fear was mixed with disgust at the driver's attitude; what a time to display temperament.

The driver had more time in the Army than any of us, but some said he was bomb-happy and he was certainly difficult to understand at times. For instance, we carried a Browning machine-gun mounted on the car and he had a fixation about enemy aircraft. At every action station he would dig a weapon pit, crown it with a ring of sandbags, set the Browning up on its tripod in the pit, lay out his binoculars which he had purloined from Jerry, light himself a cigarette and sit on the edge of the pit scanning the skies for aircraft. For a signals unit we presented a brave sight! The heavy ammunition boxes that accompanied the weapon took up already limited space, but we went along with it knowing we had a character in our midst and that we perhaps provided an additional spot of colour.

However, this was no time for nonsense. If we did not get weaving that screaming skull back there would be hastening up to badger us. Another shell landed! Wasn't anybody going to do something? It was clear Jerry had nailed us.

With gritted teeth I seized the large axe we carried strapped to the side of the car, and swinging it like a man possessed attacked the solid tree which was blocking us, hitting it low down at ground level, as if it were the driver, the officer and Jerry combined, thinking that the poor farmer was not going to like it. It was quite incredible the way that axe blade bit through the thick wood and the strength that can be generated by fear and fury. A few more strokes and the tree fell. I turned, confronting him with the raised axe.

Rugby at Alife where the author once again was carted off. *Alexander Turnbull Library*

'Now you can bloody well move, move it! Get cracking!'

Without a word the driver got back into the car and as the rest of us dragged the tree aside it lumbered on while we got off the little ridge before another shell came in.

The large, two-storied farm house built of stone was occupied by Americans and surrounded by anti-aircraft gun pits. I wondered if our driver was going to feel frustrated. Now that we had a chance to look around we found we were on a spine, at the extreme left below Mount Trocchio towering over us, running steeply down to the crossroads. To our left facing the front and the town of Cassino were the plains, and to the right steep little gullies and ridges with one or two dwellings still occupied by Italians, poor devils.

We knew the Americans had suffered heavy casualties in this area and it looked fairly well done over. We examined one or two empty foxholes but were not interested in inhabiting them as by this time buildings were considered a much better bet, no matter how dilapidated.

Walking back to where the tree had been chopped down it was surprising to find camouflage nets being draped over the vines.

'What's that for?'

'Jerry can see us here, he's down in those houses over there.'

So that was why those shells came in, they must have watched every stroke as I swung the axe. Perhaps it also accounted for the ear-bashing I had been given.

I jumped down into a gun pit to join seven or eight Americans but it was disconcerting on opening conversation with them to be greeted by silence. Then, in a Southern drawl, 'What'd he say?'

133

I could understand them perfectly but only one of them seemed to comprehend my accent, and after listening to my remarks having to be translated each time, I gave up and went looking for accommodation. I installed myself with half a dozen others on the ground floor of a small, two-roomed building, one up, one down, which had lost its roof; there was the usual outside staircase and the walls were thick stone.

We spread our blankets out on the floor and were rolling them back against the wall to sit on, when the officer's batman arrived and began setting up his boss's stretcher immediately alongside the spot I had selected. This did not evoke any enthusiasm on my part but perhaps the outburst was an isolated one. Anyway, a move was not on now because all the best possies would have been taken and a hole in the ground did not appeal.

New positions always felt strange for the first few days until a pattern emerged. Some were good — that is, reasonably free from enemy fire — whereas others were bad. Being in an artillery regiment one had to expect to receive counter-battery fire but in Italy it looked as if you could be lucky at times, especially when Jerry had more pressing targets. We would wait and see, but in the meantime something had to be done about the cold. We cut off the ends of the 25-pounder shell cases with hacksaws and since they tapered it was easy to fit them together to form a chimney, which we pushed through a hole in the wall. There was plenty of wood available from the ruins about us and once the stove was roaring hot it was reasonably comfortable. The stove was a hard-case affair in more ways than one and as heat expanded the cases they slowly pushed the stove, which was actually a jerrican, out from the wall. Later, in our blankets and the fire dead, contraction would skip the stove in little jumps back to its original position.

The first night as we were bedding down we were warned that in the withdrawal of the troops from whom we were taking over, no infantry had been left in front of our position and there was nobody between the Germans and our guns. If we had been new chums it is certain we would have stood to all night while our officers paced anxiously up and down, but in desert warfare more often than not there were never any infantry between us and Jerry because one never knew where he might be; he could come in through the back door. So what the hell! We wedged the shaky door shut, checked that the mags of our rifles were full and took them to bed with us.

A pattern did not take long to emerge, but initially there were orders that care was to be exercised in utilising our 25-pounders because High Command was not anxious to divulge that the New Zealanders had switched sides from the Adriatic Front. Such was the standard of its gunnery that at times the Division's fire had been taken by the enemy to be automatic. But with the infantry's call for artillery support the guns became busy.

Behind us to our right within our lines, or perhaps we were in theirs because they were there first, were big American field pieces getting a shell away every few minutes. Someone mentioned that the shells were visible leaving the muzzles so I borrowed a pair of field glasses and squatting down just in front of the guns trained the glasses on a spot about ten feet ahead of the muzzles; sure enough the black shape of the trajectory was visible for a split second. Tiring of this I switched the glasses to where the shells were landing on what appeared to be an empty paddock close to a row of isolated houses from which I had been told earlier Jerry was watching us.

It was difficult to determine just exactly what the Americans had in mind because the shells were blowing great holes in what appeared to be an empty field. If there were troops there I could not see them through the glasses. They were quite big guns and to the Americans ours had appeared tiny but I think we impressed them because the first time we fired an American officer seemed fascinated, remarking, 'Those are the greatest, fightingest little popguns, man, I ever darned seen.' On the other hand, some of our officers were a bit caustic about the American fire; 'Up a mile, down a mile, left a mile.'

At that moment the troop of 25-pounders alongside us opened up. Not just a shell every five minutes, but a continuous fusillade on apparently the same target. The first bunch of shells landed plumb on the end house. Several Germans burst from the front door and hared up the road to the next one. Without any apparent pause our shells started falling on this too and more Germans ran out and entered the third house. The shells followed them like a hose and we chased them from house to house right up the road until the survivors running across paddocks disappeared from view. As a demonstration of controlled firepower it was pretty impressive and not lost on the watching Yanks.

Not a great deal of enemy fire was coming our way in daylight, but there was enough to keep us on our toes at times, when we crouched behind banks and the stone remnants of buildings as wicked 88s slashed the foliage and fragments of steel and stones whizzed overhead to rattle against the gun shields and buildings. On one occasion I got caught out in the open with nothing deeper than a wheel rut to try to press into.

There is nothing worse than high-velocity shells landing just short of you, sending hideous screaming pieces of metal over your head. It was pretty hard to take because as it arrived like the roar of an express train, one felt each shot was the end and they were keeping it up. As holes and white wounds appeared in the small cactus a metre from my head and the juice began to drip I really believed this time I was going to buy it. Pinned down for half an hour with the acrid smoke stinging my nostrils I think I aged ten years.

There was another occasion when I was standing by the armoured car and a shell fragment slammed into the armour and whined wickedly away. I looked at the gouge in the heavy metal; it was six inches from my hip, about level with my navel. The Americans with whom I had been gossiping melted away to their gun pits where they usually sheltered during shellfire.

We normally crouched wherever we happened to be, if there was something reasonable to cower behind, so I stayed by the car. On my belly, of course.

But if the shelling was sporadic during the day it was a different story at night, from a big gun thought to be a 170 millimetre. There is no doubt about the prowess of the German soldier; they must be about the best in the world, but they were predictable. Every night they moved the big gun up and at about midnight or a little later the cannonade would start; shell after shell whooshing over our heads like goods trains, just clearing our already demolished roof. This would go on for an hour and a half and it was nerve-racking lying tense in our blankets on the floor speculating when Jerry would drop one to clean us out. This went on every night for many weeks. Presumably they ranged on the crossroads below us to get our transport bringing in supplies but we were directly in line of fire and many landed short in our lines. Between times, just for variety, they added horrible mortar bombs from their nebelwerfers. These were ghastly multiple mortars of large calibre which sounded like gigantic moaning elephants, and one mortar bomb which landed at the foot of the wall of the farm house certainly shook the Yanks trying to sleep on the other side of it. Another yard either way and it could have been the Adjutant, signal office, or the Sergeant Major.

Sleep under such conditions was a problem but there was plenty of rough red wine so each night we sat around the stove in the light of a hurricane lamp drinking and talking until sodden with wine we would go to bed on the floor and fall asleep. But the shelling always woke us up; no one could sleep through the noise and there was nothing we could do except grin and bear it. There was a more-than-usual grimness about this particular operation which made it worse than the Orsogna Front where, although bogged down by snow and mud, we had felt that once the weather improved we would make progress. Here, we were confronted with a task of different magnitude and we knew the Americans had suffered terrible casualties which had broken their hearts.

The area of the Gustav Line, of which Cassino was a vital part, had gained a place in history for the natural strength of its fortifications. Here in 1503 the French invaders had been beaten and in 1860 the Neapolitans were defeated. Its defences ran from Monte Cairo in the north to the Anunci Mountains in the south, and Cassino was the hinge in the centre where Monte Cassino dominated the Liri Valley. There was the Rapido River and few roads, and the Italians who had regularly studied the area as a tactical exercise, regarded it as a classical defence system which could be made impregnable and this the Germans appeared to have succeeded in doing. Not a great many troops were required to man it, and the Germans kept making it stronger.

It was also becoming obvious that instead of being used as a pursuit force we would have to try and crack Cassino ourselves because the Americans were exhausted.

We attacked along with the Indians and gained some ground but the Germans remained in possession. The Maoris crossed the Rapido River and we were on the verge of a great success when they captured the railway station but without tanks which could not cross the river were unable to hold it. Our guns kept up a cannonade night and day until the muzzles must have been red hot but we made no further progress.

One sunny morning when things had quietened down a bit we had an orange fight; us against the Yanks. The American officers were scandalised at seeing their combat troops behaving like a bunch of schoolkids, climbing on to the tops of broken walls shouting with glee as they pelted us back. They could not understand us. We were supposed to be an élite division of the British Army and had even earned praise from Field Marshal Rommel; although our gunnery techniques were impressive they considered us most unsoldierly with battledress unbuttoned, awful grey woollen jerseys, bareheaded or wearing those ghastly rolled-up knitted things called balaclavas, encouraging their men to go without steel helmets, and now introducing games and hilarity into what was a Godawful serious situation. But it did the American lads a lot of good, relaxing and laughing for the first time since we arrived.

If the American officers did not understand us, by the same token their men were a puzzle to us. On a couple of occasions we invited some along to our hovel but as the wine flowed and we all got fairly full the Americans seated on the floor with their arms around their 'buddies' became sentimental. They were much the same age as ourselves but seemed so much younger. They were deadly serious about the war, to the point where it was difficult to get a spontaneous laugh out of them. We were aware they had been through a hard time at Cassino but we had been fighting for a good deal longer and mauled about more than once. The Americans were generous and courageous but appeared to hold a romantic Hollywood image of themselves which could disadvantage them and at its worst, perhaps, lead to greater casualties. To us, gallantry was an unmentionable word and indulgence in that sort of thing not far removed from idiocy; our attitude was 'let's get on with the bloody job and no frills, please.' We were very glad to have the Americans with us, make no mistake, but after a few drinks they did get carried away, showing us their Purple Hearts in their satin-lined cases.

The wine was starting to run out and this was serious. While it would not be true to say that the only way to insensibility was through soggy drunkenness, it certainly helped. Something had to be done so permission was obtained to take a jeep and forage for it in the rear.

What a reprieve to get away down the sunken lane, revved up like kids off to a picnic! We knew a British 25-pounder regiment had moved in behind us because their first shot had not cleared the top of Mount Trocchio, but what a surprise to find them by the buildings at the crossroad! Such an obvious target!

137

We stopped for a few minutes at the Hove Dump where the sky seemed more blue. I heard birds for the first time since arriving at Cassino and experienced that delicious feeling of release that comes from being outside enemy range. We were in no hurry because opportunities like this were rare and we spent the whole day obtaining a few litres. We also purchased a bottle of brandy; at least that's what the farmer insisted but we had our doubts. It was more like methylated spirits.

'See!' he said, dropping a spoonful on the hot stove where it immediately burst into flames.

We could not afford to be fussy so purchased it. There had to be some sampling so by the time we roared up to the crossroads we were feeling pretty merry. What a place! Smoke was rising and steel-helmeted white-faced British gunners were loading wounded into an ambulance. It had received a pasting and as we charged past them towards the enemy with whoops and cheers it was easy to decipher the expressions on their faces: those mad Kiwis! They were not to know we were half drunk and hated the place as much as they did. Whoever selected the crossroads for a gun position should have been castrated.

The jeep could not be brought right up to the house so the wine was carried over the last stretch. Buster seemed to be taking an inordinate amount of time to come up the sunken lane so I went back. He was sitting against a bank, hugging to his chest two of the large glass carboys.

'What the hell are you doing?'

'Protecting these two little beauties,' he chuckled, 'I'm looking after them.'

'For heaven's sake, let's get out of here.'

Large, genial, built like Friar Tuck, he had obviously done more sampling than the rest of us and this was no place to linger. Arms round his shoulders we made our way up the lane, Buster lifting his feet high as if feeling for a swaying deck. We made the house in safety with the wine undamaged.

That night the farm house received a direct hit from the big gun. The shelling had been going on for some time when there was a hell of a crash outside but it was only one of many so we did not go outside to look. It was surprising therefore at breakfast to find the house had a hole in it big enough to pass a bus through. Striking an upstairs room, the shell had demolished a large portion of the upper wall and the Sergeant Major had had a lucky escape. We were pleased about that, for as Sergeant Majors go he was an amiable type. He had been in bed in the room but thinking the shells were getting too close for comfort had walked out as one came in; there's nothing like experience for saving one's skin.

In the afternoon we had an air raid. It was not much of one but scary, because we learned how dangerous American anti-aircraft gunners can be when confronted by low-flying aircraft. The planes came in at roof-top height and the Americans hosed them with their .5 machine-guns. As the planes swooped down behind buildings they kept their fingers on the triggers so that shot ricocheted off walls and anything else still standing. Some

138

of us somersaulted over rubble. I was beside a wall but once the gunners opened up finished with my head wedged between a rock and a large piece of concrete. There I remained, afraid to move a muscle. It was a salutary experience because we were above ground and the dug-in guns when they first dropped their fire conveyed an awfully strong impression that they were firing up between our legs. The general consensus afterwards was that to be outside in an air raid with these boys was just not on.

Another raid caught the Americans with their pants down. Not a gun was manned. About seven German fighters swept over low down, not a shot being fired until one gunpit opened up with stuttering well-directed fire. No continual hosing, but careful stuff which kept the planes moving. You've guessed; it was our driver! But on that second attempt the Germans got what they wanted. They went home and developed their film and next night really got stuck into us.

We were sitting round the fire when there was a swish and a boom outside the door. The gun was in our front yard, or sounded like it, and the shell went past so close it caught my breath. Nobody spoke. More shells arrived and they were not whooshing overhead but swishing past the side of the wall; so close they were perhaps only inches away. I had heard bullets make that sound but never shells and these were exploding in our back yard. We did not count the shots. Perhaps it lasted fifteen long minutes;

Freyberg taking the salute at the ceremonial parade. *Alexander Turnbull Library*

rapid fire by one gun. We sweated it out, holding our breaths, then it stopped.

The phone rang. The Signals Officer picked it up, cocked his eyebrows while he listened, then put it down.

'Don't know what all that was about. Signal office chaps. They say they are all right.' He shrugged his shoulders and rejoined us round the stove.

In the morning we understood the reason for the call. There were shell craters everywhere around the sandbagged hole they slept in. How they were not left with ruptured eardrums I'll never know. The Germans had brought up a tank or self-propelled gun, so just in case they repeated the performance all the packed transport and the troop of 25-pounders in the gully behind us were shifted out to reduce congestion and present a less juicy target. Jerry must have seen them go because he did not bring the gun up again but reverted to his former shelling with the 170.

I had noticed some coolness between the Signals Officer and myself since he had bawled me out over the tyre chains, but was at a loss to know why. I had stopped letting him censor all my letters and was using our green envelope system which meant communications were not censored locally. Perhaps that put him out, I don't know. It could have been anything.

I had thought he had his good points but he was a bit of a big kid and being in such close contact did not help. And it was starting to rub off on his batman. We were all becoming tired and on edge but why the batman should begin to show such enmity to me I just could not understand. He did not sleep with us and early each morning would enter and rekindle the stove, douse it with a liberal supply of petrol, and from the door toss lighted matches until there was a flash, a boom, and the stove jumped off the floor and started roaring. He would then disappear chortling to himself while we removed our heads from under the blankets where we usually sought cover during the operation. A few minutes later he would return with a cup of tea for everyone but me. The others would sit up, sip, and exchange morning pleasantries while I remained lying in my blankets. It was embarrassing, childish and extremely difficult to understand how the officer who slept alongside me could allow a situation like that continue.

It nearly came to a head one day, when rounding the back of our ruins I encountered our two cooks imbibing while alongside them the batman chopped firewood. The cooks were older than the rest of us and alcoholics. On this particular day they were stoned to the eyebrows.

'Have a drink, have a shandy,' they called out, passing me two glasses, one of red wine and the other which I thought for a moment contained water. I couldn't see this pair watering their drink, so sniffed it. Good Lord, it was pure alcohol; they were distilling the damned stuff! I raised the glass of alcohol to my lips to sip it, but the fumes caused me to gag. Another attempt was made in response to their urging but still I couldn't make it, and after a swallow of wine handed the glasses back.

140

At this point the batman stopped swinging the axe and said something to which I took exception so moved towards him. He raised the axe above his head.

'I'll kill you,' he gritted.

'Go on. Go on, have a go.'

I stepped right up to him, white-faced, trembling, axe still raised. I took another step. It was crazy taunting him because one swing of that axe, if it didn't cleave my thick skull, would certainly wound me badly. The drunks took no notice. The batman's eyes were bulging in his head and I was coiled to jump when raising the axe an inch he hurled it to the ground and almost sobbing disappeared quickly round the side of the house. The whole episode was the end product of fatigue and days and nights of strain. I did not feel so good myself; it was getting to us all and perhaps like the Americans we would soon be unable to smile.

Buster was the next one to feel it. I was called away to help on the radio, putting my lunch down unfinished. On my return it had disappeared, along with the pannikin. In a fit of rage Buster had flung the pannikin through the doorway as far as he possibly could into the rubble across the way. He helped me look for it saying, 'The bastards keep leaving food lying around.'

Smothered in dirt and stuck to the bottom the food was inedible. A contrite Buster apologised, but it indicated we were all getting on edge. As radio operators our war was not perhaps so awful as that of the infantry and people in carriers and tanks, but we endured a lot of shelling and did have our moments. Our continued survival meant it was becoming a very long war for us, and the draft of which some of us were part was in the end to serve perhaps the most drawn-out stint of any in the war. Stress over three to four years was beginning to take its toll and there were more and more days when one felt dispirited and unwell. My bowels were peculiar and it was not diarrhoea. Too many butterflies in the stomach and one felt like an old piece of elastic that had no elasticity left. I was spending more time lying down when not on duty and the Signals Officer must have noticed this. Opening my eyes one day I found the Medical Officer standing over me.

'How are you feeling?'

'Not much good.'

'You had better come down in the morning, you could be sickening for jaundice.'

I wondered whether this was so, but it could also have been the wine. It did not sit easily on one's stomach if taken regularly; probably it was a combination of booze and fatigue, with mild jaundice thrown in.

Next morning down at the Regimental Aid Post the Doc wasn't sure.

'I could evacuate you,' he said.

Too tired to reply I said nothing.

'I'll keep an eye on you.'

Poor man, he had five hundred to keep an eye on. Next day Brigadier Kippenberger stood on a mine on Trocchio just above us and was grievously wounded, leaving the doctor with more important things to worry about than me.

We seemed to have reached a stalemate and the monastery continued to loom over everything. You could not escape its presence. If the Germans were using it for observation why did we not bomb it? The trouble was that nobody knew for certain that they were. We knew we would if we were in their position. The building was of considerable historic importance; it contained valuable relics and housed refugees. Without going into the pros and cons that have since been advanced by people who were not there, it would be true to say that most of us agreed wholeheartedly with Freyberg's recommendation to bomb it. The whole theatre was beginning to resemble the mud, horror, destruction and dead of the First World War and the sooner this static phase ended the better it would be for the Allied cause.

As in the First World War there were many head injuries, the percentage considerably higher than in the fluid type of action in North Africa. Fully aware of the New Zealanders' antipathy to wearing steel helmets, Freyberg issued an order making it mandatory to carry them at all times. He possibly thought we might find it easier to wear them than lug them around but we simply slung our arm through the chin strap and went about our business as usual. New British troops coming into the area noticed it immediately.

'The Kiwis are carrying their helmets.'

A close up of D. Jones (Wellington) and J. A. Batty (Wellington) looking out from a forward artillery observation post in the Cassino area. *Alexander Turnbull Library*

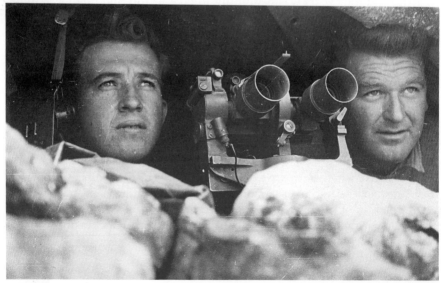

Their smile vanished as they considered the implications.

Once it was decided to bomb the monastery we looked forward to the event, feeling that it was an important milestone. The day dawned clear and sunny with not a cloud in the sky and as the first wave of bombers came in their wingtips formed vapour trails in the cold air. Because of Trocchio we could not see the final descent of the sticks of bombs being released over our heads, and could only hear the explosions. But as wave after wave came in the smoke began to rise, the vapour trails grew and merged, the sun was blotted out and the whole sky turned grey.

The bombing had been going on for some time when there were the most awful crashes behind us and we were appalled to see great volumes of smoke of volcanic dimensions billowing up from the village nestling at the foot of the mountain range in our rear.

Good God! The Americans had mistaken it for Cassino. How on earth could they do that with this inferno in front of us? It was difficult to accept but there could be no other answer; in broad daylight too! It was an unbelievable, shocking botch. The village housed the French Corps Headquarters and they suffered appalling casualties.

So much was expected from the bombing but in the end it was a disaster. The buildings were turned into high mounds of rubble, and where the rubble did not block the streets great deep craters did. Our tanks were prevented most effectively from moving through the town and out into the open. In the cellars and under the rubble the Germans went on making their fortifications stronger.

One night Peter Robson from Signal School days in Egypt visited our signal office. He was now an officer in the Maori Battalion and a very tired one at that; the old ebullience was missing. He sighed.

'We can't get at them. When we move in they call down fire from their own gunners on themselves and as they are under cover but we're out in the open, we cop it and are forced to move back again.'

I listened in on a tank frequency one day.

'This stretcher party seems to be going up and down the track a lot.'

'Have you been watching them long?'

'Yes, and I'm not sure they are carrying wounded.'

'What do you think they are doing, then?'

'They could be carrying ammunition.'

'Are you sure of it?'

'Yes, I'm pretty sure they are carrying ammunition. Over.'

The New Zealand voice came back coldly matter-of-fact, as if asking that the milk bottle be put out.

'Eliminate them.'

And then in equally level tones, 'Wilco, out.'

It was easy to visualise the scene; a tank commander talking to one of his tanks hidden in the rubble, an unsuspecting stretcher party on a cleared track now being blasted into eternity. The gunner, his finger now on the trigger, would probably be munching hard rations in a minute or two; it was nearly lunchtime.

We were experiencing a great deal of trouble in maintaining telephone circuits because the telephone wires were cut continually by shellfire or tracked vehicles passing over them. No sooner would the line party return than their jeep would be obliged to go out to repair yet another fault. They were becoming exhausted. The Signals Officer was standing outside our door as Buff and his little party returned from such an errand.

'Sorry, Buff,' he greeted them, 'the line's gone again.'

It was too much for Buff. Trembling with exhaustion and frustration, he sounded off in the roughest language I have ever heard addressed to an officer. For once I had to concede the latter did the right thing; he let Buff rave on, nodding agreement, uttering the occasional 'sorry old man' until his voice breaking, Buff turned and led his exhausted little party back over the ground they had just covered. I had been a spectator but should have got out of the way. His eyes alighted on me.

'Got a job for you. A walk will do you good. There are messages to go around the batteries. You can take them.'

Bleeding hell! He was way off court. As if he had my welfare at heart. There were despatch riders for that but I had no option other than to obey. There were no union rules. As I trudged from one position to another I wondered what would be his reaction if I got clobbered.

It could not be said that morale was low in the regiment but people appeared subdued and there was a sombreness about the whole rotten deal. Perhaps it was the dark hills, the brooding mountains, the mists on the plain, or the regiment on the left which forever fired smoke shells to blind Jerry. Or was it a smell of death? The whipcrack explosions of the 88s by day and the dull boom of the 170 at night? The slashed trees, the rubble, sour stomach in the mornings and the cold. Would it ever end?

In the desert, action had been pitilessly cruel. There was heat and glare, refracted light, smoke, flame, screaming noise which tore nerve ends, blood, metal, burning sand and the experience of naked fear. But except at Alamein it was usually over in a few hours, not this drawn-out stuff.

On one of the lowest days walking back to the rubble I lived in I must have prayed. Words of that old hymn, 'Oh God Our Help in Ages Past' were in my mind and I thought about the 23rd Psalm, 'I walk through the Valley of the Shadow of Death.' If it was a prayer the only justification I had was that I was too young and too bloody ignorant to die yet. With a false feeling of sanctuary I passed through the doorway where one was safe from everything but a direct hit. The more one saw of war the greater grew one's awareness of the fragility and vulnerability of the human body and the risks we ran. Severed limbs and organs could not themselves regenerate.

Some may consider battle experience provides greater confidence and that with this fear diminishes but I did not find it so. The reverse was true in fact. Earlier ignorance made fewer demands upon one's stock of courage. Repeated doses of action provided fuller comprehension of its nastiness. This was apparent amongst some around who had suffered wounds in earlier engagements. What experience did give was ability to distinguish real danger from the apparent, but with this came a diminished capability to go on absorbing stress.

Opportunities were being provided for people to enjoy a full day's leave in Naples; recharge their batteries, as it were. It involved three days and two nights out of the line. One moved to quarters in the rear outside of enemy range, had a clean up and a decent night's sleep, and next morning left for Naples a few kilometres away.

I departed with the others in a somewhat funny mood. To date in this war there had been no involvement with women, but there had been too many near-misses lately, and if an opportunity arose to sleep with a woman it would be taken. The matter was mental rather than physical; a state of mind, a rejection of firmly held principles. Who the hell cared anyway? The Army equipped everybody with various types of prophylactics against disease, so why mess about? In the morning before we left for Naples I dosed myself.

It was another beautiful day with winter falling behind and a growing heat in the sun. Lots of Americans were on the road because this was 5th Army country. There was a big truck following us containing two Americans. One of its rear axles complete with wheel began to emerge from its side and obtrude on to the other half of the road. It looked not only ridiculous but also bloody dangerous, trailing that great scythe, but the occupants took a lot of convincing before they stopped to check.

I had been to Naples before in transit and had never forgotten the miserable facilities provided by the British there on an overnight stop. We had arrived about 8.30 p.m. on a cold, frosty night after travelling since early morning to be told meals were off. We had insisted and received a plate of what must have been hardboiled eggs in curry but there were no eggs left, just a cold, green, milky slime which we spooned into our mouths. There may have been tea but I do not remember it. What about our accommodation, we had asked?

'There are no empty tents up,' they said, grudgingly showing us a tent crammed with other folded tents and flies. It was ten o'clock at night and we had no lights. Rummaging around in the tent I finally found a piece of tent fly. There were concrete squares spaced around which were presumably sites for the tents and also some long home-made wooden ladders. On my back, wedged between the stiles to keep me off the damp concrete and fully clad in boots, battledress and greatcoat with only the thin fly to keep out the cold and frost, I had spent a fairly uncomfortable night. If Freyberg had known his troops were being treated like that while on leave he would have erupted like Vesuvius looming up ahead.

It was hot in Naples and what a dirty smelly place it was in some areas.

Children played in the narrow streets amid rotting garbage under lines of washing strung between buildings. They were undernourished, some wizened like little old men, but indomitable and hard as nails. They would have had your bootlaces if you'd let them, and when they knew you were on to them, caution was returned with flashing smiles. It was clear that the citizens of Naples were having a tough time and easy to understand their antipathy towards the Germans and their desire to see the war ended.

I wanted to see the famous Bay of Naples. What was the phrase? See Naples and die? It had been changed by our airmen to 'See Naples and dive.' Unfortunately, however much we tried we could not get near the sea for acres of barbed wire and great mounds of military stores and equipment. In fact it was difficult even to see the top of Vesuvius from where we were. Walking around had made us thirsty so we stopped at an outside café for a drink. All that was available was Marsala and with its taste of dates it was far too heavy a drink on an empty stomach at that time of day. It left one feeling lethargic and as the sun grew hotter produced a dull headache.

We finally entered a restaurant for food and wine but there was little to choose from, only spaghetti and polenta, but we made do with it. Someone wanted a woman and for the first time I had ever known we were all of the same mind. Perhaps we had reached a milestone in our lives? In the past we had turned down scores of opportunities. There had been the odd individual like Ernie who wanted sex, but never a whole group. Perhaps the others felt the bell tolling for them too? The café proprietor would look after us so we got down to drinking and eating and as the day wore on the group diminished.

It came my turn and a youth led me down a couple of streets to a laundry where two middle-aged women were ironing clothes. Good Lord, I thought, not these two, and was on the point of beating a hasty retreat when an attractive young woman came in and beckoned me to follow her upstairs. My eyes were on her slim figure as we climbed the stairs and entering a bedroom she promptly kicked off her shoes and stretched herself out on the counterpane of a double bed. She was wearing a thin summer frock and nothing else.

I shed my battledress tunic and got out of my trousers, but what next? Surely I had to get my boots off? I bent down to unlace them.

'You don't need to take your boots off,' she said.

I had heard the expression 'boots and all' many times, but had never thought of this connotation. Was this where it originated? I continued undoing the laces. To hell with her. If she thought I was going to keep my boots on she was crazy.

In fact this whole exercise was crazy and I wished I had never got myself into this situation. I felt ridiculous trying to be nonchalant, as if I had gone through this performance many times before. She was becoming impatient and patted the quilt beside her, so down to my underwear and

Route 6 at Cassino. *Alexander Turnbull Library*

almost outside myself observing, I climbed alongside making a tentative gesture to caress her, but there was to be none of that. Get on with it. The message was clear, and with a head thick with wine and rising anger at the whole coldblooded business, I entered her. At one stage she plucked the dress from one shoulder to bare a breast, perhaps to hurry me on, but the sight of the brown flaccid nipple nearly stopped me in my tracks. It was nothing special and soon over. Without warmth and emotion it was like yesterday's fish and chips. I stood, frustrated, watching her wash and soap her hands at a little handbasin against the wall. I was completely unprepared for what happened next. Turning, she came forward, clasped my penis in her hands and rolled it between wet soapy fingers, rinsed and dried it, gave me a flashing smile and quit the room leaving me feeling like a little boy. My face must have been a study, and if anything like my mood, a pretty black one. Obviously she had been a harlot, but what did I expect? I stumbled down the stairs past the two women ironing, and returned to the café. I had been almost the last and my companions had disappeared, so I ordered more wine and food.

For a long time I sat there brooding and drinking and in the foulest of moods as the afternoon wore on. I'd have another woman! That was the answer! It would be different this time. The proprietor demurred. I insisted. He was not enthusiastic but he would fix it. Time dragged, my mood was ugly and I was attracting curious glances from other patrons. The proprietor made soothing noises; he obviously wished to be free of me. I sat glowering in a smouldering black fury and with patience almost exhausted when the proprietor came forward and himself conducted me down the street.

It was the same place and the same young woman. She gazed closely at me and her face broke into a smile. 'Ancora,' she said, pinching my cheek. If only she had known! Up the stairs again. Perhaps I kept my boots on, I don't remember but know I didn't care. It took longer and at one point there was some faint response from the body beneath me, but the wash was more perfunctory before she disappeared with the money. I was no happier but perhaps some of the blackness had dissipated.

I looked at my watch. Good Lord! It was nearly five o'clock and I had less than five minutes to find the vehicle park otherwise I would be AWOL in Naples with now almost empty pockets. I was unfamiliar with the city and had no idea where the car park was but sometimes running, turning left and right as instinct prompted, I homed in on that square as if locked in on radar. One New Zealand truck remained, engine running, and as they dragged me in over the tailboard it moved off.

Sobering up as we bowled along I reflected on the day's events. The chances of infection were pretty remote in view of the inordinate amount of precautions I had taken and would again when I got home. So what was Naples really like? I had spent most of the day inside.

There was an American jeep behind us with three stars on the front bumper and on the helmet of the geezer sitting next to the driver. It must have been a three-star general. He sat impassive, watching us.

'Must have a piss,' said someone opposite, standing up.

'Me too,' said another, unbuttoning himself.

'Bloody hell! That's an American bigshot,' said a third. 'For God's sake . . .'

Interrupting him, a fourth chap stood up saying, 'Bugger him, I'll do it in his eye,' and they stood together over the tailboard.

If looks could kill, that general would have annihilated us. The driver must have nearly wet himself and the jeep all but ran off the road. There was freezing disapproval on the general's face as the jeep fell back to a safer distance. We were lucky not to be reported.

Transport to take us back to Cassino and the regiment came late the following day and it was night in the valley as we neared Trocchio. It was like entering Dante's Inferno. Through the misty dark we could see dull red gun flashes and hear the grunts of the tank guns like rutting monsters of the underworld. For once our 25-pounders were silent and we were grateful, and then at midnight the 170 resumed its beastly shelling.

148

Chapter 11

The Pressure Eases

Rome to Florence

'You're going up into the mountains tonight,' said the sergeant. 'Take the armoured car and a crew and find the Polish Brigade. Take over their Signals Office.' Unbuttoning his revolver and holster from around his waist he added, 'And you'd better take this in case you run into trouble.'

'Hell,' I thought, 'what sort of deal is this?' I buckled the heavy thing about my waist. I wanted to ask him why he wasn't coming himself but lacked the nerve. Feeling like Tom Mix, the old-time cowboy film star, I climbed reluctantly into the car and took off.

I'm not sure how we found the Signals Office — or the Poles for that matter — but we did without incident. It was on the outskirts of a small village and we must have stumbled on it because the night was as black as pitch. The Signals Office? Just the smallest hole in the ground. We left one of our chaps there manning the telephone exchange after making contact with the regiment and blundered around looking for a place to sleep. It was a miserable little village with every building joined to its neighbour. Under an archway I opened a door and upon lighting a lantern found we were in a decent-sized room. It had a stone floor, stone walls and was filled with rubbish. It stank of urine but we could do something about that.

The rubbish was shovelled out into the street and with water heavily laced with disinfectant and plenty of flea powder we soon made the place more salubrious. We had little idea of where we were or whether there were any Germans in the village but it was late so in our awful woolly underwear we climbed into our blankets. I dropped into instant oblivion with the revolver cuddled against my cheek and without the 170 to wake us had my best sleep for weeks.

My eyes opened to broad daylight and giggles, feminine ones at that; over the top of the blanket I saw that half the village was watching. There was a food queue in the narrow passage outside and somebody had opened our door. They were gazing at us with great interest, gabbling amongst themselves and bursting into roars of laughter.

How were we going to get up and dress without displaying our hideous winter woollies? There was no alternative. I was closest to the door so threw aside the blanket and rushed and closed it. By the time we had shaved, folded up the bed-rolls and made a cup of tea the queue had disappeared. Outside, the regiment was beginning to arrive and the village in daylight proved even drearier and smaller than first supposed. It nestled at the edge of a river at the foot of a high conical hilltop on which stood a crumbling tower. There were whitewashed stone terraces and a few vines, and across the road about seventy yards away a battery of 3.7 ack-ack guns being used as field artillery was heavily dug in.

As the ground was particularly rocky, two of us elected to build a stone sangar against a little stone wall and put a tent over it. The only person really digging in was the driver, doggedly excavating another of his interminable gunpits. Hullo! What was this? He was installing a .5 anti-aircraft gun! Surely he hadn't pinched it from the Americans? What happened to the Browning? Perhaps he made a swap? I must have missed it in the dark last night, but my mind had been on other things.

The terrace on which we had placed our tent was level, and if we removed the odd rock we could have a tenniquoit court. We had just finished constructing it and were resting before having a game, studying the net and its poles, when whoomp! there was black smoke, and a shell exploded right on the edge of our little court. The bloody bastards! The Jerries must have been watching us, now perhaps laughing at us scurrying like rabbits. As I leaped for the sangar I would gladly have exchanged it for the gunpit down which the driver's head was disappearing. A few more shells in and around us, then it stopped. I could never understand the enemy in Italy. Time and again he lined us up, right on target, but instead of finishing us off he stopped. More than once I had suspected we were escaping a lot of grief simply because the Germans were being forced more and more to conserve their ammunition to resist our attacks. Not like us; as we advanced we carpeted the ground with shell holes, so much so that we were seriously eating up ammunition stocks required for the Second Front in Europe when it started. If it started! We still felt our final destination would be Berlin.

That first night in the sangar was a disturbed one because the rock wall was the home of livestock which rustled and made little noises all night long. One could live with lizards, rats and fieldmice, but I wasn't too keen on the snakes. The large black ones were supposedly harmless but I did not fancy sharing my blankets with them. In the Western Desert little snakes occasionally crept into blankets seeking warmth, but these were large enough to ask you to move over. I watched one of our chaps chase a snake; catching it by the tail he engaged in a long tug of war with it. Its head had disappeared into the wall. There was over a metre of it visible and to get a better grip he took a turn of snake around his wrist. Watching, I thought that if the snake lost its grip the head would come flying out and smack the soldier right in the face. However it was the latter who lost his grip and the snake disappeared.

A light had been observed flashing from the tower above us. Two of our officers went up taking a tommy-gun with them to investigate. It was all fairly lighthearted and they got nothing except a lot of advice from us as to how to fire the gun.

Next day I stood down by the river openmouthed as a jeep came smartly round a bend in the river and drove nonchalantly past as if jeeps did that sort of thing every day. I had hardly turned around when our driver appeared with a bazooka and some rockets. What now! Was he going tank hunting? We could barely fit into the armoured car because of his boxes of ammunition and now a bazooka. We probably had more firepower than any other signal unit in the British Army, perhaps in any army. It comprised two pistols, one issue, one not, four Lee Enfields complete with bayonet and bandoliers, one tommy-gun, one .5 automatic anti-aircraft gun, several hand grenades, one Bren gun, and now a bazooka with rockets.

'What are you going to do with that?'

'Fire it.'

'Well for God's sake be careful, it could be defective.'

I watched him walk into the trees by the river with a couple of his cronies, returning triumphantly later with a blackened face and a couple of stone chips in his cheeks. They had tied the bazooka to a tree and fired a rocket using a piece of string, so here was another piece of equipment we were going to live with. Perhaps we could offer our services to the Divisional Cavalry.

I went down to the river again. Good Lord! It had disappeared. In its place was an almost smooth gravel road. No wonder the jeep had made such easy work of it. The village was in a panic; they had lost their water supply. Apparently our engineers had diverted the river, perhaps so its bed could be used to bring up supplies. However, it came back in a couple of days so we constructed a weir with sandbags and as the river was broad soon had a sizable if shallow swimming pool. The weather was becoming warm; we thought no shell could reach us down there, and it was all very pleasant. One had to admit there were people around with innovative ideas. The Polish Brigade had replaced us at Cassino. We didn't envy them; this was immeasurably preferable.

Our wireless code signs changed daily and as wireless NCO for the regiment it was my responsibility each morning to draw new communication diagrams for distribution. They encompassed our link with Divisional Artillery Headquarters, the three gun batteries, a medium artillery regiment and the spotter plane. I had been provided with a piece of perspex with circular holes and rectangular slots and triangles, and using this could hardly go wrong. As one who fancied himself at sketching I thought I did a good job. Each morning, using a sharp pencil, I would complete them and hand them to the Signals Officer for inspection.

He would stand, not looking at me but pursing his lips and shaking his head.

Rome leave. Author on right.

'These are pretty rough. You can do better than this. Take them away. No, I'll keep them, but do them again.'

He was beginning to do this every day unless caught up in other activities. Sometimes he insisted I do them three times and as there was no carbon paper and six or seven copies required it took a good deal of time. At some stage he would nod his head saying, 'These are much better. Good. You can distribute them.'

It made me furious because the repeats were never better than the originals into which I put a lot of care. He knew and I knew they were not because I had tried him out, but there was nothing I could do about it.

One day I was at least a hundred yards away when he commenced bellowing my rank and name in his bullhorn voice. I walked smartly towards him to be greeted with, 'Corporal Blythe, when I call you, you come running.'

Who in hell did he think he was? This was the New Zealand Division, not some Gestapo outfit and it was doubtful whether even they addressed their men like that. There was a stranger present which made it more embarrassing, a man from Archives who had come all the way from Bari

152

in the south to get some 'local colour'. But what was wanted of me I never did find out, for at that particular moment the German artillery opened up on the 3.7 battery across the road. It was a savage attack and each shell was landing squarely on the gun positions; it was fortunate they were so strongly dug in.

The three of us stood watching it for several minutes. The bloke from Archives was getting all the colour he probably wanted but as his face was becoming progressively whiter it did not seem to be doing him much good. We were accustomed to shellfire and knew we were not the target this time, but it was close enough to be dramatic. The Archive chap clearly had no stomach for this type of thing and wanted to get away but could hardly do so as the officer, obviously enjoying the situation, kept him talking. When the shelling finally stopped he wasted no time in mounting his bike and roaring off down the road, no doubt giving his mates an earful on his return to base. The officer watched him beetle away and turned to me, grinning; I thought, 'You bloody oaf, you've already forgotten how you spoke to me,' and as he appeared to no longer require me, I left him where he stood.

Next day there was great activity across the road and the guns were moved higher up the valley and brought into action. As they fired, puffs of smoke emerged from the mounds across the road. What jobs some people get landed with! These unfortunates had been left behind to simulate gunfire every time the battery fired from the new positions. But they were lucky, or perhaps Jerry was not fooled because he left them alone — us too for that matter. It was a very quiet sector. So were our guns; it was almost like being out of the line.

Our two alcoholic cooks were really very good and dabs at making apricot pie. The meals were the best I had ever enjoyed in the Middle East and Italy. They slept in a hole in the ground under a heap of dirt over which grass had grown. Each morning they would surface like two tall gnomes, red-eyed and shaking as they shambled off to light the cookhouse burners. They did a wonderful job but there was one drawback to this good food; at meal times we were besieged by silent children who watched us from the road less than a chain away. One rarely saw the villagers so the number of children was surprising and many probably came from miles away with their empty tins to fill.

One girl, older than the rest, stood out. Her young breasts pushed against her freshly ironed white blouse. She invariably was neatly dressed whereas most of the children's attire was well worn hand-me-downs. Some of the chaps fancied her, especially when she surprised donors by thanking them in a Scottish accent. We learned later her mother was a Scots woman married to an Italian.

It was a problem deciding whether to eat it or to donate that last deliciously roasted potato soaked in gravy with so many eyes riveted on one. As it was, we were no longer receiving our full ration because after we finished the children would queue up while those two alcoholic softies filled their tins from what had been held back in the big dixies. Notwithstanding, everybody shared the remnants from their pannikins into the proffered tins and not once did the smallest child take a morsel for itself. Obviously they took the food back for families to share, so what could one do? Early on it all went into one tin, be it pudding or potato, but later some brought tins for each course. The saddest sight one day was old grandpa with his tin standing behind the children.

I was beginning to wonder about the precise location of our guns. They were apparently not so close to us as usual — or so I thought before I took a walk. No wonder they had not been obvious, for our gunners had really changed their style for this static warfare. It was a new technique and I do not know whether there was a forester amongst us, but from a short distance away the gun sites looked like solid log cabins sitting in the bush. With a green camouflage net draped over the protruding barrel, it was not at all obvious that they housed 25-pounder guns.

There was to be an important BBC announcement. Well, anything to break the monotony! As we stood in the sun that morning with the volume knob on the sets turned up, it came out like the voice of God.

'Allied forces have landed this morning in Europe.' They were telling us D-Day had arrived.

'American and British forces have landed on the beaches across the English Channel and are pushing forward.'

I felt so full I wanted to kneel on the ground and weep. After all this time! We had waited so long, had battered our way so many miles. Crossed seas. Mostly alone, feeling the 8th Army was carrying the can as the long-awaited Second Front mirage-like retreated as we advanced. Now at long last the war had moved to Europe. The Allied forces and the Russians must surely reach Berlin! For the very first time real hope blossomed. It could end! This war could end! We might get home? But just as quickly came thought of Japan. Yes, go home to fight the Japs.

There was other good news too; I had been included in a three-day leave party to Rome. This would be different. Purged in Naples and Cassino behind us, this would be a culture trip. There was so much to see in an historic city like Rome, I couldn't get there quick enough.

We were stocked up with cigarettes saved as currency for such an occasion and knew black market English cigarettes were fetching good prices. Our first concern was to secure good accommodation and we found it on the fifth floor of one of the many apartment houses. Two of us shared a fine room; it was big, long, with lace curtains over the windows at the far end from which we could look down into the street below. The furniture was in dark wood and well made, there were tall mirrors, a single bed against the inside wall by the door, and half way down the long room a magnificent double bed which was mine.

Each morning the lady of the house brought in glasses of strong black

Radio deception party in Tuscany. Henrietta laid just over 100 eggs before becoming a battle casualty.

coffee; real ground coffee like sweet syrup, of such flavour it tasted like a liqueur. She joked about sharing my bed with a signorina; it would have been agreeable but time was short, there was a lot of artwork to be seen, and no time for lingering in bed. It was an unbelievable experience after four years of Army life sleeping in holes and trenches, in ditches and drains, behind banks and haystacks, in sheds and stables, caves and cemeteries, to lie between crisp sheets. On my back with the taste of coffee fresh on the lips, I could luxuriate, gazing at the lavishly decorated plaster ceiling above. With its flowers, scrolls and cherubim in golds, greens, vermilions and blues, it was my own Sistine Chapel. One had to hand it to the Italians; they might not have cut much dash in the desert (although they could be worthy opponents when their hearts were in it); their hygiene in villages was questionable; but when it came to artwork their craftsmen were superb. How many ceilings would you find like this in New Zealand? Would there be a single one?

We mainly ate out, even breakfast, but we had brought a few rations with us and had one morning meal in the apartment. It consisted of sardines, Italian lettuce dripping with olive oil, crunchy fresh bread, no butter but in lieu a mild cheese, washed down with a surprisingly smooth vermouth.

The barber shops were good and an entertainment in themselves, far advanced on anything we had in New Zealand. I enjoyed a green facial mud pack, a shampoo followed by a haircut, but almost baulked when the barber brought back long-gone waves in my hair which the desert had eliminated, and finished it off with hot air blown over the scalp, and, of all things, a hair net! However if the burly Kiwis sitting alongside in adjacent chairs could endure it without losing their masculinity, so could I.

We walked through palaces, gazed at splendid fountains, looked at the Dome of St Peter's framed through the keyhole of a gate and then set off to find it. St Peter's Square was an impressive sight as were Cellini's columns and the statuary high on the facade. The tall Swiss guards standing at the great entrance lent an exotic touch with their brown-and-yellow striped doublets and hose, curiously shaped steel helmets and pikes. Under the great dome we watched people queueing to kiss the big marble toe of St Peter. There was a bridal party; it seemed odd for people to be getting married during a war. Perhaps it was the best man who, using a large silk scarf, wiped the toe with many flourishes? Notwithstanding, it still did not seem very hygienic. Someone drew our attention to the subtle difference between Italian and Scandinavian sculpture in the marble figures about us. The former they assured us were softer and I could see what they meant. Perhaps it was the curves, the smoothness and greater sensuousness; if such a phrase can be applied to marble, it certainly was softer in appearance.

The Sistine Chapel was smaller than anticipated although the height of the roof surprised. There was scaffolding in place, perhaps much the same as when Michelangelo went through the rack of painting it. It looked in need of repairs and artificial lighting would have helped our viewing, but then it was hardly the season for tourists. From pictures in schoolbooks to standing in the place itself — one almost pinched oneself. We wandered through many halls of the Vatican but there is a limit to what one can absorb at any one time and I found it easier to study famous old paintings than equally well known sculpture.

Many service people were striding purposefully down one of the wide corridors and we learned that the Pope was about to grant an audience to servicemen and servicewomen. Thinking we might as well join in and get a look at him we followed the crowd. Packed together in a chapel, several hundred of us standing, we waited and waited. The air grew foul and the heat oppressive, and although there were signs that His Eminence was about to appear we had had enough. Clutching the little medallions which had been handed to us at the door of the chapel we walked out past the slightly scandalised faces of the officials. One gathered it was not the thing to do but our time was very limited, we had stood in discomfort for an hour, and we were not Catholics; in fact we were only a couple of rubbernecks intruding on what was probably an emotional experience for the many present. Yvonne, the girl in the cipher section back home, would appreciate these tiny medallions and I'd post them to her. For some time we had been conducting a steady correspondence and her letters meant a great deal to me.

We wandered down to the marketplace, colourful with barrows of fruit, vegetables and gorgeous huge chrysanthemums, and entered the Colosseum. Although the ruins from the square were spectacular, we were a little surprised at the smallness of the arena from inside. I walked the narrow passages originally beneath the arena from which the combatants came up to do battle and mostly die, climbed high on the ancient terraces, sat down on the warm rock in the sunlight, and visualising the gladiatorial combats beneath me looked down over my raised thumb at them.

On the third day with money running low, I returned to the apartment to get some more cigarettes to sell on the black market. I was hoping the younger son had not lifted any more out of my bag. Momma had given him a rough time when I reported an earlier instance and I had been surprised and touched when she had insisted on replacing them, albeit with a lesser known brand. English cigarettes represented dollars. An obviously intoxicated British soldier was sitting on a chair in the hall outside the door of my bedroom. Momma, who appeared agitated, was laughing and exclaiming ninety to the dozen and I did not understand a word. As I moved towards my door she seized my arm and linking it to hers hugged it to her ample breast and virtually dragged me into the kitchen. She was barely pausing for breath and I knew something was up, and it was in my bedroom. However, as I liked Momma, I remained with her to her obvious relief. There was shortly a soft click as the front door closed and Momma, now all smiles, dropped my arm and rushed out. Following her slowly I entered my bedroom through the opened door, uplifted my cigarettes and went down into the street.

Getting into bed that night the sight of a used condom on the carpet at my feet confirmed my suspicions; that Momma had lent my bed to some harlot was a bit much. We had returned with a bottle of anisette to celebrate our last night and had enjoyed a happy hour in the kitchen, leaving Poppa rather merry. We were going in the morning so what was the point of raising a fuss? I was feeling a bit merry myself, and the incident had its funny side. Sober, it might have been a different matter. Carefully, with the toe of my boot I flicked the disgusting article further up the room then undressed and climbed into bed. Momma would find it when she cleaned up the room tomorrow. That would surely elicit a lot of *mama mias*?

Times were difficult for the civilians of Rome. They had to survive somehow, and one could not pass judgment. Food was short and their industry must have been in a terrible mess. I had also noticed that when one knocked on the front door, the only door of the apartment, it was never opened without a voice first asking who was there.

The Division must have moved during our absence because we were not returning to the same place, and the sight of the regiment's pick-up truck waiting where we were put down was depressing. However the mood lightened considerably when I found the Division was in bivouac, and that Johnny was our new driver. Squatting on a grassy slope under the trees he brought me up to date. Our former driver, as a time-expired man, was on his way back to New Zealand and most of his armament had disappeared with him. We were in an area in the vicinity of Arce, and during my absence the regiment had suffered casualties.

'At Sora,' said Johnny, 'we got done over by Jerry. It was our own bloody fault because we rushed in without enough care. The Germans were on to us. They got stuck in before we even got the gun trails down. I think about eighty of our chaps got clobbered.' Listening to Johnny I gathered that many of the wounds had not been serious but was pleased to have missed it.

The big item on the agenda was a gala sports day and the bulldozers worked away carving out a circular running track on which we galloped around in training, chins up, elbows in, loping stylishly along. Marquees were set up, a wine bar (even if it was only 'plonk'), and the event took place on 14 June 1945. I took part in one race. In white singlets and smart white underpants we looked very professional as we trotted to the start line. It was a big field, about the size of a platoon, and we were to do four circuits of the track. The gun cracked and we were away at a blistering pace. The finish was a comedy turn; the winner slowly jogged in with his tongue hanging out. The runner-up walked in to howls of derision, and the third placegetter and the only one left in the race was so far back he was overlooked.

Johnny was getting ready for the drinking competition which was the big event of the evening. I liked booze but did not possess a big 'swallow' and a competition involving wine sounded lethal. I wanted to get a letter away to New Zealand while Rome was still fresh in my mind so sat in the car and got on with it. Later, much later, Johnny came stumbling back to fling himself down on his bed-roll under the tree, groaning that he felt unwell.

'I told you not to go in for it, you big ape.'

'I know.'

'You don't even drink, you should have left it to the experts.'

'I know.'

'How far did you get, anyway?'

'You'll never believe it.'

'What?'

'I won it.'

'What!'

'I won it. All the way through to the final.'

Poor Johnny. He did not drink but must have had a mighty swallow. There would have been stern competition. How he suffered!

There was another casualty; a chap blew himself up on the lavatory seat. A large wooden contraption with five lift-up flaps had been installed over a large pit. The weather was hot, there were flies about, and someone must have been a bit heavyhanded with the petrol they poured into the pit and fumes had built up. This fellow had lit himself a fag and taking the first drag dropped the lighted match between his legs. At the dull boom we looked to see the big toilet askew, smoke rising and the bloke flying through the air. We laughed, but it must have been painful.

A fine-looking Italian woman in bare feet came over and gave Johnny some washing. She was accompanied by two young children. I noticed other women bearing laundry.

'Where did she come from?' I asked Johnny.

'From Sora.'

'But that's six miles away.'

'I know, but if she wants to do it, it suits me.'

There and back in bare feet twice meant twenty-four miles for a few lira. We did not know when we were well off.

In July the regiment took up the hunt again and we attacked south of Quirinale, moving to Civita Castellana about 10 July. There was action around Monte Castiglion Maggio, Monte Cavadenti, Monte Lignano and Camucine. In the vicinity of Arezzo we took over from a French Moroccan Division on 21 July in the San Donato area. There were lots of wooded ridges and below one we found the French hidden in the trees. What a

The farmer, family, and relatives on the estate near Siena who entertained us to dinner and dance.

tough-looking bunch! They must have raided the local livestock because feathers and entrails of poultry were scattered about. In view of this perhaps it would have been wiser to have declined the mug of wine they offered me. After they departed we had to listen to our harassing fire for a good part of the night.

I didn't like the place; because of the trees it was a deathtrap if we were shelled. I wanted out of there and I got it. Sometime after midnight on radio watch I began to feel terribly ill and was forced to call for a replacement. This was no ordinary pain in the stomach. Damn that wine! In the end I crawled to the first aid post where I was put on a stretcher to be looked at in the morning.

In the daylight I awoke to find the doctor bending over me before an ambulance took me to a casualty clearing station where there was a great deal of activity going on; they were all stretcher cases, but nobody seemed to have time for me. Alongside, lying on his stomach, was a member of the master race; a blond Aryan with a bullet through his buttocks. I spoke to him but sullen as hell he ignored me. Finally somebody came along, took my temperature and tied a label on me as if I were a package at the railway station. An ambulance took me to a British Camp Hospital near Lake Trasimene. The Hospital was notable for two things: the manner in which the British doctor talked down to us — he addressed us as if we were seven-year-olds — and the medical orderly in charge of our ward. He was all bonhomie as we recovered and became walking patients, and soon we were helping him with his fatigue duties. What a conman! It took four days to realise we were doing all the work while he sat on his duff. So we withdrew our services, telling him where to go. He did not turn a hair but devoted himself to the next batch of patients emerging from their beds.

Recovery from whatever it was had not left me particularly weak so I joined a group taking a walk down to the lake. There we enjoyed a swim although obliged to remain in the water longer than intended when two nurses in swimming suits came out and swam nearby; we had no togs.

Discharged, we spent a couple of days in a transit camp with grinning Gurkhas who filled us with sweet milky tea until it began to run out of our ears. On the second day we were bawled out by a Sergeant Major for not having come forward the day before when our names were called. There was now no official transport to take us back to the Division; I was placed on one of our ammunition trucks. As we ground on all day with a rather uncommunicative driver I found myself giving a lot of thought to my future.

Amongst the signalmen I had no close friend as most of the section were composed of a later reinforcement who had been together all the way from New Zealand and were a fairly tight-knit bunch. I had teamed up with Johnny but he was a gunner and could be moved away any time. The worst aspect however was this bloody Signals Officer and it was only a matter of time before we had a confrontation and I would certainly be

Divisional Signals twisting cable wire. Athol Lane and Charlie Baron of 'Beer' cable section. *Alexander Turnbull Library*

the loser. I had also missed out on becoming a sergeant because some of these jobs were now being filled by officer reinforcements dropping down to that rank in spite of having a commission. What the devil was I to do?

The ammo driver dropped me off at Rear Divisional Headquarters where locating the command vehicle I dumped my gear at the foot of its steps as an officer came out the door. I knew him, and explained I had just been discharged from hospital. 'Hang on,' turning to go inside, 'I'll make arrangements for you to be picked up.'

It was a now-or-never situation and almost without thinking it came out.

'Sir, I don't want to return to my old unit. I'd like a change. I'll go anywhere.'

He stood looking at me quizzically for a moment.

'Okay, I'll see what I can do.'

I knew that I could finish up at a sharp end, but I had had a bellyful of that atmosphere back at the regiment and didn't care. I also knew that it was probably only because of my 'go anywhere' that it was even being considered.

He reappeared.

'We're short here, we'll keep you in Rear Div.'

Good Lord! I had struck the jackpot! Not for one moment had I considered Rear Div as a possibility. This could virtually make me a tourist for the rest of the war! Furlough must come soon. I had already served a year longer than the first furlough draft. I had spent a short time at Rear Div in the desert but it had not meant much there because mobile warfare could make it a front line in a matter of minutes. It was from Rear Div I had joined the Ammo Coy for the breakthrough at Alamein.

There was an added bonus. Only a small group of signalmen remained at Headquarters; most of them had been around and I knew some of them. They were an harmonious bunch and the officer in charge was a thorough gentleman.

We were now in Tuscany where the Division was taking a brief respite before it attacked Florence. The countryside was pleasant, the weather warm and I liked this part of Italy best. Even the Italians seemed different; not so many darkhaired people as in the south, lots of blonds and tall good-looking men with faces like the heads of old Roman coins. We were quartered on an estate near the walled town of Siena. A long drive led in from ornamental gates to a cluster of little houses in the trees, a large farm house and an imposing mansion which was uninhabited and locked up. Perhaps some Fascist bigshot living there with his family had fled at our approach.

The locals did their washing at a low concrete water trough and here we used to congregate and try to strike up an acquaintance with the young women. The first night I situated myself under a tree inside my mosquito

The remains of a New Zealand truck in the village of San Michele, the scene of one of the fiercest encounters in the Italian campaign. *Alexander Turnbull Library*

net, the top of which I had tied to a branch above. Rising early we usually went to bed about dusk and I was just drifting off to sleep when laughter made me open my eyes to see three or four pairs of feminine legs; standing above me was a bunch of girls out for a stroll. I don't suppose they had ever seen an apparition like me before and I felt damned silly lying like a silkworm in my white cocoon.

The Division mounted its attack on Florence, leaving us for a couple of days to carry on a radio deception scheme, and the farmer invited some of us to dinner. All accepted except our officer and our host was clearly disappointed but fraternisation was not encouraged at certain levels and our bloke was merely being correct. He did, however, give us some slabs of chocolate to pass on to the farmer which was very generous of him; chocolate was not easy to come by and much prized by the Italians.

Thinking spaghetti would be the only food we accepted generous helpings but this was only the entrée. Instruments were produced and there was vigorous dancing but not knowing the steps we were mainly spectators. We tried, but the young Italian lads kept seizing the girls before we could get a look in, and stuffed with food we owlishly watched them perform. I thought one lad was a little free with his hands during the dancing but Poppa did not appear to notice, or perhaps ignored it. Later we stumbled home in the dark by touch.

The idyll could not last, however, and we were ordered to rejoin the Division. I was travelling in a soft-skinned ex-command vehicle when it developed a fault which I gathered from the driver was longstanding. Every mile or so the drive shaft appeared to slip and bring us to a halt at which the driver would jump down, seize an iron bar, crawl under the vehicle and belt something hard. It seemed to work because we always moved again but we got left far behind and the driver ran out of expletives. At one stage flames started issuing from beneath us and grabbing extinguishers we both let fly from our respective sides. My first burst caught the hapless driver full in the face.

We caught up with the Division outside Florence where the attack went in for three days. Nothing of note occurred in our vicinity except the incessant roar of the guns about us and the Allied fighters diving in with their guns ablaze; their cannon shells ripped the air like coarse sheets being torn apart by giant hands. I felt a little guilty lying in a steep gully eating plums from the tree above me while only a couple of ridges away people died.

Two plump civilians in dark suits and gaiters staggered down a slope and drawing puzzled glances joined our evening meal queue. Their giggling revealed they were two of our blokes dressed up and full as boots. However, top command was not amused and I'm not sure they were allowed to finish their meal.

Florence fell but we did not see the inside of the city. We raced around the outskirts and were a little annoyed when we learned that the South African Division was making a triumphal entry. 'For political reasons,' they said.

Chapter 12
Any Old Socks?

From Florence we moved in the direction of Rimini, on the Adriatic coast. The area was flat and knocked about. From appearances there had been some pretty savage cut-and-thrust in this vicinity. We halted in the grounds of a large church, school or monastery with outbuildings surrounded by a high brick wall, breached in several places. There was the dull thudding of artillery close by and no civilians; it was a scene not conducive to wandering around exploring, and it was also raining.

At lunchtime we looked for a shell hole into which to scrape our plates. Nearby was a little sunken depression in the ground where someone had already emptied scraps. I was about to do the same as others came behind me. 'Hang on!' I bent down to study a pathetic little piece of wood, perhaps from a fruit box, thrust into the ground. There was something pencilled on it. With difficulty we read two names and 'sorella', the Italian word for sisters, and the numbers seven and nine. Dear God, it was the grave of two poor mites probably killed during the shelling.

We removed the scraps of food, put in more earth where the ground had sunk and converted the piece of wood into a cross, rewriting the inscription in ink. All this while the rain fell and the sullen note of the guns came back. Nobody said a word and I had a lump in my throat at the thought that we had nearly used their grave as a rubbish dump. Who were they, the poor little beggars? Had our gunfire meant that they should end in this wet ground?

I opened an unlocked door to find a room crammed with church property. There were heaps of robes and vestments, texts and hymn books nicely bound in blue covers edged with gilt. There were also dozens of tall altar candles, and as my fingers gripped and slid around the thick smooth wax, I thought, could I? They would be fantastic in the pup tents. Only one. I would take only one. It would be marvellous to have a light again and be able to write at night.

That candle lasted for months. At the beginning, the flame almost touched the roof of the tent and the incongruity of its girth, size and the smell of incense in my humble abode aroused mirth, albeit tinged by a touch of guilt. I've never liked incense since, which I suppose is not surprising.

I was detailed to take a radio van and crew and link up with a Field Ambulance Company. The van was okay but the crew were new reinforcements who had spent a good deal of time in the Army back in New Zealand where no doubt they had endeavoured to enjoy every home comfort. They had some good things going for them and they had 'tarted' this van up. Set in elaborate silver frames above the transmitter were photographs of their wives or girlfriends, and tastefully draped along the top of the set was a large colourful paper lei and seashells. No headphones were in sight but attached to an inside wall of the van was a walnut loudspeaker. In some ways the speaker had advantages, because it eliminated the need for headphones and one could wear a steel helmet, but I was not enthusiastic about the set-up. I could tolerate the photographs but the lei and the shells had to go. I also thought the speaker was not good from a discipline point of view because the operators tended to wander around and talk and there were times when I was obliged to ask who was on duty.

I had heard that one of the film units was showing a film about a mile along the coastal road so set off to see it. It was being screened in a factory devastated by shelling and bombing and parts of the roof were open to the sky. During the film we were subjected to an electrical storm, the lightning flashes through the open roof adding a bizarre accompaniment. As I walked back along the lonely road it was an experience in itself. The thunder had ceased. I could hear breakers crashing in on the beach, and about every five seconds there would be the most extraordinary vivid purple flash which I was using to pick my way, because between times I was completely blinded.

The storm was abating as I arrived back at the Field Ambulance unit where, when I opened the back door of the van, I found the two operators chatting cheerfully inside with the radio switched off! For one mad moment I thought perhaps the war had finished.

'What gives?' I asked.

'Oh, there was too much static, we switched it off.'

Such casualness was unbelievable! These two needed putting together and I let them know. We operated our radios in all kinds of conditions and never gave up trying because people's lives and perhaps our own depended on communications. We had bounced over the desert holding the key in one hand while sending with the other. I had passed blood doing that, unable to hang on as we plunged into a crater. We had sent messages with the keys strapped to our thighs; smothered in dust and perspiration, we had done our job over and over under fire. We had fine-tuned incoming signals under the most impossible conditions of static until they became just fragile whispers in our brains and almost always we got through.

This priceless pair had simply switched the set off and sat gossiping on their backsides. What the hell did they think they were here for? Words

166

almost failed me. I reinstated the headphones immediately and angrily told them that if I ever caught them using the speaker again I'd have their guts.

In the event, Divisional Headquarters from miles behind had tried and tried to pass a message to us. In the end they had used the Division's most powerful transmitter with its own trailer generator, said to be powerful enough to reach New Zealand under certain conditions, although I had never heard this officially confirmed.

I learned the facts at dawn when the ambulance unit colonel informed me a despatch rider had made a wet and dangerous dash through that night bringing orders for the unit to move at first light.

'Must have been the storm,' I said.

Still on the Adriatic coast, our next stop was in the grounds of a sprawling cement factory on the outskirts of a town. As we moved northwards through places like Rimini and Riccione we seemed to be done with villages; 'towns' would be more apt descriptions of the places we were passing through. We parked ourselves outside something like a huge school shelter-shed adjacent to the main building. The floor was covered with straw but after one night of discomfort we got rid of it — it was full of large black fleas. The Italians told us the Germans had been sleeping there so they must have been lousy.

I was sitting in the van feeling sorry for myself when there was a smart rat-tat and I opened the door to be greeted by the grinning face of a brother-in-law last seen on final leave four years ago on the Christchurch Railway

Infantry moving up through Gambettola — the guys I left behind. *Alexander Turnbull Library*

Station. The impact of a close relative out of the blue was overwhelming. Formerly a captain, he had dropped to sergeant to reach Italy.

'I'm with 25 Battalion, told 'em I had a brother-in-law and had to see him. I've come to have a quiet night with you,' he cheerfully dumped a bed-roll off his back on to the ground.

Quiet night! He had barely sat down when we had an air raid, the first for some time. I was off duty and shouting for him to follow hared off for one of the vehicle inspection pits inside the factory, hearing this hobnailed boots clattering on the concrete behind me. Some of the pits had concrete slabs over parts of them and I don't think I have ever felt so comfortable during an air raid. Squatting on the floor and ignoring the booms and bangs, we brought each other up to date. It was therefore startling when there was a tremendous explosion directly overhead and we rushed outside to look. There was nothing to see but a small cloud of smoke in the sky above, and the only explanation we could think of was that our ack-ack had got a direct hit on a bomber and it had blown up in mid-air.

A few minutes after the raid a medium gun in the vicinity commenced harassing fire. It went on all night. This time the Germans retaliated. What a performance! We fired. They answered. It was insane, and with the noise and remaining fleas there was little sleep. As my brother-in-law shook hands in the morning his final words were, 'I'm going back to the battalion to get a decent night's rest.'

The Division was heavily engaged and suffering casualties and the field ambulance unit was the place to see them. They stitched up the bodies of the dead in our grey army blankets and laid them out in rows on stretchers to await burial. Under the tightly stretched blankets their shapes were unmistakable; they were like so many mummies. Down the driveway of the cement works came a gaggle of laughing young teenagers, all girls. I watched them pass, speculating what would be their reaction when they reached the blanketed forms. They stopped, one girl stepped forward and leaned over the nearest body. Then she screamed. They all screamed and, turning, came running back horror-stricken, uttering keening cries from mouths held open. I thought, next time you'll think twice before you go roaming through the Divisional area.

We had become involved in a grinding routine of artillery barrages and infantry attacks; pounding guns and the guttural thumps of the tanks, abrupt detonations of incoming stuff, the whoosh of flamethrowers and blackened German corpses.

Under cover of darkness we advanced to occupy a large two-storey building which previously may have been a hospital. We made it one and became an advanced dressing station-cum-operating theatre close up to the battle scene. It was near the town of Forli, Mussolini's birthplace, and there was all hell going on around us. The commanding officer and his staff were clearly worried at our proximity to the forward units. A decision was made to lower the largest tarpaulins bearing the red cross they possessed from the top of the roofs on the side facing the enemy in the hope that at daylight the Germans would respect them. This they did and in all that bedlam not a single shot came our immediate way.

Our radio van was parked outside the front door. For some time we watched two orderlies digging a deep pit between us and the door. Perhaps it was a rubbish hole? In a way it was. As the attack mounted and the night wore on casualties arrived in jeeps and carriers. Some even walked. From time to time there would be a flash of light, a door banged, and an orderly came out and dropped something into the pit. By daylight it continued; the surgeons were obviously engaged in amputations.

A few nights later I was conducted through one of the wards, an experience I never wish to repeat. There were twenty or more men in that ward and all were unconscious. Many of the beds were steeply tilted, some bodies suspended on wires in strange positions and connected to tubes. They were all enclosed in white mosquito nets stretching to the ceiling, seemingly caught in ghastly cobweb. It was weird. I had heard wounded screaming or moaning more than once, but nothing like the scream from this sedated silence. There is a verse in Les Cleveland's *The Iron Hand: New Zealand Soldiers' Poems from World War Two*. It's from 'Autumn 1945: Sparamagos: Riccione'.

> The wounded strung on surgical wires
> In wards like winter-bleached landscapes
> Are racked on loving engines of repair
> While pus drains daintily from deep wounds
> And bone-scraping nightmare meticulously
> Mangles them with blunt knives
> Some die after months
> Cursing Life.

The orderly showing me round was no ghoul, just interested in his job. Many of these medics were anti-war and possessed strong religious principles. I remember standing at Cassino as the guns raged when one of their companies arrived and began to erect pup tents. As the tents went up we read the religious tracts on them. One in particular I remember, printed in large letters. It said 'Safe in the arms of Jesus'. Listening to the thumping hell of our bucking guns I hoped its occupant was not going to be disillusioned.

'He won't last to morning. He's had it. That one might. This one looks as if he is already gone.' Acutely conscious of having all my working parts, I wanted to be out of the place. Almost all were dying, and the greenshaded lighting on the waxen faces already made them look like corpses.

In the vicinity of Forli we were recalled to Rear Div and as we entered the town it was a new experience to be directed to park in the front garden of an imposing three-storied home. It was fenced by iron railings set in concrete and the gate proved too narrow for our great lumbering vehicle. As I attacked the gate post with a sledgehammer, four pairs of eyes watched from a basement window. The barbarians were breaking up their home; the Germans had been right after all.

I knocked away only a few chips and it was enough, although more might have to come away later if we were to get the vehicle out. Momma from the other side of the window breathed a sigh of relief.

We walked over tiled floors and peered into empty rooms while the family cringed in the basement where they had locked themselves in. The door to one large room upstairs was locked; probably because of possessions stowed in it. We let it be. Most of us were not looters. The house even had a chapel. We checked out the bathroom with its bidet and found no water but by filling buckets from a well in the garden were able to flush the loo.

We chose a bedroom on the top floor: how strange it was to be sleeping in a modern and almost functional house again.

The family consisted of Momma, or perhaps I should say Madame because she was very much the grand dame and was always addressed as Signora; her older daughter and son-in-law who was a doctor at the local hospital; and an attractive child of about eleven years, Maria Theresa. As for father, apart from referring to him very respectfully, Madame shied away from the subject and we suspected he must be of the Fascist order, either in hiding or in custody.

For some time the family would not venture out of the basement except the son-in-law who went daily to work at the hospital, but as we gained their confidence Madame returned to her kitchen during the day and Maria Theresa to her great delight was allowed to play outside the side door at the back of our truck.

A Divisional Signal communicating by telephone from the ruins of Faenza.
Alexander Turnbull Library

I was invited down to the basement one night to spend the evening with the family. There was barely room to walk between the beds in the basement and Madame and I sat on the only two chairs. The elder daughter fed tiny slivers of wood into the cheerful red-tiled stove, just sufficient to keep a spark alive. The family were obviously suffering from the cold. Madame was wrapped in a long purple dressing gown; in fact I don't think I ever saw her out of it. Outside the weather was bitter, so cold that rain turned to black ice as it ran down the canvas canopies of the trucks. The bare trees were covered in hoar frost, taking on the appearance of white salt. They would have presented a pretty sight if it had not been so cold and dark.

Although all the shops were closed, Forli was a good town to be quartered in during this kind of weather. It had not suffered a great deal of damage and the paved footpaths and cobblestone square and streets permitted us to walk around without great muddy birdnests adhering to our feet. The main street sported a large marble male statue; it was a typical Mussolini effort, bespattered with stains and chipped by bullets and outside a building whose front was mainly glass. The film unit had selected this for its cinema and I was sitting there at a five o'clock session thinking what a hell of a place it would be to be caught in during an air raid, when there was a rattle of small-arms fire, the 'bumpin' of Bofors, cannon fire, and a dark shape rushed past the glass. It was over before I could rise from my seat.

The five o'clock cinema sessions were popular and every time we had a raid. It was crazy. Each evening a bit after five, down the main drag would scream a German fighter at roof-top level with guns blazing. The bored gunners sat behind their guns waiting for the plane, and as it arrived on cue all hell let loose as we cheered and ducked for cover. Heavens knows what the pilot's motives were unless he wanted to die young.

It was always, 'Look out! Here's the Mad Major!' We got used to him and it became the event of the day. Perhaps he lasted a fortnight and then the raids stopped. Shot down? Probably, and we missed him. Poor old Mad Major, the guy had style!

How cold it was! We were developing nagging aches. We covered our bed-rolls with our gas capes but it wasn't a good idea. In the mornings the hollows in our blankets were soaked with condensation enough to fill mugs. Then Jerry started shelling the town in the evenings; long-range stuff. His target was the airfield at the rear of the town. Unfortunately the hospital was in the flight-path of the shells and it could not have been pleasant for the patients and the nurses. It was perhaps the first and only time some of our nursing staff found themselves under fire.

One of our chaps was struck by a fragment in the face and we all trooped into the hospital to see him. It seemed absurd visiting someone in hospital, just like civvy street, marching down the ward. Unfortunately since he did not smoke there was nothing we could take except a tin of bully beef which would not have been appreciated. He surprised us by telling us he had also been hit in the stomach and had not realised it until he complained of a stomach ache and someone found another fragment in his tum.

Besides its good streets, Forli had other facilities including a stadium where the final of our rugby championship was played out. We made a good target but who cared? Freyberg came and sitting in the grandstand it was like Saturday afternoon at Athletic Park. The 25th Battalion were out of the line and I watched the game with my brother-in-law. Walking home we met one of his friends from the battalion, a reinforcement lately arrived from New Zealand. He had never been in action and was all fired up.

'We're going in tonight! I have been practising my reloading and timing it to see how quickly I can do it!'

He was dancing around on his toes parodying fitting a fresh magazine into his tommy-gun, his face alight. As we left him I asked my brother-in-law whether he was married and finding he was, shook my head. He died that night.

My old friend Don from Maadi Camp days was still a survivor and working now as a medical orderly in the 25th. I went to one of their parties hoping to see him but because of his musical ability he had been commandeered by the officers who were also holding a party. These parties were pretty lethal; about the only drink was straight vermouth and although a certain amount of moderation was exercised early on, as a party progressed it was quaffed like beer. I went back to the 25th next morning to see Don and found him unconscious on a stretcher.

'He's okay,' said the doctor, cheerfully sponging his face.

'We filled him up last night, it was a good party.'

Poor Don, like Johnny he was no great boozer and that morning he looked like a corpse. I never saw him again.

It was New Year's Eve; another year gone by and we no longer celebrated them. What was the point? We were sitting quietly gossiping when our driver walked in. He was pretty full and mumbling on about something.

'What's that?' we asked.

'The Bren. The bloody Bren. I'm gonna fire the Bren, the bloody Bren, at midnight, that's what I'm gonna do.'

Looking at his condition, I thought not if I can help it. He disappeared and we hoped he had flaked out. Not him; at midnight, wild-eyed and barely able to stand, he appeared in the doorway, a loaded Bren in one hand a spare magazine in the other, weaving around.

'Don't point the bloody thing at us!'

As he staggered outside in the street I was really worried. In his condition he could spray everybody in sight. The fire of the Bren would bring faces to the windows and somebody could get it between the eyes. I rushed after him, shouting that I'd help him fire it.

'Don't want any bloody help.'

5 Field Regiment moving forward, first day after the fall of Faenza. *Alexander Turnbull Library*

He cocked it and let go with a burst. I grabbed him and with arms wrapped round him and the gun we wrestled in the street as I forced the barrel skywards. The noise was shocking at that time of night. I thought emptying the gun would have been sufficient but no, he insisted on reloading. I held on but he was determined. As the gun thundered and clattered empty it was like an orgasm and he collapsed at my feet. We carried him unconscious into the house.

I was due for leave and packed my bag for a fortnight in Florence, something I had really looked forward to for a long time.

'You're not going on leave,' said the officer at breakfast. 'We're sending you and Mac back to Bari to do a tour of duty, you'll probably be acting sergeants and teach procedure. There's a big reinforcement from 3 Pacific Division arriving.'

Mac and I looked at him aghast. We had no procedures; we had thrown them away years ago. What we did use would take no more than five minutes to explain. How the hell could we spend weeks teaching something which did not exist? Especially to troops who had probably suffered a bellyful of tuition over the years. They could possibly teach us a thing or two. If I was furious, Mac was even more so.

'How can I teach procedures, I have a stutter, I'm not going to bloody do it and where's my bloody leave?'

He did indeed have a slight hesitation in his speech at times which perhaps in a lecture room could prove troublesome. Sadly we watched the leave truck depart for Florence.

This probably meant the end of the war for us, at least in Italy. There were still the Japs, but what a way to end. What an anticlimax; I had

173

never thought it would finish this way. I had been up to the next town, Faenza, a few times and stood by our 25-pounders belting away but this was it! They'd never bring me back to the Division again. Not in Italy. I was time-expired. No longer did I have the sickening, hollow-gut feeling concealed from everyone, going mechanically about my duties. It had been a way of life, stimuli and ennui, stimuli and ennui; it had gone on for years. Only now was one approaching the zombie stage. Those people back there at base probably thought they were doing us a favour, but if I had not been so mad about missing Florence I think I would have felt sad. I went inside to tell Madame what was in store for me.

'La guerre finito pour vous,' she excitedly mixed French and Italian, our usual mode of communication, and burst into tears. She asked me what I would do when I got home and I said I would probably try to go to University and finish my studies as I had heard people being discharged from the Services were encouraged to do this.

At my mention of studies, she was all smiles again, asserting I'd study to be an officer, correct? That did it! No wonder we were becoming paranoid. Why, oh why, did everyone even as far back as the days in Cairo, assume that because we were not officers we were virtually uneducated? What they failed to realise was that although the New Zealanders performed like professionals they were mainly civilians caught up in a war.

There were more tearful farewells; I thought how afraid they had been of us when we first arrived. In something of a daze I boarded the waiting truck. Not going to Florence. Not going to Florence. There was no feeling of relief at the thought of putting so many miles between me and the sharp end. The family back home would be pleased to hear of my new job. But there was no elation. The war wasn't over.

Mac was still simmering and in the hours we sat in the truck there was plenty of time to kick the idea around about presenting a united front and refusing to do the job. They would surely strip our rank but that would be no great loss. In the early days I had been ambitious but not any more. For too long I had been deprived of the right to think for myself; enforced discipline in one's formative years retards development. At the time I think we held low opinions of ourselves and had temporarily lost our confidence. A good deal of my exhaustion was also due to vitamin deficiencies but I was not to know that until after my return to New Zealand.

At Ancona we boarded the 'Brazilian Packet' and had just settled ourselves in a large comfortable deck cabin when the officer in charge apologetically asked if we would mind vacating it to some South African sergeants. We were a mixture of NCOs and signalmen and the Boks were pulling their rank. As we filed out they came in. Not a glance passed between us. Much more democratic, I am certain if the boot had been on the other foot we would have let the situation stay as it was.

The wind was piping thirty knots as we left the shelter of the harbour to be greeted by whitecaps and big green seas; I didn't think the Adriatic could get so rough. I survived the first night but in the morning the Indian crew served lukewarm baked beans and fatty bacon swimming in grease and that was the end; we dry retched to Brindisi where a waiting truck delivered us to base camp a few kilometres out of Bari.

Next morning we went before the Signals Major to learn our duties.

'Not going to do it, Sir,' says Mac.

I thought about our agreement.

'I'm not going to do it either, Sir.'

He looked taken back and obviously had not encountered anything like this before. He had spent years pushing people around and here were two refusing to be pushed; it was virtually mutiny, a nasty word. He patiently explained that there were many things people did not want to do but they did them. We knew the rules, we must know we had to obey orders. Mac was adamant. I supported him and in the end we were waved out of his office. When I think about it, if the Major had come up with some kind of training programme for us to implement I would have accepted it, but instead we found ourselves backed into a corner.

Next morning I was summoned before the Bari Camp Commandant. Where was Mac? I had visions of a provost jeep calling for me. They marched me into the orderly room and from behind a desk a red-headed Major looked up at me.

Good God! I knew him! Knew him very well!

Getting up, he came round his desk, hand outstretched, his face breaking into the same old slow grin.

It was 'Ham'! We had been good friends at secondary school.

'What's all this trouble I hear about?' he asked.

I explained, or at least tried to, and he changed the subject. I was embarrassed. Perhaps he was also. There is an awful gulf between a corporal and a major and after chatting for a few minutes I excused myself, which seemed the natural thing to do. He could not offer me a drink or even share a cup of tea and it was a ridiculous situation for two contemporaries to find themselves in.

If charges were contemplated he must have buried them because Mac and I were left alone to sweat it out. Nobody took any notice of us so we joined keep-fit groups, played basketball, and put ourselves on leave to Bari as we wanted.

Two chaps we knew arrived after graduating from OCTU at roughly the same time as the reinforcements came in and finished up doing the job we were supposed to do. Whether their arrival was fortuitous I did not know but one did ask, 'What the hell have you two done, you're as popular as pie dogs?' I did not enlighten him.

Then Mac and I were paged one day. So they were aware of us! Within the hour we were on our way to take over a telephone exchange in a small town near the coast. We still had our stripes. The town was drab, full of flies and boredom, and previously had been occupied by the Americans.

The locals regarded us as their poor relations. There was a café where we ate out sometimes, although the only dish was eggs, fried, for which we paid the equivalent of fifty cents. On one occasion when two Americans came back for a meal we were swiftly adjured by the proprietor who spoke English.

'Don't tell them you pay fifty cents, I charge them one dollar, plenty money!'

It hurt our pride, but fifty cents was okay by us.

'Si, si,' we agreed.

Many of the local girls, and there were some nice looking ones, showed off engagement rings the Americans had given them. Perhaps we had the wrong idea, but it seemed a little heartless to us. How many of these supposed fiancés would return? We knew how our authorities viewed permanent liaisons with Italian girls, and the obstacles they placed in the way. We could not imagine the American Command being any different.

Mac came back from one of the laundries in the town with love bites on his neck.

'What goes?' I asked.

'Gee man, this dame, you ought to meet her.'

I did later, but could see little to get excited about, finding her on the plump side. One of our chaps had already established a relationship and did not come home every night. He was a married man but these, in my experience, chased after women more than the single ones did. It had been the same in Cairo although Ernie had been an exception; I wondered what had happened to him.

Behind the telephone switchboard was a small room about the size of a pantry containing a single bunk. Our two predecessors manning the exchange for twenty-four hours a day had shared it with a girl. They changed shifts at one a.m. and all three used the same bed. Talk about hot bunking!

Somebody decided to liven the place up, get to know the local talent and into the social swim if such a thing existed. A dance was organised in a hall and our officers were good about it. There was music, food and wine, and all the girls available were invited. Many turned up chaperoned by their mothers. The music had everyone on their feet and it was going with a bang when one of our blokes arrived with his 'new girlfriend'!

There was an immediate freeze, the dancers stopped, there were dirty looks and muttering, and all the mommas got up and walked out dragging their protesting daughters with them! Unfortunately, the new girlfriend was a lady on the town and a notorious one at that, whom this great galah of ours had brought in off the street. There she was, dancing around enjoying herself, just the two of them on the floor until the music faltered to a stop. We polished off the food and went home early. There were no more dances.

For a night of variety I took over a hotel. There were forty-seven bedrooms and looking at the keys I had some difficulty making a selection. The empty hotel had previously been occupied by the Americans and the only thing they had left behind was a huge carton containing hundreds of prophylactics. So there I was with forty-seven bedrooms, plenty of stock, and no one to share them with. I slept under my mosquito net but it was a mistake. There was mesh on the windows, the hotel was airless and it took some time to get going again in the morning.

We spent several weeks in the town going to the beach occasionally in togs we manufactured from tea-towels. Mac even brought his girlfriend and in the surf it was nice to feel like a civilian. But too soon it was back to Bari Camp where the reinforcements had moved out to join the Division in the vicinity of Trieste. In their place were quite a few old-timers so perhaps something was in the wind. There was also one addition I could have done without; the Signals Officer from the regiment. I met him standing talking to one of our sigs and stopped because it was obvious he was in a draft going home and common courtesy demanded I acknowledge his presence.

He looked at me then gazing at his feet continued talking while I stood a couple of feet away. Gorge rising I took off to hear him say, 'John, I'll see you later.'

Not if I can help it, I thought, and was pleased we did not meet again before he left.

Did I want to go to Rome? Well, why not. Bari was beginning to pall. I was getting sick of standing around the waterfront watching fishermen

Soldiers of 21 Battalion saved their issue of chocolate and purchased sweets to entertain Italian children at a party held in Muccia. *Alexander Turnbull Library*

pounding small pink squid on the pavement until they reached a colourless transparency. The locals ate them raw. Everywhere you looked was the strutting Italian male, still in uniform, with a girl on his arm. I suppose I was envious but they got my goat, parading around like peacocks. Weren't we supposed to be the victors? It took me back to the beautiful Austrian blonde I had met in a Bari laundry on an earlier visit. Everything seemed to happen in laundries.

We had been waiting to pick up our washing when this absolutely gorgeous creature strolled in looking like an American film star. My companion had exclaimed, 'God I'd like to sleep with her,' but in cruder terms. I was hoping she did not understand English when she turned and addressed us with just the slightest of American accents. You'll never guess what this vision wanted; my old grey socks!

The truth was she worked for the American forces and was knitting herself a grey cardigan but wool was extraordinarily difficult to procure. New Zealand soldiers wore grey socks of exactly the right shade and whenever she could she endeavoured to buy some, secondhand of course. The thought of this really beautiful woman wearing my used socks was almost too much for me. I knew I had two new pairs back at camp and eagerly promised to bring them into town on my next trip. We fixed a date. It was a strange feeling going into town to keep a rendezvous with my beautiful lady but I knew I was kidding myself. Working for the Americans there would be no lack of escorts, probably about colonel level. She was there waiting, gratefully accepting my socks and wanting to pay. I declined, the fatuous look on my face lost in those blue eyes and smile. Like a cat looking at a queen, how sadly I watched those gorgeous legs trip elegantly away. What the hell was I doing anyway? I needed those socks!

But did I want to go to Rome?

Chapter 13

The Road Home

Rome — North Africa — Indian Ocean — Dunedin, New Zealand

It is an awfully long way from Bari to Rome by road, sitting on the steel tray of an Army truck. We made it to the Hotel Quirinal which Freyberg had commandeered for the New Zealand Forces Club. I spent the first night in the lounge with an Australian airman on the last day of his leave. He kept going on about the wonderful time he had spent with three sisters.

'They are really nice, it's just like being at home and you can take your pick which one you take to bed with you.' He wanted then and there to ring them up and get me introduced but I declined. Nevertheless he wrote out directions how to get there, telling me I would never regret it.

I wandered around Rome, saw marvellous paintings in the Borghese Gallery and did all the usual things but felt constantly tired and my nose to my embarrassment bled most of the time. Fed up, I asked an operator to connect me to the telephone number the Australian had given me but my Italian was not up to conducting the sort of conversation I had in mind so in the end I decided to find the house myself.

I had no trouble with the directions, they were so explicit. These were terrace houses, with iron railings, a patch of grass and a dove on a little fountain. When I knocked on the front door again my Italian was not equal to the task. A smiling young matron answered the door, a mixing bowl in her hand, but she didn't seem to know any young Australian or three sisters. You couldn't say I was enjoying any success in these essays of mine. I wandered back to the market amongst the stalls of fruit and vegetables feeling slightly ashamed of myself.

The next night, standing under a street light, I had just finished telling a streetwalker to shove off when people in an Army truck roared up, shouted and threw a bundle of newspapers at my feet. I pulled a paper out of the bundle and there it was before me in great black screaming headlines: 'WAR IN EUROPE OVER'.

God! They were in Berlin! It was really over! And there was I, mouth open, alone, in Rome on a dark night. Not a soul in sight. No wonder they had chosen me to unload their papers. Anybody with any sense would be inside on a night like this. I headed for the Club. There would be great goings-on there. Perhaps they were tearing the place apart? I mustn't miss this, I thought, half walking and half running all the way back.

The bored receptionist looked startled as I rushed in the main entrance. The place was like a tomb. A New Zealand officer came in with two Tuis and they walked quietly up the stairs to the officers' quarters. This was unbelievable. Back in New Zealand I understand they threw files out of windows and people danced in the streets.

Standing there in the foyer I realised that this was really a repeat of what happened in North Africa. As Alan Moorhead wrote, 'No special event marked the moment.' Dismally I went to bed while others in cafés, I imagine, sipped their drinks and heavily absorbed the news, too tired to care.

Next morning we left for Bari. I don't think anyone even mentioned that the war had ended. I bled all the way from Rome to Caserta, but when they put me into hospital that night I felt fine. In the morning when the truck came past I was at the gate waiting, feeling better than I had for days.

We made one stop between Rome and Caserta, at Cassino. How it brought back memories! My God, what silent tokens of horror were the pulverised buildings moulded into bizarre shapes. Great bomb craters were filled to the brim with green slime. Did they still hold bodies? Across from where we stopped the huge war cemetery was filled with our dead and many from other nations. It drew me like a magnet. I walked purposefully down one of the main aisles for about fifty yards, turned right past several rows, right again, taking in three graves, then faced in and stopped. I do not believe I am superstitious but what coincidence led me so directly to that particular grave? I think there are about four thousand buried at Cassino. I read the inscription.

Private Richard Bagrie. Killed in Action. It was Dick! Perhaps carrying the Bren again?

There had been only him and his dad back there in Invercargill. He stood so clear in my mind; tall, dark, and good-looking. The poor bastard; so he hadn't made it. He had come a long way though. In Les Cleveland's words:

> . . . and instantly I feel
> the thump of shrapnel pillaging
> my temporary brother's flesh:
> he cries out for help, and grips me
> in a child-like hold;
> I break his arms from their embrace . . .

I walked back to the truck. Had I stayed in the infantry that probably would have been my lot!

Bari Camp appeared even more run-down on our return but the usual ennui had been replaced by animation and people everywhere were speculating about our future. It was clear we would be heading to the Pacific but whether home or to fight the Japs we could not be certain. But surely we would see New Zealand first? In the meantime a delicate situation existed in Trieste, where the Division was having a confrontation with the Yugoslavs; we hoped nobody was going to do anything silly. I had no great enthusiasm for partisans and partisan armies; they usually contained a sanguinary element of assassins and people seeking revenge and tended occasionally to get carried away. If they took on our blokes they would surely get a bloody nose and the thought of more casualties at this late stage was obscene.

We were going back to Egypt. 'Pack your gear!' Just like that, and the strange thing is I cannot remember a single incident, hour, or how we got there. It was by sea of course, but I must have been switched off.

Maadi Camp had not changed but we certainly had; we were definitely older, had more grey hairs and we were aware of them. We beetled off to Cairo, back to the horse dung, Turkish tobacco, spices, Packard cars and Stella beer. We even visited the old Globe beer hall but the girls had changed. The rest of the time we sat on our beds in a tent and played cards interminably.

We had a Maori in our tent. On this particular afternoon during the siesta period he had stripped down to just his boots, with no socks, and was fiddling around with a great green Egyptian flag on a pole. Heaven knows where he had got it from; perhaps he had pinched it from Farouk's palace? He also had a red fez, and placing it on his head stood to attention and raised the flag over his shoulder. Giggling, he said, 'I'm going over to the Orderly Room, they'll like this.'

We looked at each other and at him, starkers except for his boots, the fez, and the flag. We watched him marching across the parade ground, arms swinging to regulation height, thumbs pointed down, fingers clenched, certain he was having us on. We waited for him to wheel away at the last moment; instead, he disappeared straight through the doorway of the administration building.

'He's bonkers,' said someone and we resumed the game.

Our emissary, or whatever he thought he was, returned shortly and collapsed on his bed shaking. We couldn't get any sense out of him, just helpless guffaws.

Large numbers were beginning to come into the Camp from Italy and as old friends made their appearance it was reunion time. The Sixth and Seventh Reinforcements had been withdrawn from the Division and we would all go home together. That was official!

The long troop train left Maadi in the afternoon. There were many stops and starts but we did not mind because campaigning had endowed us with endless patience; we got there when we got there. Towards dusk the train stopped once again as we approached the tall slender towers of the Citadel. I thought again of the myth of Saladin jumping his poor horse from the high walls to escape, and the feeling that we were passing into history was incredibly strong. There was an acute sensitivity, an extreme awareness of the moment. Memories of our first arrival in Cairo were strikingly vivid. The wheels began to say *going home, going home, going home.* Incredible, but I had made it! I was going to live, LIVE, LIVE! Once home they would have a job prising me out into the Pacific.

At Tewfik on the end of the Suez Canal the *Strathaird* was waiting and we went aboard. It was completely unreal, just like a dream. I examined the ship, 28 000 tons and plenty of room. It had required a 47 000 tonner, the men packed in like sardines, to bring our single reinforcement and now two drafts were returning in a ship almost half the size. About a quarter of us were coming home; the lucky ones.

I found another relative on the ship and we became companions. He was madly in love with a photograph. Sam had become friendly with a South African who had given him his sister's address in Capetown and after endless letters and photographs he was going to South Africa as soon as he could make it. I told him about the girl in the cipher section who was still writing to me, showed him my photographs, and together we dreamed.

We slept anywhere, on the decks where the fire hoses woke us at dawn, or on a table in the sergeants' mess. The ship must have rolled heavily one night because, flat on my back on the hard table, the bulky lifejacket under my head, next morning I couldn't raise my chin.

We sailed for Ceylon escorted by a cruiser but two nights out from Colombo all lights on the blacked-out ship came on and the radio blared that Japan had capitulated. The war was finally over. I suppose we cheered. But did it matter? We were more concerned about the many Japanese submarines we knew were in the Indian Ocean and we felt that they were taking a lot for granted in lighting us up like a Christmas tree. If we had had anything to do with it we would have continued blacked out. Just because Japan had capitulated was no guarantee that one would not have a crack at such a juicy target. When you consider how individual Japanese soldiers refused to give up in the Islands, I think the fears were justified. We went to bed feeling horribly vulnerable.

Next morning the escorting cruiser came alongside with her crew dressing the decks. They cheered, we cheered, and as the cruiser fell astern to bear away I knew this was the final act, the beginning of the great wind-down, the reversion to civilian status.

We were not allowed ashore at Ceylon but sat out in the stream. They said there was a famine there and perhaps there was. We had thought we might have enjoyed a ride through to Kandy but no such luck. We gazed instead at the red tiled roofs half hidden in the trees, and listened to the mynah birds and their interminable racket. We marvelled at the cranky little fishing boats, like a log awash, in which fishermen on their own put miles out to sea.

Some of the New Zealand graves in the Cassino Military Cemetery, Italy.
Alexander Turnbull Library

It was wonderful weather for cruising and for weeks we sailed south-west. The world was flat, we would go on and on, until the ship fell off the end. In the late afternoon, following the sun, my favourite spot was on a metal canopy housing one of the winch motors, with our backs against the foot of the bridge. From there we could watch the flying fish rising forward of the starboard bow to wheel in wide arcs before falling back into the sea. My God, the Indian Ocean is enormous. We sailed with a permanent lean to starboard day after day, suspended in balmy blue space.

But the weather had to change, and as we sailed slowly up Port Philip Bay to Melbourne it was cold and blustery.

At Flinders Railway Station we looked for a bus, Sam and I, to take us to an uncle's home. On the bus he continued talking to me in the 8th Army vernacular, a mixture of Egyptian and Italian.

'But I thought they were New Zealanders,' a teenager whispered to her friend.

'It's Maori,' said the other.

Sam kept it going but in the end we had to ask the driver in English where to let us off.

We sat in the kitchen not even bothering to close the fridge door while we drank Richmond beer until my aunt, pink-cheeked and out of breath, came bustling in. She had been in the city and seeing New Zealanders in the streets had thought I might be amongst them and hurried home. The last time I had seen her was on a honeymoon visit to New Zealand when I had sat on her knee.

They took us out to dinner. Leaving the restaurant tables and passing the cashier my arm was suddenly wrenched and I was violently swung around. The cashier had come out from behind her desk and was berating me loudly for not paying. Since there was no apology it was not exactly a good introduction to Australia but obviously others must have tried the dodge more than once.

It rained the whole twenty-four hours we were in Melbourne, stopping only as we pulled away from the wharf. Of course there were latecomers, risking their lives by diving into the sea in near proximity to the huge screws of the ship, much to the Captain's disgust. A certain amount of jockeying went on and then we were out in the Tasman Sea where the big swell came up green. Yes, these were home waters, no more sovereign blue.

'Land ahead,' and there was Egmont, just a dark smudge ahead in the dusk. It was all very moving when we reached Lyttelton in the morning and piercingly cold to our blood which had thinned again in Egypt. There was a crowd on the wharf and welcoming signs with one particularly long banner held by somebody's relatives and friends. Freddy Jones, our Minister whom I had last seen in Tunisia, was telling us over the ship's amplifier system what a good job we had done but nobody really listened. We did not even go around saying goodbye to the North Islanders continuing on in the ship to Wellington; sticking together, we determined to stay that way on the troop train to Dunedin. Johnny still had his great canteen of cutlery and I was going to take turns roosting on it.

The train stopped for a few minutes outside Burnham Military Camp. Three small figures in battledress were standing at the edge of the distant trees when one suddenly broke cover, long hair flying as she ran to meet one of our passengers galloping towards her. They met in the middle with such force they both reeled back before embracing to hold each other and remain locked together. The whole troop train to a man cheered and whistled. My eyes moved on. What ridiculously big horses there are in this country, I thought. A couple of Clydesdales grazed with their huge feet, so different from the slim Arab ponies. Towards evening at a station north of Dunedin, Johnny was out the door in a flash reappearing at the dark window, his family behind him. I passed out his box of silver and gold purchased from a thieving Sergeant Major in Italy for three months' pay.

Night, and the old familiar lights of Dunedin Railway Station with its long platform. Another one of those mental blanks left me standing alone in front of the main gate. It had all been highly organised and we had remained in our seats until called.

'There he is!' came the delighted shouts of my family, the closed gates opening for a moment to let them through. Clasped in the arms of my sisters and mother, pulled forward to stumble over the kitbag dropped at my feet, we nearly all fell in a huddle on the platform. But who cared?

A taxi appeared like magic, its door opening; seated I realised we were driving slowly through a cheering, waving throng as if we were royalty.

'What's going on? Do they always do this?'

'Yes, it's for you people coming home.'

Tears and laughter, cups of tea and plates of cakes pressed upon already full hands. My eldest sister sitting in my lap hugging 'her little brother'.

Later in a bedroom they all stood around my bed.

'How is your bed?'

'Absolutely marvellous, it's like sleeping on a cloud.'

It was. So different from those tables in the sergeants' mess or the windy decks where the grinning Lascars woke us at first light with their fire hoses sluicing water and shouting, 'Wakey, wakey.'

In the morning they came with cups of tea.

'Why are you sleeping on the floor, wasn't the bed comfortable enough?'

'No, it was too comfortable, too soft, I couldn't sleep.'

Like my first night in Egypt I remembered, but there the sand had been hard.

Walking down Princes Street still in uniform heading for the Hospital and my medical discharge, I found myself screwed up with sudden fibrositis and barely able to straighten my back.

'What a splendid medical record you have,' said the first doctor.

'My word yes, you'll be right as rain in a couple of days,' beamed the second.

'A-1,' they both agreed, stamping my discharge.

'Bloody no-hopers,' echoed me, as I headed for the exit.

The back might have earned a pension; instead I became the recipient of a row of unengraved war medals and an income tax demand!